D0227257

LIBR/

TAHRIR
THE LAST 18 DAYS
OF MUBARAK

000000513274

TAHRIR
THE LAST 18 DAYS
OF MUBARAK

ABDEL LATIF EL-MENAWY

GILGAMESH
PUBLISHING LTD

Tahrir: The Last 18 Days of Mubarak

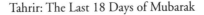

Published by Gilgamesh Publishing in 2012
Email: info@gilgamesh-publishing.co.uk
www.gilgamesh-publishing.co.uk

ISBN 978-1-908531-12-4

© Abdel Latif El-Menawy 2012

Printed and bound in the UK by CPI Antony Rowe

All rights are reserved. No part of this publication
may be reproduced, stored in a retrieval system or transmitted in any
form or by any means, electronic, mechanical, photographic or
otherwise, without prior permission of the copyright holder.

CIP Data: A catalogue for this book is
available from the British Library

DUDLEY PUBLIC LIBRARIES	
000000513274	
Bertrams	27/02/2012
962.16055	£12.95
	DU

CONTENTS

ACKNOWLEDGEMENTS

When I finished writing this book I thought, "OK, I think now I have put in all the characters that led to the acceleration of events." But that can never be the case. There are others who played a role. Like the first in a line of dominos they are way in the back but no less important than the ones near the front. They set off the chain of events that led to the climax of this book. I thank them all. My wife Rola, and our children: Marwan, Omar and Haya, without whose total confidence and support none of this would have been possible. My parents, who taught me in my first years how to act in times of difficulty and put into my heart the qualities a man needs to make choices in a time of need. Colleagues in Maspero who stayed in the building under life-threatening circumstances because they believed in me and believed in serving our nation with the highest level of professionalism and the maximum loyalty: Nihal, Mohammad, Abdelrahman, Moustafa, Omnia, Dina, Hamed, Sherif, Amr, Manal, and Safwat, and many more that I cannot mention here but who have my full respect. I have started with the ones back home, but Alex, I did not forget about you – thank you for being my voice to a Western audience. Finally, Max Scott and Claudia Shaffer, without whose good guidance and support this book would never have come out the way it is now.

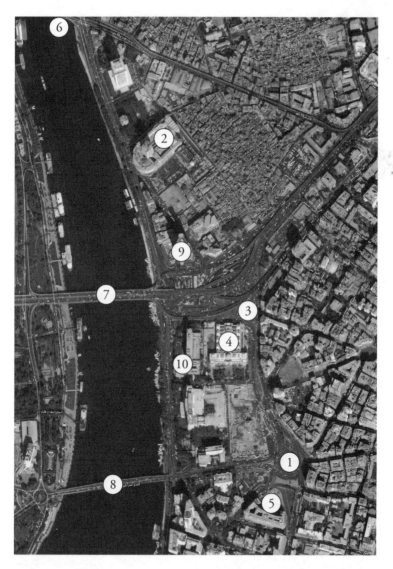

1. Tahrir Square
2. Maspero building (TV & Radio Tower)
3. Abdel Moneim Riad Square
4. Egyptian Museum
5. Mogamma Building

6. 26th July Bridge
7. 6th October Bridge
8. Qasr El-Nil Bridge
9. Ramses Hilton
10. National Party Headquarters

FOREWORD

For 18 days in 2011, the world's eyes were on Egypt. From the moment on 25th January when angry, frustrated Egyptians began to pour into Tahrir Square – ordinary people determined to voice their contempt for a regime that was treating them with contempt – until the brief 38-second broadcast by the dour Vice-President Omar Suleiman announcing the resignation of President Mubarak on 11th February and the handover of power to the armed forces, the world held its breath. Would this extraordinary, spontaneous uprising bring freedom and democracy to the Arab world's largest nation? Or would it end in bloodshed, revolution and the seizure of power by Islamist extremists or a military junta?

To many outsiders, the momentous events, centred largely on the square that has since become the symbol of the Arab Spring, came as a surprise. Policy-makers in Washington, who for 30 years had counted on the loyalty and stability of President Mubarak's Egypt, had failed to see the slow-burning resentment of a nation that was strangled by corruption, angered by the arrogance and extravagance of the rich and desperate at the plight of the poor, without jobs, without opportunity and without hope. And as Western capitals scrambled to protect their interests, their allies and their democratic ideals, outsiders watched with bemusement as students with mobile phones, middle-class professionals with minds of their own, Islamist activists, and ordinary Cairene workers outwitted and eventually overthrew one of the strongest and most heavily-policed regimes in the Middle East.

With hindsight, everyone now says they saw it coming: the fraudulent parliamentary elections of November 2010 that mocked any semblance of democracy, the routine police brutality that led to the death of a young man, Khalid Saeed, in June 2010, the lack of jobs, price rises, urban squalor and, above all, the general sense of stagnation, despair and futility. All this was slowly turning a normally-peaceful, sentimental, happy-go-lucky nation into a country on the brink of a social explosion. The ruling clique, fixing the rules to benefit their businesses, cocooned the ageing President, once a popular war hero, in increasing isolation from reality. The bureaucrats basked in sycophantic indolence. And meanwhile the young Facebook generation, educated and losing its fear, suddenly saw in Tunisia a way of bringing down a dictator.

When it became clear that the "Day of Rage" in Tahrir Square was the start of a real confrontation, few knew how to react. The outside world dithered, issued statements, called for peaceful change. The cabinet hard-liners, including Habib Al-Adly, the hated Interior Minister, wanted a crackdown. The police summoned their thugs to break heads in Tahrir. The Army waited, its elderly, conservative leadership proud but uncertain, and determined to avoid an explosion. And Mubarak himself remained aloof in his palace, ignorant of the mood, refusing to believe rumours, assured by his loyalists that all was well and manipulated by his ambitious son Gamal, who desperately feared the "inheritance project" (his own future accession as Pharoah) was slipping away.

One man was caught in the thick of it. As Undersecretary of State and President of the News Sector at ERTU (Egyptian Radio and Television Union), a consummate professional who for years had struggled to maintain the media's credibility and honour despite censorship, restrictions and propaganda, Abdel Latif El-Menawy suddenly found himself buffeted from all sides. His political bosses wanted television to ignore the protests, to carry on with the old routines, to put out reassuring but mendacious bulletins. The radicals gathering in Tahrir wanted to proclaim their demands but turned instead to Al-Jazeera, the ambitious Qatari station with little love for the Mubarak regime. And Abdel Latif himself, who insisted he was neither a stooge of the regime nor an enemy of Mubarak, simply wanted to do his best for his country: to broadcast the truth, to maintain balance, to fend off the opportunists and political schemers and to help Egypt find a way out of the growing chaos.

His story is the inside story of what happened. It is a magnificent, astonishing and often wryly bitter record of bumbling, confusion and missed opportunities. Determined to stay at his post, he soon found there was no escape: the state television centre was surrounded by protesters who made sporadic but ominous attempts to storm the building. He lived, ate, slept and worked round the clock in his office. Increasingly exhausted, he also found himself increasingly forced to take radical decisions of his own as his political bosses made ever more unrealistic demands. In the end, it was he who played the pivotal role in negotiating between factions and urging Mubarak to quit. He went to see the old man when others feared even to disturb him. He drafted the speech of resignation, which would have lent dignity to the final hours, had Gamal and the last-ditchers not disastrously recast it and withdrawn the offer to resign. He persuaded the stooges that the game was up and that media lies could no longer save them.

History seen from the inside is often revealing in the haphazard details that change the course of events. While the White House was earnestly weighing the messages it would send to Cairo, those in the thick of the melee were too preoccupied to listen, caught up in the momentum that no one could control. Events that were unplanned threw everything off course: the furious camel owners, who charged into Tahrir from the Pyramids, angry at the loss of tourist income; the young Google manager, Wael Ghonim, who became the voice of the crowd; the hapless Prime Minister, Ahmed Nazif, who early on lost his bearings; the Mubarak sons, quarrelling furiously as the regime caved in; and the mysterious aide who accidentally blundered into the picture as the improvised broadcast recorded the military takeover. Perhaps the most poignant moment, revealed here for the first time, was the final refusal of the President's wife, Suzanne, to leave her villa, delaying Mubarak's departure for three hours while she wept uncontrollably on her bed, keeping the world waiting and wondering what had happened.

Abdel Latif relates it all with verve, honesty, occasional shame and a quiet pride that he played a big role in ensuring Egypt's most fateful three weeks for a generation did not end in tragedy and bloodshed. If only there had been television directors with the same dedication and professional conscience in Libya, Yemen and Syria.

Michael Binyon
December 2011

CAST OF CHARACTERS

Hosni Mubarak

Mohammed Hosni Elsayed Mubarak was born on the 4th of May 1928 in the village of Kafr Meslha, Mounofia, Egypt. He married Suzanne Thabet. They have two sons Gamal and Alaa. Mubarak, a fluent speaker of Russian and English, gained his commission as a pilot officer on the 13th of March 1950 after undertaking part of his training in the then Soviet Union. Mubarak served in various Army units before joining the Air Force Academy as an instructor in the late fifties. Mubarak was appointed Air Force Academy's commander in November 1967 and was credited with doubling the number of pilots and navigators in the Air Force in the years preceding the 1973 war. Two years later he became Chief of Staff for the Egyptian Air Force. In 1972, he was appointed Deputy Minister of Defence, whilst keeping his position in the Air Force. The following year he was promoted to Air Chief Marshal after the 1973 War. In April 1975, President Anwar Sadat appointed him Vice President. Mubarak became the fourth President of the Republic on the 14th of October 1981, following the assassination of Sadat, after being confirmed by a referendum. Upon assuming the presidency, Mubarak crushed an Islamist insurgence in Asyut and jailed over 2,500 members of militant Islamist groups. He executed a handful, had others sent to prison, and gradually released the rest. He also released the more secular political figures whom Sadat had indiscriminately jailed in the September crackdown that helped provoke his assassination. Since then he also held the positions of The Supreme Commander of Egypt's Armed Forces and President of the National Democratic Party, the NDP. Mubarak won the controversial first multi-candidate presidential election in 2005. He almost served five terms in office. During his rule, Mubarak survived 6 assassination attempts, the most notable being in Ethiopia, 1995, when his entourage was attacked by gunmen. He survived thanks to his armoured Mercedes. He stepped down on the 11th of February following 18 days of protests centred around Tahrir Square.

Anas Al-Feky

Anas Ahmed Nabieh Al-Feky was born in October 1960 in Gharbiya, Egypt. He graduated from Cairo University in 1983 with a Bachelor of Commerce. He worked marketing Foreign Encyclopedias, rising to become a Marketing Director. He went on to establish his own marketing company in 1985. In 2002 he was appointed Head of the General Organization for Cultural Mansions. In July 2004 he was appointed Minister of Youth, part of the government of former Prime Minister Ahmed Nazif. He also held the position of Minister of Information from February 2005 until he resigned on the 12th of February 2011, the day after Mubarak stepped down.

Ahmed Nazif

Nazif was born on the 8th of July 1952 in Alexandria, Egypt to a wealthy former sailor who owned a sea shipping company, Mahmoud Nazif. His grandfather Mohammed Bey Nazif was Undersecretary of the Ministry of Health in the days of King Farouk. He graduated from Cairo University in 1973 with a Bachelor of Science in engineering, majoring in communication and Electronics. He gained a Master's degree in electrical engineering from the same university in 1976 and a PhD in Computer Science in 1983 from McGill University, Canada. He returned to Egypt to work as a professor in the Faculty of Engineering at Cairo University. His first public achievement was supervising the National Number Project and the mechanization of the Civil Status Department. For nine years, from 1989 to 1998, he ran the Cabinet Information and Decision Support

Centre, which collects monthly economic statistics for the benefit of ministers. He also supervised a central computerised identity card system. Nazif was appointed Minister of Communication and Information Technology in October 1999. In 2004 Nazif was appointed Prime Minister by President Mubarak, receiving a formal vote of confidence from parliament. His cabinet was dismissed by Mubarak on the 29th of January 2011 in light of the protests of the 25th of January. Nazif, who is the youngest Prime Minister in the history of Egypt, speaks fluent French and English and fathered a daughter in 2011 with Zeinab Zaki, Vice President of the Information Technology Industry Development Agency (ITIDA), whom he married in February 2010, stirring controversy in Egypt. He also has 2 sons from his previous wife, who died in 2009.

Ahmed Shafik

Shafik was born in Cairo in November 1941 and graduated from the Egyptian Air Force Academy in 1961. Later in his career he gained a masters degree in military sciences and a PhD in the national strategy of outer-space. Shafik is a fighter pilot who served as the commander of the Egyptian Air Force between 1996 and 2002, and was appointed in 2002 as Egyptian Minister for Civil Aviation. During the 1973 October War, Shafik was a senior fighter pilot under Hosni Mubarak's command. From 1984 to 1986, Shafik was the military attaché in the Egyptian Embassy in Rome. He was later appointed Commander of the Air Operations Department before taking the position of Air Forces' Chief of Staff in September 1991. In April 1996 he became Commander of the Egyptian Air Force. In 2002, he was appointed Minister of Civil Aviation. He remained in that post until the 29th of January 2011 when he was appointed Prime Minister. His premiership lasted just over a month, until he resigned on the 3rd of March due to pressure from protesters and the opposition. He is considered a potential candidate in the 2012 presidential election.

Gamal Mubarak

Gamal Al-Din Mohammed Hosni Elsayed Mubarak was born on December 27, 1963. He is the younger of the two sons of former Egyptian President Hosni Mubarak and former first lady Suzanne Mubarak. In contrast to his older brother Alaa, Gamal enjoyed an active public profile as a politician and former head of the policies committee in the then ruling party (NDP). He was educated at Mrs Woodley's Primary School and St George College in Cairo, before attending the American University in Cairo. Gamal graduated with a business degree and went on to earn his MBA from the same school. Early in his career, he worked in the Bank of America in Cairo, moving later to the bank's London office. He married Khadija El-Gamal on the 28th of April 2007, followed by a private ceremony in Sharm El-Sheikh on the 4th of May. They have one daughter.

Although Gamal's high profile was mostly related to the National Democratic Party, he initially appeared in public life in the 1990s as the chairman of the Future Generation Foundation (FGF), an NGO focusing on professional training for young people.

Gamal joined the National Democratic Party in the year 2000, going on to hold a series of key posts. In 2002, Gamal became head of the influential Policies Committee, which was responsible for planning policies applied by the Egyptian government and revising draft laws. In November 2007, the young Mubarak was appointed Deputy Secretary General of the party. Due to his rapid rise within the party, it was widely speculated that Gamal was being groomed to be his father's successor as the future head of the NDP and, more importantly, the party's candidate for the 2011 presidential election. The term "Inheritance" was coined and dominated Egypt's political life.

Gamal Mubarak began to promote himself in earnest in 2002 when the first NDP general conference was launched under the slogan "New Thinking", in reference to a reform movement driven by Gamal. In a few years, the Policies Committee grew to be the driving force behind the NDP in planning major public policies. At the time, there was speculation that a power struggle was taking place within the NDP. This struggle involved on one hand, the "Young Guard" led by Gamal and a number of younger businessmen and politicians, and an "Old Guard"on the other, composed of politicians who had been in the cabinet for decades.

On the 3rd of February 2011 Vice President Omar Suleiman announced that Gamal Mubarak, who had never held an official government post but rather a party position, would not seek election.

Alaa Mubarak

Alaa Al-Din Mohammed Hosni Elsayed Mubarak was born in 1960. He is the elder of the two sons of former Egyptian President Hosni Mubarak and former first lady Suzanne Mubarak. In contrast to his younger brother, Alaa strove to maintain a low public profile. Like his brother, he was educated at Mrs Woodley's Primary School, St George College and the American University in Cairo. He is married to Heidy Rasekh. They had two sons, Mohammed and Omar. Mohammed died on the 18th of May 2009, aged 12, after suffering a brain haemorrhage. Alaa was primarily a businessman, not involved in politics. The director of Bullion Company Ltd. in Cyprus, Alaa was accused of international arms trading, corruption and bribery scandals in Egypt, which led him to put himself out of public for some period.

Ahmed Ezz

Ahmed Abdel El-Aziz Ezz was born in 1959. In 1982, Ezz graduated from Cairo University with a degree in Civil

Engineering. His first passion was playing drums, which he satisfied by joining a small band that performed in hotels and private parties. An engineer by profession, he inherited his father's business in scrap and iron, becoming the most prominent businessman and politician in Egypt in the last decade of Mubarak's rule. In 1996, Ezz owned two modest factories manufacturing steel and ceramics. Ezz founded the El-Ezz Porcelain Company. He also was the Chairman and Managing Director of Al-Ezz Dekheila Steel Company Alexandria SAE. Ezz served as the Chairman of Ezz Steel (Formerly Al-Ezz Steel Rebars) until May 17, 2011 and served as its Managing Director.

The turning point in Ezz's life was on October 1996 during the Middle East and North Africa Conference in Cairo. After a distinguished appearance alongside Gamal during the conference, he embarked on a journey to the top of Egypt's political and economic pyramid. Ezz was a parliamentary member representing the districts of Sadat-Monouf-Sers al-Liyan in Monofuyia from the year 2000 to 2011. He became NDP Secretary for Organizational Affairs before being elected chairman of the Budget and Planning Committee. This committee was responsible for presenting a number of economic legislations, which the public viewed as little more than a means of easing business for the wealthy. He also played a leading role, along with other officials, in brushing aside reports of corruption and financial irregularities within state institutions.

The boom in Ezz's business career came when he managed to take control of the Al-Dekheila steel factory. Using his Dekheila shares, he was able to apply for bank loans and expand his business. Opposition parties, parliamentarians and other groups accused Ezz of monopolizing the steel industry in Egypt by holding more than 60 percent of the market share, describing it as a state backed monopoly. He was also blamed for the 70 percent hike in steel prices. Ezz resigned from the NDP on 29 January 2011. On the 15th of September 2011 he received a sentence of 10 years in prison and a shared fine of 660 million Egyptian pounds.

Rashid Mohammed Rashid

Rashid Mohammed Rashid was born in 1955. He graduated from Alexandria University with a Bachelor in production engineering in 1978. He received further education at Stanford, MIT and Harvard in the US.

Rashid had a prominent career, spanning more than two decades in international business. He is the founder of Fine Foods which became Egypt's leading foods brand. He also held many international positions with Unilever after joining the multinational in 1987. Rashid served as Chairman of the Alexandria Development Centre, an NGO that seeks to develop and mobilise resources for the regional development and revival of Alexandria. He also acted as Chairman of the Board and as a consultant for a number of multinational companies based in the United Kingdom. His international activities included his membership of the Executive Committee of the Arab Business Council, the World Economic Forum, and the Investment Advisory council in Turkey, under the supervision of the Turkish Prime Minister. Within Egypt, he sat on the board of various NGOs and business councils.

In July 2004, Rashid was appointed Minister of Foreign Trade and Industry in Egypt. He was dismissed as part of Ahmed Nazif's government on the 29th of January, though he was offered a new position in Ahmed Shafik's government. He refused and left the country. He was later tried in two cases and found guilty in absentia. In September 2011 he received two sentences of total 15 years in prison in addition to a fine of 1,414 million Egyptian pounds for embezzlement and squandering public funds.

Yousef Boutros Ghali

Yousef Raouf Boutros Ghali, the nephew of the former Secretary General of the United Nations Boutros Boutros-Ghali, was born in Cairo on the 20th of August 1952. In 1974, he graduated from Cairo University with a bachelor of science from the economics and political sciences faculty. He then worked for a year as an assistant professor in the economics and political sciences faculty in Cairo University. In 1981 Ghali finished his PhD in Economics at MIT (Massachusetts Institute of Technology) in Cambridge, Massachusetts, United States. In 1981 he became a senior economist at the International Monetary Fund, based in the US. He first worked for the government in 1986, as an economic advisor to the Prime Minister. After working as a professor of economics at the American University in Cairo, and then as an advisor to the Governor of the Central Bank and member of the board at the Egyptian National bank, he began his government career in 1993, when he was appointed State Minister for International Cooperation, becoming State Minister for Economic Affairs in 1996. In 2004 he rose to the position of Minister of Finance and a member of the General Secretariat of the National Democratic Party. He also became a member of the Policies Committee at the National Democratic Party.

He was dismissed on the 31st of January 2011. Then, on the 4th of February 2011, the IMF reported that Boutros-Ghali had resigned the Chairmanship of the International Monetary and Financial Committee (IMFC). He left the country on the 11th of February prior to Mubarak's resignation. On the 4th of June 2011, Ghali was tried for corruption, found guilty in absentia, and sentenced to 30 years imprisonment. His wife Michaela Khalil Habib Sayegh died of a heart attack in London on the 29th of October 2011 caused by stress and anxiety. They have three sons.

Habib Al-Adly

Habib Ibrahim Al-Adly was born on the 1st of March 1938. After graduating from the Police Academy in 1961, he joined the State Security Investigations Service in 1965. He rose through the ranks at the Interior Ministry, including a two year stint at the Foreign Ministry. He became Assistant Interior Minister in 1993. He replaced General Hassan Al-Alfi as Interior Minister after the November 1997 Luxor massacre. He was dismissed on the 31st of January 2011. On the 5th of May, 2011, Adly was found guilty of fraud and money laundering and sentenced to 12 years in prison.

Suzanne Mubarak

Suzanne Saleh Thabet was born on the 28th of February 1941 in the Al-Menya governorate in Egypt. Her father, Saleh Thabet, was an Egyptian surgeon and her mother, Lily May Palmer, was a nurse from Pontypridd in Wales. The two married in Islington, London on the 16th of March 1934, while Saleh was a student at Cardiff University and Lily was working at an infirmary on the Camden Road in North London. Suzanne has an older brother, Mounir Thabet, a former President of the Egyptian Olympic Committee. Suzanne met her future husband Hosni in the late 1950s when she was 16 years old. Her brother was one of Hosni's academy students. The two married when Suzanne was 17 years old in 1958. She returned to school 10 years later, after the birth of their two sons, Alaa and Gamal. She graduated from the American University in Cairo (AUC) in 1977 with a bachelor's degree in political science and then received a master's degree in sociology from AUC in 1982. During the tenure as first lady of Egypt, she supported countless programs that aim to improve the quality of life of individuals from birth to adulthood. She has received numerous awards, decorations and honorary degrees nationally and internationally for her contributions to public service. She was the first lady of Egypt until the 11th of February 2011 when her husband resigned.

Zakaria Azmi

Zakaria Hussein Mohammed Azmi was born on the 26th of June 1938. He graduated from the Faculty of Military Arts in 1960 and began his career as an officer in the Armored Corps. In 1965 he was transferred to the Republican Guards while at the same time he received a bachelor of arts in law from Cairo University. And in 1970 he acquired a diploma in criminal sciences from the faculty of law. Two years later he received a diploma in international law and a doctorate in international law with the subject of "Protecting Civilians During Armed Conflicts". In 1973 he became Assistant for Political Affairs at the Presidential Office for National Security Affairs as well as a member of the Presidential Secretariat for Information. He was the National Democratic Party's (NDP) deputy in the El-Zeitoun district in eastern Cairo and Chief of the Presidential Staff. He had joined the NDP following its establishment in 1978, was elected to Parliament in 1987 and appointed chief of the presidential staff in 1989. His overtly critical approach in the People's Assembly Debates led many observers to dub him "the representative of the NDP opposition wing in parliament". Azmi spoke against the terms of US economic grants to Egypt, corruption in city councils and pollution in Cairo. Azmi was promoted to the NDP's Secretariat-General in 1993. He served as former President Hosni Mubarak's Chief of Staff from 1989 until his resignation.

Omar Suleiman

Omar Suleiman was born in 1935 in Qena in Upper Egypt. He graduated from the Military Academy in Cairo in 1955 going on to receive additional military training at the Academy of Frunze in the Soviet Union. Suleiman saw action in the war in Yemen in 1962 as well as the 1967 and 1973 wars against Israel. In the

Armed Forces, he served in various positions until he assumed the post of Chief of the General Planning Department in the Armed Forces Operations Authority in 1992, his final post before his appointment as director of the Military Intelligence on the 22nd of January 1993. While head of the Egyptian General Intelligence Service (GIS), former President Hosni Mubarak also assigned him to handle the dossier of the Palestine question, which saw him assume the task of mediation on a deal to release captured Israeli soldier, Gilad Shalit from Hamas. He handled many negotiations between the Palestinians and Israelis, and helped negotiated the truces between Hamas and Israel. He also assumed some diplomatic missions in a number of countries, including a number of tasks in Sudan. In 1995, his advice to use an armoured car saved Mubarak's life in an assassination attempt in Ethiopia.   In September 2010, a popular campaign was launched calling for Omar Suleiman's candidacy in the upcoming Presidential elections. On the 29th of January, 2011, Mubarak appointed Suleiman as Vice-President of the Republic ordering him to hold a dialogue with the opposition on constitutional reform. A couple of days later a failed assassination attempt on Suleiman left two of his bodyguards dead. On the 11th of February, when Mubarak handed over power to the Supreme Council of the Armed Forces, Suleiman's brief tenure as Vice President ended.

Hussein Tantawi

Field Marshal Mohammed Hussein Tantawi Suleiman was born on the 31st of October 1935 to a Nubian Egyptian family. Field Marshal Tantawi won his commission on the 1st of April 1956, joining the infantry. Tantawi has a Masters Degree in Military Science and a Fellowship from the High War College. He served in the Suez war of 1956 as well as the wars against Israel in 1967 and 1973. He held various commands in the military, including an assignment as military attaché to Pakistan. Field Marshal

Tantawi has served as Commander of the Republican Guard, and Chief of the Operations Authority of the Armed Forces. In 1991 he commanded an Egyptian army unit in the Gulf War against Iraq. On the 20th of May 1991, following the dismissal of Lt. General Youssef Sabri Abu Taleb, Field Marshal Tantawi was appointed Minister of Defence and Military Production and Commander-in-Chief of the Armed Forces. A month later he was promoted to Field Marshal. Former President Hosni Mubarak handed over power to Field Marshal Tantawi as President of the Supreme Council of Armed Forces on the 11th of February 2011 in his last act before stepping down.

Fathi Sorour

Ahmed Fathi Sorour was born on the 9th of July 1932, and is married with three children. Following his studies at Cairo University (Bachelor of Law and Doctor of Law), and at Michigan University, USA (Master of Comparative Law), Dr Sorour started his professional life as Assistant Attorney General in 1953. After a string of legal and academic posts he was appointed Minister of Education in 1986, later becoming a Member of the Political Bureau of the National Democratic Party. He also spent some years in the Egyptian diplomatic service, serving as Cultural Attaché at the Egyptian Embassy in Switzerland in 1964, Cultural Adviser at the Egyptian Embassy in Paris from 1965 to 1970, and Permanent Delegate of the League of Arab States to UNESCO from 1972 to 1978.

During his parliamentary career, he has been active in the field of basic freedoms and other human rights. He has held numerous positions within Egypt and abroad, as well as winning various awards domestically and internationally. Dr. Sorour has directed over 30 doctoral theses in law and published many works on individual freedoms, criminal law and education, including a book on Constitutional Legality and Human Rights.

Safwat El-Sherif

Mohammed Safwat Yousef El-Sherif was born on the 19th of December 1933 in Gharbia governorate. He graduated with a bachelor's degree in military sciences in 1952. He also finished military studies at the Armed Forces Institutes in the fields of planning, management and communication. After studying in Britain and West Germany, he was transferred to the General Intelligence Service GIS in 1957. He is considered one of the founders of the Spying department at the Service, recruiting and training officers for the department. In 1968, he was put under house arrest in an apartment in Zamalek charged with intelligence deviation. He was cleared of all charges as he was not even a direct witness to events under investigation. However, he left the force and opened his own private import and export business. In 1975 he closed his company to join the State Information Service, the SIS, becoming chairman of the SIS from 1978 to 1980. The late President Anwar Sadat then appointed him President of the Egyptian Radio and Television Union in 1980. In 1982 he was appointed Minister of Information by former President Hosni Mubarak, a position in which he remained until 2004.

In 1977 he was a founding member of the NDP and since then he has been a member of the Political Bureau of the NDP, serving in many positions within the party. On the 20th of April 1993, El-Sherif escaped an assassination attempt by Gamaa Islamiya with few injuries. From 2004, El-Sherif was Speaker of the Shura Council and the President of the Supreme Press Council until he resigned from NDP on the 5th of February 2011.

El-Sherif is the founder of the Egyptian Media Production City EMPC which is known as the 6th of October Media City. He was also the founder of the Egyptian Satellite Company, Nilesat in 1996 with the purpose of operating Egyptian Satellites.

PROLOGUE

It was almost five o'clock when a well-built Republican Guard officer in bulletproof body armour, carrying his gun, entered my office, flanked by two soldiers.

"The television building is fully under our control. It is totally secure against protesters' attempts to storm in, all live studios are under heavy security," he declared, "any movement in or out of the building has to be in coordination with us."

It was dusk of Friday the 28th of January, a day known as the "Friday of Rage" by revolutionary Egyptians. In the office, people's eyes were red, streaming with tears from the stinging tear gas penetrating our building following a day of police activity in the square. As the day turned to night we could still see the scenes of confrontation and conflict between protesters and the security forces. We had just seen a CCTV feed of police bombarding protesters with tear gas and water cannon atop the Qasr El-Nil Bridge, one of many that stretches across the Nile.

Thousands of protesters faced thousands of policemen in a constant game of hit and run, until the police finally gave way and a wave of protesters swept across the bridge towards Tahrir Square. Within seconds, the police were gone. It was as if they had never even been there.

It seemed that Egypt's institutions had disappeared; all that remained was the army out on the streets and the three remaining offices where we worked, on the 5th floor of the state TV building in downtown Cairo. Neither I, nor any of my colleagues or assistants had any idea what was going on that night.

It was the longest night Egypt had ever known. Egyptians lived under the threat of attacks by prisoners who had managed to escape the country's prisons, as well as criminal thugs who put fear and horror into the hearts of the country's citizens, taking advantage of the sudden disappearance of the country's police.

We were the last and only resort for the many Egyptians who called us up in tears begging for help with no one else to turn to.

The heavy footsteps of the Republican Guard officer, which pounded the floor of my office louder than the noise of the protests outside, did not offer a way out of the chaos. It was only the beginning of a chain of sharp and tumultuous developments, which I will describe throughout this book.

These events started on the 25th of January, the official start of the Egyptian revolution, and lasted until the 11th of February when Hosni Mubarak stepped down, after nearly thirty years of rule, leading to the collapse of his regime.

From my position as the head of the Egyptian state media's news service, I was witness to the fermentation of this revolution and the state's preparations for it, according to the information available to them at the time. I saw how the Egyptian State managed the biggest crisis in its history – how those managing the crisis for the government degraded the 25th of January protests and their participants. I could see the hubris and over-confidence at work. I was constantly in touch with the small group led by Gamal Mubarak, the son and potential heir of the President, and saw their response to the crisis at first hand.

There were many questions that arose over those 18 days, and quite a few of them have still not been answered. Why was the army deployed in the streets? Where did its loyalty lie? Did the army's position change with the unfolding of events or did it stick to the same plan from the start? What kind of alliances were forged among the key political factions in Egypt? How did that affect the struggle inside the state's body between Gamal's "inheritance" camp and those who opposed him? How did that struggle affect the way things turned out, pushing events in the direction we witnessed? What is the map for political powers inside the regime and when did each group make up its mind and define its choices? Why was Mubarak always late in addressing the nation, why did he alter his first address and who ruined his last one? Why didn't he step down until he was alone in Sharm El Sheikh without his wife, his son and all his men?

Mubarak came close to surviving after addressing the nation on the 1st of February. He was able to win the public's compassion and sympathy in a manner that surprised even some of the powers within the regime. However, the next day blood was shed in Tahrir Square in a pitched battle between anti-government protesters and pro-Mubarak supporters. This battle was plotted hours after President Mubarak's speech the night before, when all the factions within the government schemed to use the state TV as a tool for achieving their own ends. Known to the media as the "Battle of the Camel" after scenes of mounted camels storming the square made it around the world, that day announced the end of Mubarak's rule, even though he would cling on to power for nine more days.

Since the beginning, I was a key contact in the media for the government; caught between various powers, I had to make some pivotal decisions which would have major ramifications as the uprising continued. During the first days of the crisis, one of these decisions was against the President's desire to keep Interior Minister Habib Al-Adly in his job, which would have worsened the unrest. I did not give the Presidential Palace the military's statements before my broadcast, something which they demanded that I do. Had the situation continued, the confrontations would have been far more damaging.

I cannot profess to know the whole truth about what happened at the beginning of 2011 in Egypt, but I know what I saw and experienced, from my own perspective. I suddenly found myself in the middle of the most radical period of change witnessed by the country in the last 45 centuries. Throughout those 18 days, I slept in my office inside the television building, under constant siege by furious protesters determined to break in. I was leading a group of colleagues who all believed, as I did, in what we were doing.

This book is an attempt to answer some of the questions which have arisen since the beginning of the revolution. Since I started my job, in 2005, I bore witness to the turmoil within the government, as it slowly began to fall apart, under the weight of its own corruption. Too weak to hold together, it finally collapsed when Egypt's people took to the streets, and cut off its blood supply. I did not see everything that happened, but then, no one did. However, I managed to see first hand many of the decisions taken on high that were never revealed to the Egyptian people. This book will not seek to justify why the government, the media, the protesters, the international community and most importantly, the people did what they did during those 18 days, but to explain the reasons.

INTRODUCTION

A little bit of history

Forty-five centuries ago, at the end of the sixth dynasty in Egypt's Old Kingdom, Egypt witnessed what historians consider the first revolution in known human history. At that time, Egypt's Pharaoh Pepi II Neferkare ascended to the throne at the age of six, ruling until he died at the age of one hundred, keeping his grip on power for a full ninety-four years, the longest reign of any monarch in history.

His death ended the rule of the sixth dynasty of the Old Kingdom in ancient Egypt. Weakened by old age, he could no longer subdue the powerful princes of Egypt, who, hungry for power, stopped paying him tributes. The ageing Pharaoh led the country into ruin, as its ancient institutions collapsed, and the public suffered as he imposed his cruel laws and taxes. The door opened to pretenders and opportunists who exploited the public, robbing them in every possible way and exposing people to poverty, humiliation, hunger and oppression. The society was stratified, and the people became stuck within their social classes. The poor got poorer and the rich got richer. People lost hope.

Egypt's only real revolution took place 45 centuries ago. Change crept up from the bottom of society because of the corruption and weakness at the top. There followed 299 years of chaos, as the Old Kingdom collapsed, and Egypt was carved up by squabbling kings, all vying for influence up and down the Nile. When this dark age ended, Egypt entered a period of unparalleled wealth and prosperity – what we know today as the Middle Kingdom.

It was the first revolution that Egypt went through. Throughout the following centuries, uprisings would occur time and again. There were invasions by the Greeks, Romans, Muslims and Ottomans. There was the Orabi Revolt against Khedive Pasha in 1879, which led to the British invasion of 1882. Egypt was to experience two revolutions in the 20th century, once in 1919 and then again in 1952. All these events shook Egypt to its very foundations, but one could argue that these were not total revolutions.

Since I began my career in journalism, and my interest in political affairs grew, I always used to remember this story. I thought it an illustrative case study of Egyptians in revolt, even though it happened several thousand years ago.

Egyptians like to give the impression that they are as calm as the waters on the surface of the Nile, the banks of which we have been living on since the dawn of civilization. But if you look a little deeper into the water, you will see underneath a plethora of whirlpools and currents.

The fatal error committed by former President Mubarak's regime, and its predecessors, was that they never grasped the true essence of the Egyptians. They never expected Egyptians to protest, let alone pull themselves together to oust a ruling president. Egyptians will force that change, even if it may be followed by years of chaos and instability, like the days that followed the destruction of the Old Kingdom, in the hope of the wealth and prosperity that comes after.

• • •

Up until April 2011, I worked in one of the most recognisable buildings in downtown Cairo. It's a huge place, and it sits on the banks of the Nile. The lower part of the building is a massive circular edifice about 10 stories high, a rectangular tower rises above it, through the centre, making the whole thing 28 stories high. On top of it, a radio mast adorned with satellite dishes and aerials of different shapes and sizes stretches up, high above the city. We call it the Maspero building, after the famous French Egyptologist. I don't know why 43,000 people work there. In reality, there only needs to be a tenth of those people, but that's the way Egypt works. Egypt was a socialist country, the government had to find a job for everyone. The television station was one of those places onto which they could load extra employees. Like many government departments and businesses, it was a family business. For every journalist you found working there, it wouldn't be unusual to find his children, his brother or his wife there too. That's the way things work in Egypt.

Egyptian TV has nearly 20 channels, three main ones, the rest specialised or regional. The Egyptian state radio, 75 years old, also broadcasts out of the same building. It's the same model as the BBC. The difference is that here, the Minister of Information has the highest authority. The ERTU (Egyptian Radio and Television Union) is part of the Ministry of Information, and part of the government.

I joined the ERTU in 2005. Before that I was a newspaper journalist. I'd done a few current affairs and news programmes on state TV before, and I think they liked what I'd done, though I was an outsider. In the February of that year, President Mubarak announced for the first time that there would be direct multi-candidate elections. There had been elections in Egypt before, of course, but they didn't amount to much. In these "Egyptian Presidential Confirmation Referendums", the parliament's approved candidate would simply stand before a public vote, and the electorate was asked the simple question, yes or no. The candidate was always Mubarak and his confirmation was always won with an overwhelming majority. Back in 1999, he was approved with 93.8% of the vote. These elections, if you could call them that, were merely a formality.

The new system that year was to be a direct election. For the first time, the opposition parties would put forward their own candidates and the public was to decide, it was to be our first taste of something resembling democracy. A week before the election was announced, I was asked to participate in the process, to make a media plan to cover and discuss the changes in the constitution and to produce and host a televised debate between the candidates. They needed a proper journalist working for the state broadcaster, and I fitted the bill nicely. I got on well with my colleagues at the station and with the Ministry of Information.

Two months later, much to my surprise, I was asked if I would be willing to take charge of the entire news bureau of the ERTU. I accepted the mission.

This was my first official position with the government. I never knew who nominated me. They had never had a journalist come from outside to take on the job before. It seemed to me to be the perfect opportunity to help reform the state media. After all, they were going to reform the political system, surely the media would have to be reformed as well.

I, along with a few others, wanted to change the ethos of state television to the concept of public television. Just as the BBC is responsible to the public, rather than the government, I believed that we could instil a sense of public ownership at the ERTU.

When I arrived, my office was large, windowless and dull: a prime spot for secret meetings, and possibly for sleeping too, but not for much else. I couldn't work there. I scouted out the building and found a much nicer spot to inhabit. Admittedly, it was smaller, but at least it had windows. It looked out onto the Foreign Ministry and a bit beyond that, the Nile. On a sunny day, you can catch the sun glittering on the water's surface. This was my home away from home, for at least 12 hours a day, 6 days a week. There was a little room next to my office, not much more than a cupboard, perhaps 2 metres across, and about 3 metres long. It had a sofa, a television and a fridge. The sofa would prove useful, for it was where I slept during the unrest that would grip Egypt in

2011. Throughout the uprising, my staff and I were unable to leave the building, surrounded by soldiers, barbed wire, concrete blocks, and hundreds, sometimes thousands of angry protesters trying to smash their way in.

I had three and a half thousand people working under me. In truth, I only needed three hundred and fifty, such is the problem with the ERTU and over-employment. Like most of Egyptian society, there was a hierarchy of age in the ERTU. Seniority is derived less from skill or qualifications, but by virtue of being older than one's colleagues. This would be an issue for me. I was younger than the youngest senior manager at the station by a clear ten years. Still, I had a job to do, and would approach it in the professional manner in which I approached all of my work.

I also had a very important man above me. Anas Al-Feky was the Minister of Information, and worked from an office on the 9th floor. He was essentially my superior and would issue various orders and directives as dictated by the Presidential Palace. His hair was thin on top, and his rounded features were bordered by his stern mouth and sharp glasses. He was very close to the President and his family, and, consequently, a very loyal minister, the President's voice. We got on, and I was very honest with him, never bothering to make up excuses for him if I was unhappy with one of his orders.

I wanted to get across the idea to my peers providing news for three stations at the Union, and the public at large, that the TV news was a public good, not just another tentacle of the state. Before I started, the first news item on every bulletin was something to do with the President. On an inconsequential day, it would be a five minute segment. Depending on the significance of his daily activities, these segments could last anywhere up to half an hour. I changed all that. The news order was to be defined by the importance of the day's events, regardless of whether the President had anything to do with them. I changed the timings as well. Within the bulletin itself, no item could take up more than three minutes. This is the way that professional news organisations operate. For the first time, there were current affairs programmes broadcast live on TV, something that would never have been contemplated before, at least not in such a risk averse and censorship-minded place as Egypt. I even had the name of the bureau changed. Before, it was simply known as the "News Sector", now it's the Egypt News Centre.

Despite all the challenges inherent in working in such an unwieldy organisation, the changes stuck, and the powers that be did not object. Unfortunately, I was to discover that when the government talked about reform, it didn't necessarily mean that we should expect it to happen.

President's Mubarak's era, from 1981 to 2011, was one of lost chances. There were various opportunities to push forward reform and spark a renaissance of the Egyptian state throughout his rule, but these chances were never seized upon.

The first of these chances came in 1982, when the then new President pardoned all opposition activists who were rounded up by his predecessor, Anwar Sadat, in an infamous Egyptian September, which contributed to his assassination on the 6th of October 1981. It was the perfect opportunity for Mubarak to win back support of the Egyptian opposition, yet he was never able or willing to establish any kind of cooperation or even understanding with them.

The second chance was after an assassination attempt on his life on the 26th of July 1995 in the Ethiopian capital Addis Ababa. Having almost lost his life, Mubarak won sympathy and support from his citizens. However, his inner circle managed to turn the incident into a farce, forcing Egyptians across the country to take part in mass organised rallies welcoming him home from Ethiopia. Instead of using his brush with death as a base on which to build, the enforced pageantry turned the whole event into a national joke.

Egypt's battle against terrorism throughout the nineties was another missed opportunity. In the face of terror, Egyptians rallied behind the government. Such support should have been used to unify the state and the public, the two of which had for so long been detached from one another. Instead, the extensive Egyptian security apparatus used the threat of terrorism to extend the state of emergency.

Historically, there has always been a great respect within Egyptian culture and society for the country's national security. As a result, the country's police force became something to be respected and feared at the same time. In the three decades of Mubarak's rule, particularly in the last few years, the police came to dominate Egyptian society. The regime was party to their spread in influence, as they resorted to handing many issues and problems, which should have been dealt with politically, to the police.

While Egypt's political system, civil society and economy was weak, the police remained strong, and could always use the ever-present threat of terrorism as an excuse to further empower themselves. Its leaders would pose as the guardians of Egyptian civilised society, valiantly protecting the country from all manner of insidious threats as they kept Egypt stable.

The leaders of the police began to show signs of hubris and contempt for the rest of the country, and this attitude filtered down through the police force. Many policemen began to show arrogance and disrespect to ordinary citizens. Admission to the Police Academy became highly sought after among Egypt's youth. There were stories of the bribes for admission reaching as much as 200,000 EGP, (£20,000 sterling).

At the same time as Egypt began to resemble a police state, the political change which we had been promised failed to materialise.

The 2005 elections, the reason I had been hired in the first place, was yet another missed opportunity for change. It was another sham, which saw the National Democratic Party rig the results. The Islamist organisation, the Muslim Brotherhood, though banned in Egypt, came second with 88 seats. President Mubarak went on to win the first multi-candidate elections that year with 88.6% of the vote.

However, the biggest mistake the government made was the 2010 election. A decision was made to take the Muslim Brotherhood out of the political equation, whilst at the same time push the more radical Islamists, the Salafis, onto the streets.

The National Democratic Party took 95% of the seats. This never happened, neither under Nasser nor Sadat. The NDP had the feeling of power, they didn't expect any response. The latest in a long line of missed opportunities for change in Egypt.

As the government became less politically astute, and Hosni Mubarak headed towards his 80s, Gamal Mubarak ascended the ranks of the NDP.

Gamal Al-Din Mohammed Hosni Al-Sayed Mubarak was born in Cairo in 1963, to the then airforce officer Hosni Mubarak and his wife Suzanne Mubarak. After attending Mrs Woodley's Primary School and St George's College, he went on to major in Business at the American University in Cairo.

He initially began his career working as an investment banker at the Bank of America, before setting up a private equity fund in London.

Gamal Mubarak joined the National Democratic Party in 2000, becoming its Deputy Secretary General in 2007. A number of political powers saw his sudden rise as a step towards his "Inheritance". The term came to dominate Egypt's political life; it had been assumed for many years that he was being groomed to succeed his father as President of Egypt, thus creating a new Egyptian dynasty.

The "inheritance project", as it became known, alienated many of President Mubarak's closest allies. They saw it as a childish and hypocritical pursuit. Some newspapers launched campaigns calling for a rejection of the whole project. The government, however, would ignore these complaints, and Gamal would always weakly deny that he had any ambitions for the presidency.

I first met Gamal Mubarak in 2006. I found him to be very sharp, choosing his words carefully and mindful to cite his sources of information. He was very much his mother's boy rather than his father's son. His obsession with detail and preparation are characteristics he inherited from her. She was well-known for being meticulous. She used to draft all her speeches more than 10 times before she would actually make them, which her speechwriters always used to complain about. The same thing went for Gamal; I had to have an extensive meeting with him going over all the points we would cover in the interview before we actually conducted it. This was a constant complaint from whoever was writing her speech. The same went for Gamal Mubarak, before a televised interview where he was my guest. I had a separate meeting with him to discuss points of debate and I remember telling him during that discussion that the issues of social justice and fighting corruption were the keys to winning over the public, not the billions being pumped into the economy that he was talking about. While the economy may have been growing, the youth still had no more than fifty pounds in their pocket.

One of Gamal's closest confidantes disclosed to me that Gamal's problem lay with his inner circle. He had surrounded himself with a few men whom he trusted, and would listen to no one else. When it came to economics, he deferred to former Trade Minister Rashid Mohammed Rashid and former Minister of Finance Youssef Boutros-Ghali. As for politics, he deferred to Ahmed Ezz, a man who used to be a drummer in a pop group before becoming a powerful yet deeply unpopular politician and businessman.

Economically, working with Rashid and Boutros-Ghali, Egypt actually managed to achieve a respectable level of economic growth and reform. But it was limited reform, as it lacked any social dimension. It did not address Egypt's considerable poverty and social tensions. The economic reform was driven by the provision of investment opportunities for the rich, and resulted in rampant corruption.

One issue that affected Egypt's political life during Gamal's rise to power was the relationship between Gamal and Ahmed Ezz. A short man with a fondness for high collar shirts and platform heels, Ezz used his closeness with Gamal to dominate the National Democratic Party. Using his considerable people management skills and his outstanding wealth, Ezz sidelined the NDP's old guard, usurping them and taking control of the party. He managed to attain a mythic status among the NDP, and create a situation where his assistants became more influential than other top ranking party officials. Despite his influence within the party, on the Egyptian street, Ezz was despised.

Up until 1996, Ezz was nothing more than the owner of a couple of steel and ceramics mills which he had inherited from his father. That year, Ezz started moving up the country's political ladder. He used his new found political power, first as NDP Secretary for Organizational Affairs, then as chairman of the People's Assembly's Budget and Planning Committee, to draft economic laws designed to make conditions more favourable for businesses, specifically his business. He was accused of using his influence to brush aside allegations of corruption and financial irregularities.

He lobbied for the privatisation of the government-owned Al-Dekheila steel company, then promptly bought it himself, without even paying for it up front. He was the only one who had permits for the production of certain types of steel, which forced Egypt's businesses to trade with him. He managed to eliminate anti-monopoly laws, allowing him to tighten his grip on the country's steel industry, going on to personally own 67% of it. When the international price of steel skyrocketed between 2004 and 2008, he made a huge profit. There were unsuccessful attempts by some MPs, and particularly Rashid Mohammed Rashid, former Minister of Trade and Industry, to limit Ezz's power over the national economy, but Ezz managed to shake them off.

Whenever I had the chance to talk with somebody close to power, I would try to explain how damaging Ezz was to the party, and how the public regarded his relationship with Gamal as strange. My criticisms would be met with agreement, but resignation. They had no hope of getting rid of him. The government was unable to deal with its own internal problems.

For other problems, particularly issues that proved to be emotive for the public, the government was not simply unable, it was unwilling to bother with them.

The story of the death of Khalid Saeed was indicative of how the government neglected to tackle important issues, letting them fester until they grew into something much worse.

Khalid Saeed was a young man whose death in Alexandria in June 2010 outraged many Egyptians, including many opposition activists who used it as a weapon against the regime. A Facebook page appeared, *Kulona Khalid Saeed* (We Are All Khalid Saeed), which would go on to attract millions of members.

On the 6th of June 2010, the 28 year old Khalid Saeed lost his life, in what many believe to be an act of brutal torture, at the hands of two police officers who demanded to search him in an internet café, using the emergency laws as justification. When he asked for a reason or a warrant, the officers dragged him away and began administering a savage beating.

Although eye-witnesses reported that the young man was ferociously beaten to death, an official statement from the Interior Ministry claimed that Saeed died from suffocation during his attempt to swallow a packet of hashish while he was resisting arrest.

His death attracted international and national condemnation, sparking protests in Alexandria and Cairo. Matters were made worse when a post mortem photograph of his mutilated corpse found its way onto the internet.

I first heard about Khalid Saeed on the 9th of June 2010 when news spread of angry protests being mounted in Alexandria. We put news of the protests, and the death that preceded them, into our news cycles. I called the assistant to the Egyptian Interior Minister, quite a few times, pushing for a detailed statement to answer questions about the case, and to find out any measures they would be taking to investigate the incident. The assistant played down the issue, claiming that the young man was a drug addict and the case was being blown out of proportion. I got the same response when I tried other government officials. The government did not seem to care, treating public opinion with arrogance and disdain.

The government failed to take any action on the issue, until I learned that Dr Mohammed El Baradei, the former head of the International Atomic Energy Authority, asked for a moment of silence at a meeting he was attending at the London-based international affairs think tank Chatham House. Baradei described Saeed as "Alexandria's martyr," before launching into a savage attack on the government. I informed the Minister of Information about El Baradei's public act of remembrance. Evidently, Anas Al-Feky made some calls to some important people, as the state suddenly engaged in a flurry of activity.

We were notified that the Ministry of Interior was going to give a statement on Khalid Saeed's death. I was, naively, expecting a contrite statement, giving details of the death and promising an enquiry, perhaps even throwing the two policemen into prison.

The statement was a provocative disappointment. It failed to address the beating in which the young man lost his life, instead labelling him a drug dealer and a deserter.

I remember seeing the anger and astonishment on the newscaster's face as he read it out on television. The statement ended with a staunch defence of the police force, which it described as being under attack from malicious rumours.

This was how the government would usually deal with its problems, only taking action on domestic controversies once they were raised internationally. Once they did so, they treated the public with derision. However, the image of Khalid Saeed's dead body was crystallised in the public mind, becoming something that would haunt the regime until the dying days of Mubarak's presidency.

As the government was consistently alienating the public, Egypt's nascent new opposition began to grow. New groups and NGOs were forming, and had to look abroad for funding, due to the constraints of the political system. According to a leaked US embassy cable, the United States spent millions in recent years supporting Egyptian organizations promoting democracy. The report, leaked from the American embassy in Cairo on the 6th of December 2007, stated that the American Agency for International Development (USAID) planned to spend $66.5 million in 2008 and $75 million in 2009 on the promotion of democracy and good governance in Egypt. This money was distributed to NGOs throughout the country.

The Egyptian government was infuriated by the support that the US government gave to groups within the country. Another leaked embassy cable described how the Minister for International Cooperation, Fayza Abu Al-Naga sharply rebuked American aid to Egyptian civil society, in a letter to the US State Department, which the government considered a violation of its sovereignty.

Another leaked embassy cable revealed that back in 2008, Gamal Mubarak aired his concerns about American funding of Egyptian civil society with US Ambassador Margaret Scobey, apparently at one point moaning: "Our job has become much more difficult because of you."

Two of the most famous movements in Egyptian civil society that would play leading roles in 2011 were the April 6th movement and the Kefeya (Enough) movement, though there were many more.

The Kefeya movement emerged in 2004, coming to prominence a year later in and around the elections of 2005. The movement was a broad coalition of groups, campaigning against corruption in the government and calling for social justice, though its most vocal attacks were against President Mubarak himself. In some ways, Kefeya was a predecessor to the youth movements, as it had an older leadership, and many of its members had been involved in traditional opposition parties, yet its calls for direct action were a tactic of the youth. The important achievement of Kefaya, however, which was mirrored in the uprising in 2011, was the way it managed to bring together a wide array of disparate groups under their banner, using broad, shared aims.

Plenty of movements had sprung up in Egypt in the last few years, collectively known as *the youth*. These movements tended to be made up of younger activists, in their 20s or early 30s, who were far more at home with the internet and social media than the political movements of their parents' generation. Whilst they may not have been seasoned political campaigners, they understood concepts such as branding and networking: powerful political tools. Some of this new generation of activists had received training and advice from European and American civil society groups on how to network and develop their online skills. Many youth activists had not been politically inclined previously, though they were educated, and some came from fairly affluent backgrounds. The April 6th youth movement was probably the most high profile of them all.

The April 6th group took their name from their first action, a call for a general strike on April 6th, 2008, on a Facebook page, supporting striking textile workers in El Mahalla El Kubra, an industrial city near the Nile delta. Gradually, the movement grew, attracting tens of thousands of members as their political aims broadened to include calls for protection of human rights, free speech and economic reform. The group went on to adopt a defiant raised fist as their symbol, the same logo as the Serbian *Otpor!* group, which campaigned against Slobodan Milosovic in Serbia back in the late 1990s, a group from which they had drawn some inspiration.

When Ben Ali was toppled from power in Tunisia, the aftershocks were felt in Egypt. The new, young civil society had learned lessons from similar groups throughout the world. Writings on resistance were freely available on the internet, techniques shared in a giant global skills exchange. Mubarak's government had provided the core ingredients of state antipathy (corruption, arrogance, economic disenfranchisement) and Egypt's young civil society had learned the recipe for political change. Tunisia showed Egypt, as it had shown the world, that Arab leaders could be felled by the power of the public.

In spite of all that, I don't think anybody, least of all the government itself, foresaw what would happen next.

JANUARY 24TH – MONDAY

January in Egypt has a taste of its own. Its days are usually warm and the sun is bright, though not burning, and while the nights are chilly, they are far from freezing. January in Egypt is a time for holidays. The schools and the universities break up for mid-term, and most Egyptians use the time to visit relatives, head down the Nile or out to the coast.

January is an important time in Egyptian politics, and sees through several important anniversaries. Egyptians always remember the Great Fire which swept through downtown Cairo on the 26th of January 1952, setting in motion events that led to the Free Officers ousting King Farouk later that July. On the 18th and 19th of January, 1977, protesters were out in force, demonstrating against the Egyptian government's economic policy and the price of bread. Egyptians called those protests the "Public's Uprising" while President Sadat called it the "Thieves' Uprising". The protests were successful, and Sadat was forced to concede to the demands and reintroduce the price controls the government had previously removed.

This particular January in Egypt had started tragically. Only minutes into New Year day 2011, at 12:20 exactly, Alexandria witnessed a horrific bombing in front of Al-Qidessain church, that had killed 21 Coptic Christians and injured up to 79 others. The regime used the fallout from the terror attack to deflect attention away from the scandal of the rigged election the previous November. The attack and the government's response to it (which was criticised as being insensitive) raised the spectre of sectarian tension in Egypt. For the first time since Amr bin Elass brought Islam to Egypt in 641AD, Egyptian Copts demonstrated in condemnation of the attack, demanding equality and the return of their "lost rights".

As Copts marched through the centre of Cairo along the Nile, I watched them from the windows of the Maspero building. The protests were dominated by sectarian language, apparent in their slogans and banners. The threat of sectarian conflict arising in Egypt scared me. I went over to the Cathedral, looking for Pope Shnouda III, head of the Egyptian Coptic Church. The Cathedral had opened its doors to mourners that night. I hoped to convince the Pope to come on television and urge the Copts to prevent an escalation of violence.

I had been warned not to go by a high-ranking security officer, who told me that the Copts had posted young guards at the church armed with petrol bombs. I ignored him. I went in and found the Pope in the main hall receiving mourners with a few bishops and the like, many Coptic figures and businessmen. There were also plenty of government officials, including six ministers. I sat beside the Pope – we have known each other for many years and got on well. We began to talk and it turned into a large debate, with everybody there taking part. We ended up talking for an hour an a half, during which the pope agreed to be interviewed by me on television. It was a great interview. We put it out on the 3rd of January. I hope it went some way to diffusing the tension between the two communities.

There has been a great deal of discord between Muslims and Copts in Egypt in the last few decades, something the government has always struggled to manage, unaware of the sensitivity with which the issue should be treated.

The events that followed the bombing of the Al-Qidessain church did not, however, cause Egyptians to forget about the rest of Egypt's problems. Egyptians were still angry about the rigged November election, rising fuel prices, unemployment and poverty. They hadn't forgotten about the almost daily humiliation some of them suffered at the hands of the police.

The youth opposition groups had called for a demonstration on the 25th of January. They chose the 25th because it was a National Holiday, Eid Al-Shurta "Police Day". The day commemorates a battle in Ismailia between Egyptian policemen and British soldiers, which left 50 policeman dead and another 80 injured on the 25th of January, 1952. It had only been a national holiday since 2008. It was a concession to the police, reflecting the spread of police power in society. The police were much more influential in society than they should have been.

On the 18th of January, the people of Suez took to the streets after Friday prayers, staging demonstrations against the government. Egyptians call the ancient city of Suez the "Brave City", as it has always been at the forefront of Egypt's wars. The residents of the city, however, face the same common hardships all Egyptians suffer from: youth unemployment, poverty and corruption. The protesters were from all strata of society in Suez. After marching on the police station, the police responded with tear gas and rubber bullets. Three protesters were killed.

Inspired by Mohammed Bouazizi, the young man in Tunisia whose act of public self-immolation was the catalyst for the Tunisian revolution, several young Egyptian men attempted to set themselves alight in public in the week leading up to the 25th of January. One succeeded, dying in hospital on the 18th of January.

The Minister of Interior, Habib Al-Adly declared that the security services had apprehended those responsible for the bombing. Although the Police announced that they would hand suspects over to the Attorney General, that never happened. The names of the bombers were never released, and many Egyptians did not believe that the police or the SSIS (the State Security Investigations Service) had caught anybody. During their investigation into the bombing, the police had been accused of torturing to death an innocent 30 year-old Salafi (a Muslim who adheres to a strict, literalist interpretation of the Koran) resident of Alexandria called Sayed Belal.

The 25th of January would be the day for Egyptians to stand up to the police and the Interior Ministry. There were also basic economic and political demands such as the raising of the national minimum wage to 1,200 EGP per month (£120 sterling) from 35 EGP (£3.50 sterling), a figure set in 1984, as well as the repeal of the decades-old emergency laws. In reaction, the Interior Ministry sent a stern warning to the country's political parties, stressing that permits were necessary for demonstrations and threatening legal action against demonstrators if no permits were obtained beforehand. Of course, no permits were acquired by the protesters.

The Muslim Brotherhood officially declared it would not be taking part in the protests, though it did not prevent its members from participating in it by themselves. The more established opposition parties distanced themselves officially from the protests, while the newer youth movements threw their support behind them.

A workshop was organised by the April 6th youth movement, attended by 50 activists nominated to lead the demonstrations. The attendees were briefed on tactics, means of confronting the security forces, and their legal rights in case they were arrested. In parallel, Egyptian expatriate activists announced plans for similar organised protests in the USA, Canada, and United Kingdom, in solidarity with protesters inside Egypt. The National Society for Change issued a statement fixing the main spots of the protests, which were the headquarters of the Permanent Egyptian Mission at the United Nations in New York, the Egyptian embassy in Washington, the quarters of Toronto's city council in Canada and the Egyptian embassy in London.

That Monday, the day before, there were a smattering of protests, about 12 in all, around the country, mostly voicing economic frustration.

On the morning of the 24th, I asked my staff to prepare a studio. I wanted about 30 people, all sitting around in a circle, like those "town hall" style debates you see on television, where the audience was the panel. I wanted the audience to be mostly made up of people from the youth movement, those that were planning and organising out on the streets. I asked my assistant to get into contact with the right people for the debate. To provide some balance and insight, I had in mind maybe three or four older politicians and writers for the show. As the preparations were under way, I went to Anas Al-Feky and asked him to allow some members of the youth opposition movement live on air.

The Minister refused straight away. However, I got on with him, and understood the way he thought. I sat in his office and talked him round to the idea of letting these people on TV. He thought about it for a while, and agreed. It wasn't quite so simple though, and he told me that he had to call Gamal Mubarak. I sat outside the office in a waiting room as the Minister made the call. Gamal was having a meeting with the "big six", the most senior members of the party, in his office in the NDP building just a few hundred metres away on the Nile. As was Gamal's habit, the simple question of whether to allow a few campaigners on TV became a matter for a conference call, and he called upon the top party officials to help him decide. Twenty minutes later, Anas came out and told me that the request had been refused. Apparently, they believed that putting these people on TV would amount to "recognition" (he even used the English word) of the youth movement as a legitimate political force by the government. He went on, telling me that it would make them seem bigger than they really are.

"This is a huge mistake," I told him, before I turned around and headed back to my office, ready to tell my staff to cancel all their preparations.

I went back to my office to tell my colleagues to stop calling representatives of the opposition, and told them the reasons I had been given not to allow those youths to appear on television. I didn't name any names, I never had to, they knew who called the shots.

It was another example of the government's inability to take sensible decisions when it attempted to mitigate and manage crises. Many of the solutions and policies that they instigated to defend themselves would end up causing new problems for them in the future.

For example, two prominent opposition leaders were previously members of the National Democratic Party's influential policy committee presided over by Gamal Mubarak. One of them was promised a high profile position in media, but the promise was never kept, so he turned against them. Another opposition leader left the party and became an opposition leader because he was continuously passed over for promotion within the party, having to sit back and watch less talented and less experienced politicians rise ahead of him. Gamal allowed this to happen because although the politician was charismatic and talented, Gamal was too selfish to work with people that he either did not like personally, or that would make him look poor in comparison.

There was always a feeling that Egyptians would never revolt in such numbers and that they would never be an existential threat to the regime. To them, the public at large would never have the nerve to stand against the government, submissive to the dominance of the National Democratic Party.

However, the new youth movements were far better organised than the opposition movements that had come before. The new generation of activists employed tactics that had not been used by the opposition in Egypt before. Some of these skills included the use of social networking to reach more citizens (probably the most famous aspect of the unrest in Egypt was the role played by Facebook and Twitter), and generalising the reasons for the protests, to attract 40,000 rather than 40.

They used social slogans rather than overtly political or ideological chants so they would be able to canvas a much wider spectrum of political opinion. The protests on the 25th of January would therefore use the emotive issue of torture and police brutality, as well as the sacking of Habib Al-Adly, the Interior Minister, as a rallying call. Khalid Saeed, the young man beaten to death by two police officers in Alexandria became a symbol of the revolution. The Facebook page, *Kulona Khalid Saeed* (We are all Khalid Saeed), which attracted over a million members, became a major hub on the internet for spreading calls for the demonstrations, as well as a powerful networking tool for the protesters. Likewise, protesters could provide instant updates to each other through their Twitter feeds.

An anonymously penned booklet also began to circulate in Cairo, named "How to Revolt Cleverly," (the Arabic title *Keif Tathur Bihadi'a* employed colloquial Egyptian). The book contained information on how to protest, instructions on what clothes to wear, how to mobilise and how to avoid the security services. It used simple diagrams, explaining how to tire out the police, even suggesting the use of spray paint against riot police whilst being attacked. One of the key suggestions that the booklet made was for the protests to begin in smaller side streets, from whence the protesters should march to a pre-ordained central point.

At the time, I was writing a book about political changes to Egypt since constitutional amendments were introduced in 2005. On the 21st of January, I made some notes about the upcoming protests for my book after talking through the issues with some colleagues.

Here's what I wrote:

• Unlike previous demonstrations organised by one group with an organisational head, these protests are being called for by multiple groups. There are many calls for protests issued through the internet and by word of mouth. These groups want to echo what happened in Tunisia.

- Leading groups include the Kefeya movement, the 6th of April movement, and Ayman Nour's Tomorrow party. Some members of these groups have attended training programmes both within Egypt and abroad, learning skills such as leadership, lobbying and citizen journalism.
- The Muslim Brotherhood did not make a public statement until today [21st January], which stated they would not take part, though they don't mind if their youth participate in their own capacity, though not under the name of the Brotherhood.
- The organisers of the protests will not map out specific points in which to protest, rather they will use any available place or chance to gather.
- The 25th of January protest will not be the last, the organisers will plan for more, especially if this one proves successful.

I knew something big was coming. There had been demonstrations before, of course, but these usually consisted of no more than a few thousand people, and they would peter out after a couple of hours. Amongst the government and the security services, people thought the same would be the case.

I couldn't sleep that night. I couldn't remember such a great build up to a demonstration before. They were more organised, more powerful and enjoyed wider support. Nobody in the government seemed to share my concern. I mentioned my worries to Anas, but he just he brushed aside my fears, telling me that the Ministry of Interior had everything under control.

I wasn't so sure.

JANUARY 25TH – TUESDAY

I woke up on the 25th of January with bleary eyes and my mind racing. It had been a rough night. It's hard to stop yourself running through all the possible worst-case scenarios when things look so uncertain. Things had been building up for weeks, months, even years. I just didn't have any faith in the government. They handled crises and adopted policies with such myopia, I couldn't trust them.

Though it was winter, it was a sunny day, about 20 degrees, with a slight breeze in the air. It was a quiet morning, there wasn't the usual hustle and bustle on the roads as it was a holiday. The schools, universities and offices were all shut. Moreover, with protests expected across the country, many families just stayed at home where they would be safe. In Egypt, there's always a risk that things could turn violent during elections, referendums or protests. As such, many people would rather stay home than potentially get caught up in a riot.

There was another reason people didn't get involved. There was a pervading sense of futility and apathy amongst the Egyptian public. The government hated it when people got politically active on the streets, and, regardless of public opinion, would carry on as they had done for decades. Street protests wouldn't change that. Sure, there were a few exceptions, but so many attempts by people to effect change in Egypt had turned out to be in vain. Many simply didn't see the point in going out and protesting.

I went to the office early. I always tried to get in early on the busy days, the days when I knew something big was going to happen. The government newspapers were all talking about how the Interior Ministry had captured the 19 militants responsible for the bombing of the church in Alexandria a few weeks before, dutifully reporting that President Mubarak had thanked the police for their work. The other papers, the ones which weren't controlled by the government, were flagging up a different story, the coming "Day of Rage".

The front page of Al-Ahram, a state-owned national daily, was dominated by a lengthy interview with Interior Minister Habib Al-Adly. Most of the interview dealt with the successful police operation against the church bombers. There was a question about the coming protests, to which he responded, "I say to public opinion, that Facebook calls for these protests were issued by the youth. I call upon the country's intellectuals to raise the youth's awareness on how to love the country they will rule one day. How can these youths destroy their homeland?" He went on, "The fact that youths will be out on the streets will have minimum effect, security forces are capable of controlling any illegal action. Any attempts to harm the citizens' security, or public and private property, will be treated with a firm fist. As for those who want to express their opinion and participate without trouble, the police will protect you and welcome your choice of the day to celebrate your martyrs and express your opinions."

Al-Adly was due to have his annual interview with Mofeed Fawzi, a famous journalist here in Egypt. It was part of an annual ritual the Minister had. He was a man of habit, and perhaps a little bit superstitious too. If he had his interview with this particular journalist at the beginning of the year, he reasoned that it would be a good year. We were supposed to air the interview that evening. Ironically, the Interior Ministry was to launch a PR campaign to improve its image with the public on the 25th of January, with Al-Adly's interview as the opening centrepiece.

There were reports too that the NDP (the ruling National Democratic Party) had tried to organise a counter rally, a "Day of Loyalty", to give thanks to Mubarak for guiding Egypt so benignly over the past 30 years. Thankfully, it didn't come to pass. The security services told the NDP in no uncertain terms that such a demonstration would lead to clashes and open conflict in the streets between the two sides.

In the car, on the way to the Maspero building, I could feel the tension in the air. Perhaps because it was a quiet day in Cairo, something of a rarity. When I got in, I went to the Minister of Information, Anas Al-Feky's office. He didn't seem particularly bothered, he was confident the day would pass like any other. All day, Anas was in constant contact with Al-Adly, regularly engaged in marathon phone calls with him. On the other side, Al-Adly was taking his orders directly from the Presidential Palace. Apparently, Al-Adly said something about this being a good day for his interview, he wasn't concerned at all. Maybe it was because he was always on the phone with Al-Adly, but Anas didn't appear worried either.

I understood that Mubarak was being kept abreast of developments over the phone as well. I noticed that he was being given the usual story, that everything was under control. It was obvious they were careful not to involve him in the details, though for that matter he didn't seem to mind. He ceded authority to Gamal and Al-Adly.

In the morning, the sense of relief among the decision-makers was palpable. They had the same attitude as most in the higher circles of power back then. They couldn't conceive of anyone, least of all these youths, standing against the government. The traditional opposition was very weak and this new youth movement was considered a bunch of opportunists. All it took, they reckoned, was for one of them to be arrested, and surrounding crowds would flee.

Even though the protests were growing larger by the hour, the big news of the morning wasn't the protests in Cairo. They'd just named the new Lebanese Prime Minister, Najib Mikati, to replace

Saad Hariri. Clashes erupted across Lebanon. We were running with it as our major story of the day. Anas called me in my office. He was in high spirits, joking that "even Lebanon is playing for the regime".

He was glad we had the perfect excuse to put Lebanon first in all the news coverage, and it wasn't just us either, the big news channels like Al-Arabiya and Al-Jazeera were all broadcasting live from Lebanon. Evidently, the "Day of Rage" had been bumped. Within Egypt itself, the local protests were running second or third down the running orders in the news bulletins. They were treated as little more than a gathering of various political factions calling for economic reform and improved wages. However, soon enough, the balance was to shift, and as things calmed down in Lebanon, the situation intensified in Egypt.

Anas told me about a meeting he'd been at a few days before with some senior ministers. The issue of the day's protests had come up. President Mubarak was at the meeting, and had given instructions that the demonstrations were to be dealt with peacefully. The security services were not to set a bad example. The government was perpetually concerned about its image abroad, whether it be in the foreign press, international organisations or in the eyes of Western governments. As they reviewed preparations for the protests, it appeared that Al-Adly gave his colleagues his assurance that he had everything under control. He promised them he would use only peaceful means to handle the crowds until the demonstrations were over. In spite of this, they also spent time reviewing procedures for the control and potentially severing of the internet and communications services, should things get out of hand.

From the early hours of the morning, security forces were deployed throughout central Cairo. The streets and squares were filled with armoured cars, fire engines, ambulances and trucks laden with soldiers. The police had erected steel barriers to control the crowds. Many were adorned in full riot gear. At around midday, the protests really started gathering momentum. The protests were taking place right in the heart of downtown Cairo, not far from the Maspero building. I could hear the slogans from outside my window, I kept hearing the word "Batal" shouted over and over. In English, it means "void". They were talking about the new parliament, and as far as they were concerned, it was void. Another slogan that was echoing across the streets was "Hubz! Hurria! Adala Agtimaiah!" – "Bread! Freedom! Social justice!" We had cameras out in the city, broadcasting what was going on.

Sitting in my office, I heard a slogan I didn't quite understand. I'd been involved in politics for years, and had been to a few protests back in my student days, and I thought I knew all the slogans people shouted at these rallies. I sent out one of my assistants to find out what it was. He came back and told me, "They are saying 'Al shaab yureed isqat al nizaam' – 'The people want to overthrow the regime,' but it wasn't quite shouted in the Egyptian dialect. It wasn't the words or the meaning that was hard to understand, it was the vocal inflections, the diction. It was a slogan from Tunisia.

It was just after midday when the Supreme Court, right in the centre of Cairo, was targeted by a group of protesters led by former MPs and candidates who had run in the 2010 parliamentary elections and failed to win a seat. All the while, they were shouting "Null and Void!" A few meters away, inside the Egyptian Bar Association, the crowd kept chanting "I swear with its skies and soil, the NDP wreaked havoc on it!"

On the next street along, another crowd marched past the Judges Club (The Egyptian judges' syndicate) chanting the same word again and again: "Freedom…freedom…freedom," without any banners or placards. Security forces were perplexed as the cries of freedom reverberated between the buildings. They tried in vain to keep the latest crowd from joining the swarm outside the

Supreme Court, throwing their bodies between the two masses. The chants grew louder as the three groups of demonstrators converged to form a single, heaving entity. As the horde expanded, they pushed on to the nearby Al-Galaa Street, incessantly chanting "freedom," as they marched on to Tahrir Square.

Another group began to congregate next to the Maspero building, where we were, chanting anti-media slogans and accusing it of misleading the public. They then moved towards the Ministry of Foreign Affairs, shouting the word "loser". On Al-Galaa Street, they rallied in front of state-owned newspapers; Al-Ahram, Al-Gumhuriya, Al-Akhbar, chanting "Where is the press... here is the Egyptian people," before marching towards Al-Atba Square, one of the busiest commercial districts in Cairo.

Thousands joined the legions of protesters as they proceeded towards the centre of the city. In overwhelming numbers, and chanting the whole time, they managed to break through security barricades around Tahrir Square with ease, rushing inside once it was breached. They were continually joined by passing citizens, enraptured by the moment who found in it the perfect opportunity to express their anger and suppressed frustration. The crowds continued to swell as the unrest spread to Abdel Moneim Riad Square, the main gateway to Tahrir Square. All the security cordons which guarded the entrances to the squares surrounding Tahrir Square were easily overcome by the sheer mass of people who surged through the barriers and security cordons. The ever expanding flood of bodies marched on to the headquarters of the Interior Ministry. However, the impenetrable block of police surrounding the Interior Ministry pushed them towards Qasr El-Nil Bridge, on the Nile.

On the bridge, protesters, estimated at over 2,000, were joined by another group of demonstrators coming from the nearby districts of Dokki and Mohandiseen from the other side of the Nile. They forged ahead towards the National Democratic Party headquarters on Corniche El-Nil Street, sounding anti-NDP slogans.

On the ground, one could find political parties, unions, protest movements, civil society organizations, think-tanks as well as unattached individuals with competing ideologies. In addition, thousands of Egyptian University students participated for the first time, declaring their rejection of the deteriorating economic, social and political status.

Tahrir Square really started to fill at around 2pm when protesters gathered from downtown Cairo, the Supreme Court and Bar Association, as well as areas like Shubra, Dar Elsalam, Boulak Eldakrour. They kept chanting, "The people want to overthrow the regime" and "Down, down, all corrupt!", "Welcome, welcome Change!" and the slightly more poetic "O, loaf where are you? Unemployment comes between us."

The question of why ordinary citizens joined was one that the former government totally failed to address. They didn't notice any of the warnings. On the 25th of January, not only in Tahrir Square, but across downtown Cairo, Egyptian citizens gathered, from all walks of life, from young children to the elderly. They all joined in the Day of Rage, even though they may not have previously considered any political affiliation or adhered to any ideology.

Each one of those protesters could reel off tragic stories from their lives, detailing countless instances of economic disenfranchisement and political disillusion. People were talking about spending the night inside the Square to keep the demonstration going until their demands were met even "if it went on for days".

Many of those who went out on the streets to protest felt that in the eyes of the government, they had no value. In order to make their government pay attention, they needed to partake in protest and direct action for the first time in their lives. It was those ordinary people, for whom this was a completely new experience, who caught the attention of the media.

One newspaper provided some examples of these unseasoned dissenters. In the article, the journalist described how he found a number of young people sitting away from the main gathering:

We thought at the beginning that they were security men working undercover in the demonstrations, especially as one of them was wearing a white coat similar to that usually worn by the informants in Egypt. After standing next to them a while, we found that their discussion suggested otherwise. They indulged us with a discussion on their reasons for participating in the demonstrations.

We found out that the young man with the white coat was called Ahmed Abdalbasser, 35, graduated from the Higher Institute of Social Services, with no political affiliation. When we asked him why he was here, he said: "I graduated nearly 10 years ago and up till now I could not get a job or any kind of work that would provide me a decent life; I worked in a pastry bakery, and as a salesman and in any other available job, but yet I have not settled on enough income. My salary does not exceed 500 pounds, what do I do with it? Shoes are 200 pounds, and trousers cost 150 pounds which means that I work all month to buy shoes, pants and a shirt?"

"I have submitted my CV to dozens of jobs, but I failed each time because of nepotism, in addition to what the government is doing to us in the form of humiliation and contempt. Several weeks ago, I was stopped by a police soldier in the street and he insisted on doing a full body search for no good reason. And when I asked him why he was doing it, he said 'This is what I have to do. I can also put you under arrest till someone asks about you. Did you forget about the emergency law?' So I decided to shut up and obey him, because I knew he could follow through on all his threats. I will not find a defender against him, but I will never forget the bitterness I felt then," said Ahmed with clear sadness.

Regarding his political affiliations, he said he does not belong to any political movement, "I'm not convinced of any of those, as there is nothing personal between me and the State's leadership, starting from the President and his son, to the smallest official." He added "We just want them to provide jobs and stop the humiliation."

Ahmed had a realistic vision. His ambition did not go beyond the demonstration, saying that he was not optimistic about what happened in Tunisia, and did not want to see it repeated. "Because the magnitude of the loss would be greater than in Tunisia; we just want tonight to be the beginning of a change in Egypt, or even a baby step towards change."

Next to Ahmed, in the white coat, sat another skinny young man with a small moustache dressed in a janitor's uniform. They had no previous acquaintance but they were brought together by the same agony and the same demands. I asked him his name.

"I am Hassan Abd Al-Fatah, 26 years old. I left education after middle school. I work as a janitor in a company," said Hassan

Hassan is originally from Beni Suef governorate. He moved to Cairo 8 years ago where he lives in a crumby room near downtown. When he learned that protesters were gathering in the square asking for change he decided to leave his job and protest with them as he also suffers from poverty, need and despair.

"I work 7 hours a day for 350 EGP a month ($58), which isn't sufficient to cover my personal expenses, let alone support my family back home. Therefore, I started working two shifts for 18 hours and I get 700 EGP ($117), which is again not enough. That is why I decided to join protesters, hoping for a change that will raise our salaries or reduce prices," said Hassan. When asked about any fears of arrest or detention, he responds "Even if they lock me up I will at least be guaranteed a free meal. Prison will not be worse than the outside world," said Hassan spontaneously.

The journalist elaborated on the scene on the ground, saying that among the crowds a lonely child standing by himself stood out.

He looked really young and his clothes were all torn. He was holding a piece of wood that was taller than him. When he was asked about the reasons behind his coming to the square he replied in a manly tone "I came to take back what is rightfully mine." His words caught the attention of a large number of people surrounding him who gathered to listen to the boy.

His name is Moustafa, 11 years old. He never went to school because of his father's tough financial circumstances. He works in shops to earn a living. He comes daily from Embaba to downtown where he works.

When he was asked to explain what he considers rightfully his, he replied:

"I want to get my rights so that I will not turn into a thief," said Moustafa

When asked about the wooden stick he was holding, he said "the police officer hit me for no good reason and I hit him back with a stone and ran and I am holding this stick to hit back at anyone who tries to beat me."

Ahmed Khamis, another protester, shared the same story with most people in the square. He graduated from law school nine years ago and has not found a job since, "I still get an allowance from my mum, after failing to get a job. I could not survive on 150 pounds monthly in return for working as a trainee lawyer," said Khamis. "I have no place of my own or a salary. I have no income and I came here to protest against all that I am going through, instead of setting myself on fire in the street like many did in the previous days. We have no dignity inside our country or even outside."

Khalid Kamal is a shop owner in Omrania. He came along with his wife to protest what he called 'injustice and corruption' stressing that they have nothing to fear, including arrest or death, before saying in a loud voice "Death is better than a life with no dignity".

His wife asserted that women have the same role as men and that she experiences the same injustice and the worsening circumstances that everyone else feels. She insisted on going on with the strike until everyone's demands are met, saying toppling the regime is the solution.

A young girl sat in one of the corners alone, her name was Amal, she graduated from nursing school and she works in a hospital. Concerning the reasons behind her attendance in the protest alone she said, "I asked all my friends to join but they refused in spite of their desire to participate because of their families' rejection of the idea, girls don't go to demonstrations." When asked about why her family didn't object, she said "My parents died and I work to support my five brothers and sisters. I participate in this demonstration for them, to provide them with a better living, to get them their rights back, which guarantee them as orphans not to be deprived of anything."

By seven thirty that evening, five hours after their commencement, the protests really began to take shape, both physically and politically. Some demonstrators gathered to form a leadership committee at the headquarters of *Al-Ghad* or the "Tomorrow" party, lead by the charismatic dissident Ayman Nour. They agreed on their final demands. These demands were later announced through a loudspeaker by Dr Osama Al-Ghazaly Harb, head of the oppososition Democratic Front in Tahrir Square. Harb was a leading member of NDP and a member also of the political committee of the party which was headed by Gamal Mubarak before moving to the opposition.

The demands included four main points:

- President Mubarak was not to run for another term.
- Gamal Mubarak was not to run for the presidency.
- The resignation of Ahmed Nazif's government, dissolution of parliament, the Shura Council and local councils.
- The appointment of a national salvation government for 6 months, paving the way for a new constitution.

After Harb finished his announcement, the crowd began to cheer, with those who scaled the traffic lights and lampposts encouraging the noise from their elevated vantage points. Protesters chanted "Raise! Raise! Raise your voice!…those who protest will not die!" and "Oh you Egyptians, answer us…are you with us or against us?!"

The exact numbers of police out in the streets were difficult to gauge; some estimates put them at almost 30,000. Most were in uniform though there were many plain clothes officers scattered amongst the crowds. When the crowds got too raucous, the riot police used water cannons, tear gas, and even rocks in an attempt to disperse them. The violence escalated. Minor clashes were reported across Cairo and also in the other provinces around the country where protests had been staged. Most of these clashes ended with injuries inflicted on protesters, with others carted away by the police. A number of police were also wounded.

There weren't any religious slogans or chants until about 3pm. The Muslim Brotherhood, hitherto thought of as the largest opposition movement in Egypt had decided not to participate in the day's protests. However, as the momentum of the day grew, it was clear that they didn't want to be left out. By mid-afternoon, Muslim Brothers started sporadically appearing on the streets. You could see them praying in the streets and hear some of their Islamist rallying cries. Only then was there any religious flavour to the demonstrations, though again, the main tide of the protest was still focused on the country, the economy and for the most part, last year's election.

The one thing that united everyone out on the street was their anger at the 2010 election. There were NDP members, opposition party members, Muslim Brothers and ordinary Egyptians who all had anger to vent over the ballot the previous November. Political power in Egypt rests on the size of one's family. That's also the way it worked out on the street, so many of those who felt aggrieved brought their families and supporters with them, that's how the protests began with such momentum. There was also a section of people there who hadn't been involved in politics. These were people who felt that they'd been treated unfairly, that they couldn't afford to live at a respectable standard. As became clear, these protests were led by the youth of Egypt. They weren't simply out on the streets demanding work, many of them had jobs, they went out wanting a good job, a job which they could do with self respect and provide them proper wages to live on.

The street protests that day were the fruits of Gamal Mubarak and Ahmed Ezz's labour. Gamal and his advisor, Ezz, had long sought to rule Egypt using Mubarak senior's presidential authority. Of course, the ultimate responsibility lies with the President for leaving everything to his son and his cronies. However, even when they spoke to the President, to tell him what was going on, they always gave the impression that they had more control over Egypt than they really did. This had been going on for years. They never wanted to disturb the President, they wouldn't give him the bad news, they wouldn't pressure him, they would always try and sort out problems before they went to him.

Late one night, back in November the year before, I got a call from one of the President's private secretaries when I was heading home in my car. The President was in the United Arab Emirates, on an official state visit. "Al-Basha wants to speak with you," said the voice down the line. That was what the immediate circle around the President used to call him, "The Pasha" harking back to the old days of colonial Egypt. The President wanted to talk to me about the opposition politicians whom we'd had on television. It was around the time of the parliamentary election, so we were regularly broadcasting political debates featuring opposition politicians and representatives from the ruling party, the NDP. Mubarak called me after he watched the programme on TV. He said the speakers we had on TV were very weak. He said, "They don't know what's going on in the country, they don't have all the information."

"This is all we have Mr President," I said to him, "this election is all we have to give the civil opposition the opportunity to become part of the system." I accepted what he said, but took the opportunity to ask him what he thought of some news events that day. I asked him what he thought about what the Prime Minister of Ethiopia, Meles Zenawi had said in the morning. The Ethiopian leader had just launched a savage attack against Egypt in a dispute over the Nile, full of vitriol and threatening to sever relations. He accused Egypt of sponsoring rebel groups within Ethiopia and declared that if Egypt went to war with upstream countries over the Nile, it would lose. The President simply responded by asking me "What did he say?" I couldn't believe it. After I explained to him what had been said, he just dismissed it and said, "Oh, he's just talking, don't worry about it." But that wasn't the point. It was incredible that no one had even bothered to inform the President of one of the most inflammatory statements made in years by one of our closest neighbours. It was left to me, when I managed to catch his ear by chance, 14 hours later.

I had only interviewed him once before, in late 2009, a few months after his grandson's death. Apparently, he asked for me personally. The President and his wife respected me, and in turn, I respected them. I was never that close to them, but there was definitely mutual respect between us. I never had the same chemistry with Gamal. He would often try to have interviews with other journalists ahead of me, though it was his interviews with me that people remembered.

The interview with the President took place down in Aswan, on top of the high dam; it was the first interview he'd done on television since the death of his grandson. I'd flown down to Luxor and taken a car to Aswan. It was a long trip. When I arrived, I sat waiting for him to finish his morning meeting. Before we got started, I was told not to pressure him, not to push him, and just cede control of the interview to him, and if he wanted to stop the interview, I was to stop. His advisers and those close to him just wanted him to be kept in his comfort zone. When I finally sat down with the President and got the interview started, there wasn't any need for any of that. We just sat and talked for 45 minutes. Even before and after the interview, he was just telling me stories. He started going on about how he'd been everywhere in Egypt, personally visited every part of the country. He said that there was just one place he hadn't been, Wadi Gadid, but he would go there someday. He was proud of how much he knew Egypt, how he knew every inch of its sky. Looking back on it now, I realised that the man was never in touch with Egypt, or at least, hadn't been for a good few years. The people around him were overprotecting and, in the process, isolating him. It was always in the name of security, everything was about security, especially since his predecessor was assassinated.

I kept asking the people around him, "Why don't you just let him talk to people?" In Egypt, Friday prayers is a huge deal. People don't pray all the time, many aren't even that religious, but Friday prayers is still important to the country. Somebody could be robbing a bank in the morning and they would still turn up to the mosque for Friday prayers. I asked "Why don't you let Mubarak go to a mosque, in any one of the towns in Egypt?" But they wouldn't have any of it. They wouldn't let him talk to anybody. In some ways, he did little to get back involved in the day to day running of the country. I don't think he could have even if he tried.

It really boils down to two major incidents in the last couple of years of his presidency. Back in 2010, he'd had an operation on an inflamed gall bladder. He'd had the procedure done in Germany, and it was deemed a success, but he was never quite the same afterwards. The other event was the death of his grandson. The boy, his grandson through Alaa, was twelve when he died, back in 2009. The two of them were very close, in the way that grandsons often are with their grandfathers. The government didn't say how he died at the time, only that it was related to an existing condition. It turned out to be a brain haemorrhage. From then on, he just delegated everything to Gamal.

Throughout the day, I was having regular meetings with Anas Al-Feky. I kept him updated with the latest developments picked up from our field reporters throughout the country. I briefed him on the escalating situation in Suez, where there were increasing reports of clashes between the police and protesters, as well as worrying news of serious injuries inflicted on both sides. Demonstrations in Alexandria were gaining strength, with more opposition leaders unexpectedly taking part. He didn't seem particularly surprised by these developments. I had the feeling I was telling him things that he already knew, as he was in constant contact with the Interior Minister, Al-Adly.

Just before sunset, Anas made an attempt to defuse the crisis by contacting some of the leading opposition figures involved in the protests. He intended to initiate a round of negotiations between the opposition and the government. Initially, his attempts seemed promising, as three opposition figures accepted his invitation and arrived in his office. Among them were Mohammed Moustafa Sherdy, the former Wafd Party MP for Port Said who withdrew from the 2010 parliamentary elections in the second round, and Rami Lakah. Lakah was a wealthy businessman who had recently returned to Egypt after years of self-imposed exile with a settlement deal to pay back his loans to Egyptian banks. Shortly afterwards he joined the Wafd Party and ran for the 2010 parliamentary elections but lost due to Ahmed Ezz's questionable election management skills.

For more than two hours, Anas discussed with his guests their demands but could not resist imparting some slight criticism of their participation in the protests, telling them that it was a trivial event for them to be getting involved with. He stressed in the meeting that specific steps towards reform would be taken, especially in relation to court rulings concerning MPs' fraudulent votes in parliament. He also stressed the importance of dialogue with them and with other legitimate opposition politicians in the future.

Contrary to the reports of the meeting that appeared in later months, the atmosphere was fairly cordial. His guests expressed willingness to take Anas's proposals into consideration. Anas dutifully reported what had been said over the phone to the President and his senior advisers.

However, in spite of Anas's attempts to open a dialogue with some of the government's opponents, the protests had taken on a life of their own and lasted far longer into the night than anyone had expected. Tensions rose among crisis managers at the top of the government, and phones started ringing off the hook as they all chased each other, trying to mitigate the unfolding predicament. In spite of the panic, there was an unmistakable air of confidence among the decision-makers, brought on by Al-Adly's repeated assurances that he had everything under control.

By evening, the Interior Ministry issued its first statement since the protests began that morning and as usual it lacked political intelligence and stuck to its traditional tone of addressing previous minor protesting actions.

"In a bid to give a better chance to protesters to express political or categorical demands through the previous period, in line with the road to democracy, and to allow freedom of expression and despite the provocative approach used by instigators of the 25th of January gathering, claiming it as the means to escalate their demands and led by the Muslim Brotherhood group, what is called 6th April and Kefaya movements as well as the National Association for Change, protesters were permitted to organise protests. The protests centred in the cities of Cairo, Alexandria and Al-Gharbia. Other governorates also witnessed limited gatherings which ranged from a hundred to a thousand. Police forces were committed from the beginning to secure these protests without obstructing them, in spite of them turning violent. Some of these marches in downtown Cairo brought the traffic to a complete halt and pushed it into alternative roads. Leaders of these gatherings insisted on this incitement and refused calls to evacuate the square even after they were given a full chance to express their opinion."

The statement ended with what I believe to be the biggest mistake they made that day:

"Despite all that, by 6pm, the Muslim Brotherhood group mobilised huge numbers of its members to go to Tahrir Square in Cairo. The number of protesters exceeded ten thousand and some of them threw stones at police forces on Qasr Al-Aini Street, and others were involved in riots and damaged public property which caused injures in the lines of police forces."

Complete rubbish. Anybody watching TV on any of the stations covering the demonstrations could see that they patently weren't being directed by the Muslim Brotherhood. OK, some Muslim Brothers were participating, but there were people there from every opposition movement in Egypt. Just before sunset, they started gathering in Tahrir square. There couldn't have been more than 10,000 of them. The police started marshalling them, telling them to go home and so on. The protesters were having none of it.

Towards the end of the day, after hours of provocation, some protesters started hurling stones at the police. Others tried to calm the situation, calling in their fellow demonstrators to stop clashing with the police. Some groups formed human shields in front of the security forces chanting "Selmia…selmia" – "Peaceful… peaceful".

After security forces retreated to Qasr Al-Aini Street, which leads south out of Tahrir Square, protesters tried to break through the security blockade to reach the Interior Ministry and Parliament which are just off Qasr Al-Aini, a short way down the street. Police responded immediately with tear gas, forcing the instigators to call off their attack and remain within the square.

As the day faded into night, at around 8pm, more protesters flooded into the square from across the Nile, coming from places like Embaba, a notoriously poor and run down district in north-west Cairo. The demonstrators greeted their newly arrived compatriots with applause and chants, yelling, "Here they are!... The Egyptians…here they are!"

Some of the more well-known political personalities tried to exploit the circumstances and the captive audience and give speeches to the crowd. Most refused to listen and carried on chanting: "Bread…Freedom…Social Justice".

There were growing calls from within the square for the protesters to unify their demands and start an open sit-in until they were met. At that point, some demonstrators decided to draft a statement, laying out their demands and their positions. Committees were formed to direct and organise the demonstrations in Tahrir Square. These committees provided logistical support for protesters in addition to keeping the protesters supplied with food and water.

Missions were specified and assigned to different groups, or rings, of protesters. This division of labour enabled constant protests in the square. Some protested in front of security barricades, some would be chanting or singing, while others rested or slept. It was ensured that each protest ring would receive a meal that night. Later on, blankets were brought into the square in preparation for them spending the night there. When the blankets arrived, they were greeted with cheers and applause from the protesters.

At around 10pm, one of the protesters had managed to climb onto one of the traffic lights holding a microphone attached to a huge speaker. He announced that he was, "Change Radio…from Tahrir Square!" It began with some songs by Sheikh Imam, a blind singer famous in the 60s and 70s for his politically-charged music. Instructions were given to the demonstrators through the speaker to stay until morning, whilst reiterating calls for solidarity between protesters. Before midnight, hundreds of protesters were chanting patriotic songs in time with "Change Radio".

Under the circumstances, I did not think it would be wise to broadcast the usual two-hour interview with the Interior Minister. The streets were crowded with protesters. There was some real anger out there. Anas refused. He told me that a pre-recorded interview with the Minister had to be broadcast on "Police Day".

We started broadcasting it at around 10pm. It was a lengthy interview, recorded two days earlier, addressing a number of issues, including the Alexandria bombings and the status of Egyptian Copts, the Muslim Brotherhood, and the Salafi Islamic movement among other things. Generally, he seemed confident and in control, presenting himself as a man without whom Egypt couldn't survive.

Al-Adly stressed in his interview that there was a possibility of blocking certain websites, which were used to recruit the youth for terrorist operations. He added that the block might only be temporary, as a permanent block would be impossible as most of these sites are run by overseas foreign entities who could circumvent such measures. He also declared that there were cases of Egyptians being recruited by Al-Qaeda.

In relation to the recent revolution in Tunisia, Al-Adly stressed that there were no comparable circumstances, saying that what happened in Tunisia was "destruction and ruin." He said that Egypt did not shake because of what had happened there, and neither did its officials. He repeated that there was no possible comparison to be made between Tunisia and Egypt, as the whole world believed in Egypt's stability. He added that freedom of expression has its boundaries, though the state allows and ensures freedom of speech.

The timing of the interview, along with some of the Minister's more contemptuous statements, was appalling.

At around the time the interview ended, at midnight, the police had had enough with those in the square. The police were reorganising their lines and mobilising large numbers of reinforcements. Since sunset they had been issuing frequent warnings to break up the demonstrations and evacuate the square. They gave the crowd a deadline. They were to disperse by midnight. Sure enough, the deadline came and went. The police started resorting to the old tactics. Tear gas was launched into the crowd and shots were fired.

Security forces were launching teargas canisters through cannons to give them further reach inside the square. Faced with the hail of streaming gas shells, spewing out their acrid fumes, the crowd fled in different directions into the streets surrounding the square. Some attempted to throw the teargas canisters back at security forces. Within minutes of the deadline passing, over 100 gas canisters had been launched into the crowds. It was impossible for protesters to hold their positions inside the square, as some fled, others were forced into clashes with the security forces.

Security forces retained control over Tahrir Square and established numerous security points around the area. Though the square had been cleared, there were still large numbers of protesters scattered throughout Cairo's central streets and the smaller Abdel Moneim Riad Square. The police hunted them until a large number gathered in front of NDP headquarters at Corniche El-Nil Street, on the banks of the Nile. Demonstrators attacked the building's main gate and smashed its windows. The strike at the party headquarters provoked fierce retaliation from the police, resulting in running battles between the police and protesters. Another group gathered in front of the Maspero building, where we were based, cutting off the road and preventing cars from getting through, while destroying the police traffic blocks on the road. Microbus drivers joined in the clashes, in solidarity with the protesters, helping set fire to the blocks, following them to Abdel Moneim Riad Square. In front of the Egyptian Museum, on the south side of Tahrir Square, a group of protesters managed to stop a police car, forcing the police inside to flee as they set it on fire.

Finally, after hours of protesting, and later outright fighting, the crowds began to dissipate in the early hours.

By the night's end, after the police had finished with the crowd and the square was cleared, Habib al-Adly ordered his driver to drive through Tahrir Square. Anas told me about it; he said that Habib was happy, as if they had accomplished something. I was disgusted, I told Anas "He's not invading a foreign country. There was no victory. It was a demonstration." I had a bad feeling about it, the idea that one of our ministers would take his car to the site of protests. Habib was telling everyone around him, boasting about it. I didn't think there was anything to boast about.

JANUARY 26TH – WEDNESDAY

We finished at around three in the morning the night before, after everything had been settled and the air in Cairo was filled with the unmistakable acrid smell of tear gas, seeping in through our windows.

I came into work slightly earlier than usual, at around half past seven in the morning. The mood in the street was still not quite back to normal, there was a hint of tension in the air. I went to my office, and started checking in with my reporters. I had correspondents in Cairo, Alexandria and Suez. They told me that all the demonstrations were nearly the same, small groups gathering in adjoining streets before marching towards a central focal point in their respective cities. When the police moved in on them, they would disperse, only to move back again to areas which the police had left open. It was tiring for the police. There were individual leaders directing the protests, but nobody knew who they were. When the masses move, all they need is one loud voice to mobilise them. The masses of people were angry, depressed and annoyed. All those organising the protests needed to do was throw out some slogans and the protests gathered momentum by themselves.

The biggest demonstration we had had in Egypt in the last few years, organised by the April 6th movement, had consisted of no more than 5,000 people. One of the leaders of that movement was recently called up to do his national service. The general in charge of the section he was posted to told me of a conversation he had had with the young man about the recent protests. He told him that when they organised the demonstration on the 25th of

January, even the organisers were taken by surprise by the large numbers they attracted. The original plan was to have a protest on the 25th of January, then another one on the 6th of April and then a larger nationwide demonstration on the day of the presidential election, which was supposed to have been held in September. Nobody expected the protests to take off like they did. Though it seems so entrenched now, the whole idea of an "Arab Spring" had not really emerged yet. The Tunisian President had fallen, but Tunisia was never a great powerhouse or trendsetter in the Middle East.

These protests had touched a nerve. They were the voice of the collective anger which had built up over many years. People were fed up, and the government had been blind. The protests were very much an uprising driven by the long silent middle class of Egypt. The revolution in Tunisia had been largely driven by the educated middle class over there, and suddenly we had been reminded of the disenfranchised middle class we had here in Egypt.

Looking back over the previous day's events, reviewing the footage and reports from our correspondents, it became clear that the government had made two major mistakes. Firstly, they blamed the whole thing on the Muslim Brotherhood. The second blunder was the way they dealt with Suez.

Suez is an old city, continuously inhabited since the days of the pharaohs. Despite the fact that Suez is towards the north of the country, it is very much an Upper Egyptian city. The people in Upper Egypt have more fire in their blood than their cousins to the north. Incidentally, when we refer to Upper Egypt, we mean the south of the country. Many Egyptians from Upper Egypt live lives enriched by tradition, and place great value on ancient conventions relating to death, family and honour.

The security forces handled protests in Suez poorly. They were insensitive, they were arrogant. Two demonstrators were killed in Suez by the police that day.

There is a very strong tradition in Egypt, and throughout the Islamic world generally, that commands the dead be buried as soon after death as possible. It also ties into very strong notions of respect for the dead that date back to our ancient history. When the families of the dead protesters appealed for the return of the bodies of their loved ones from the authorities, they were refused. I'm not sure where in the chain of command the refusal came from, whether from the governor or some ill-mannered police commander. The insult infuriated the demonstrators more than anything that had gone on that day. It could possibly have been more divisive than the reasons for calling the Day of Rage in the first place. Not only was it an insult to the grieving families, it was also an insult to the very culture of the people.

Suez would remain a real hotspot for protest over the following days. Even when unrest died down in other parts of the country, tempers would still run high in Suez. Hafiz Salama, a respected leader of popular resistance in Suez, tried to intervene and have the corpses of two protesters released, though the negotiations were not immediately successful. Even though the bodies were subsequently returned the families, a wound had been opened. A wound that would not heal as the crisis dragged on.

The demonstrations continued on the Wednesday, though in much smaller numbers. Many people had opted to return to work and carry on with their lives. The day before, the protests had managed to attract people who weren't politically involved at all. However, on Wednesday, the protesters mostly consisted of the core activists. Tuesday was a holiday, Wednesday was not. People had jobs to go to. Even though people had returned to work, Cairo remained in chaos. The markets had been thrown into disarray and the stock market crashed.

The Muslim Brotherhood also had to make a big decision on Wednesday. I have some good friends in the Brotherhood, and some good journalistic connections too. Throughout my career,

I've always been interested in Islamic politics and have done a great deal of investigative work on Islamist groups in Egypt. When I called around my connections, they explained to me the situation in which the Brotherhood had found itself.

The Muslim Brotherhood had decided to throw their support behind the protests, and, more importantly, to continue with them to the end. When the Interior Ministry announced that the Muslim Brotherhood was at the forefront of the unrest, the Brothers felt their backs against the wall. They decided to take action because they believed that if the government remained as it was after the uprising was over, they would use the recent civil disorder as an excuse to crack down on the Brotherhood harder than ever before. The Brothers had to force some kind of change in the government in order to survive.

The Brotherhood has an international network, it receives some funding from the Gulf and some sympathisers based in Europe and the US, and has links to various sister organisations set up in other Middle-Eastern countries. The Brothers strongest ties were in Gaza, Sudan, and Yemen, all areas with large numbers of Islamist activists and sympathisers. Hamas, the Islamist government of Gaza evolved out of the Gaza branch of the Brotherhood. The Brothers would call on these logistical and financial resources in the coming days. The Brothers would take part in all the demonstrations, although they would refrain from chanting and displaying the more overt Islamist slogans or banners. For the Brothers, it was a matter of life or death.

I met up with Anas in his office, shortly after he arrived in the morning. He told me how Habib Al-Adly had boasted to other senior ministers in the government the night before about driving his car around Tahrir Square after the police had cleared it. The major players in the government, particularly those around the President, were still confident that Al-Adly and his Interior Ministry had everything under control.

Gamal, Zakaria Azmi and Anas had concocted another plan. In an effort to counter the bad publicity the protests had aroused, they resolved to spread all the government ministers and party officials across Egypt's TV stations and news programmes. It was to be an all out media assault. The schedules were packed with NDP leaders: it was almost an occupation. Each of these ministers would laboriously put the government's case to the public, while at the same time decrying the anti-government protests. It was a curious tactic, as it had often been very difficult to get anybody to speak on behalf of the government, before the start of the unrest.

The government also began bringing its ministers home. Safwat El-Sherif, the General Secretary of the ruling National Democratic Party was abroad at the time, as his wife was undergoing treatment for cancer. He was called back. Ahmed Ezz, one of Gamal's key allies at the top of government, was also called back from overseas.

Upon Safwat's return, he was instructed to comment over the telephone during some of our current affairs programming. His tone was slightly more conciliatory, acknowledging economic problems, but still warning the youth not to protest, and, importantly, to stay away from political movements which the government considered unsavoury. He even appealed directly to the political groups that had been active in Egypt. On one talk show, *90 minutes*, he made a particularly provocative statement, saying, "Please, raise your hand against our youth – don't spoil them. They are keen, they are good, we understand what they want and we will do it for them." It was a provocative statement, and particularly dismissive of those calling for protests. All the while, he reiterated that the party was still powerful, and would not be shaken by this recent civil unrest.

I went up to Anas's office again before lunch with a view to convincing him that it still wasn't too late to get some of the youth leaders on TV.

"Look, I know it's complicated," I told him, "but we still have the time to do it."

"I know, I know, trust me, I understand what you're saying," came his reluctant reply, "but you saw yourself that we have instructions from them [the Presidential Palace]. The youth should not go on air. We will stick to this."

Anas had received further instructions from above. As part of the new media offensive on every television channel, state and commercial, there was to be programming attacking the Muslim Brotherhood.

Anas made a few phone calls in front of me with managers, directors and presenters in privately-owned TV stations, lobbying hard to keep everybody on message. While the Interior Ministry was accusing the Brotherhood of leading the movement, the media would seek to undermine the Brotherhood's image in the public eye. Curiously, even the private commercial stations and news organisations agreed with Anas and approved of the plan to attack the Brotherhood. It was a patriotic, almost instinctive reaction to support the country which they perceived to be under threat, a common reaction of the media in many countries at a time of crisis.

They were even repeating old programming simply on the basis that it was critical of the Brothers. That night on Channel One, it was decreed that we were to air the first episode of a 30-part docu-drama on the history of the Brotherhood, "The Group". It had received high viewing figures upon its first broadcast; it was well shot, critically acclaimed and written by Waheed Hamed, a very famous writer in Egypt. Naturally, it was not sympathetic to the Brotherhood; Waheed Hamed has long been an outspoken critic of the group. They even repeated a lengthy interview with the writer after the episode was rebroadcast.

Unlike many of the other journalists, I had access to the decision-making process, and was highly sceptical of it. I told Anas that I would not join in this attack on the Brotherhood. I didn't really think it would be the right thing to do. Regardless of my opinions of the Brotherhood, such a tactic could only prove counterproductive in the long run. If I was going to go on air, I resolved, I would just discuss the real problems of Egypt, with real people. I wanted new faces, not old ones. That would surely be a better way to tackle the problems the country faced, out in the open.

In my broadcasting career, my work was slightly more in-depth, and I tended not to handle the sensationalist stuff. It's one of the perks of having had a long career in journalism before turning to broadcasting. Whenever a senior minister or a notable political personality, opposition or government, wanted to do a comprehensive interview, they would ask me to do it.

I had a programme on that night, a discussion show where we usually had three guests and a chat about current affairs. I told Anas that I wouldn't go on air that night if all I could do was drone on about the Brotherhood. He backed down, and let me do my show the way I wanted to.

The guests on my show that night were somewhat unknown to the public, though I liked to call them "the nation's wise men". Dr Samir Radwan, a liberal economist, who would later be appointed Minister of Finance, Dr Gamal Abd Al-Gawad, Head of Al-Ahram Center for Strategic and Economic Studies and Dr Amr Al-Shobaky, an expert on Islamic movements, known for his Nasserite tendencies.

What follows is a translated transcript of my introduction to the programme:

"We must admit that there is a crisis. A crisis that poses dozens of questions for the government, and the nation's wise men. These questions revolve around economic and political reform, around communicating with the Egyptian street, around containing that anger and to understand what happened. Why did it happen? Why did it exceed our expectations? Who participated? The most important question is what will the government do next? This nation is not exclusively for the opposition or the government; it is a nation for all Egyptians. And to preserve this nation, we must have dialogue with what I call the nation's wise men, who do not hold a political position, though they are still politicians concerned with the future of this nation."

We talked about how the protests began peacefully the day before as well as the demands of the protesters. There were calls for economic, social and political reform as well as raising the minimum wage, lowering prices and providing employment opportunities.

I explained that the protesters had made it clear that their main goal was to deliver their message peacefully to those in power. I continued by stating that the national expression of disillusionment with the government was appropriated by various disparate groups who, at the least, sought to promote their own ideologies and at the most, sought the overthrow of the government.

Meanwhile, on commercial television, other stations were busy attacking the Muslim Brotherhood. However, at the same time, they were also attacking the ruling National Democratic Party, so the government wasn't quite able to control the media's response to the protests the way they had hoped.

As the government and its allies in the media attempted to tilt the balance of public opinion back in favour of the government, the government's critics also began to mobilise their media campaign. Al-Jazeera, the world famous international Arabic news station was very sympathetic to the protests and had long been indignant with the Egyptian government.

On Wednesday, Al-Jazeera broadcast the previous day's demonstrations, without quite making it clear that the footage was recorded. The implication was that Egypt was still caught in the throws of protest, when in actual fact, the major protests wouldn't start again in earnest for a couple of days. These broadcasts were being made from Al-Jazeera Mubashir (Al-Jazeera Live). This live channel featured a news bar along the bottom of the screen and a bar displaying text messages sent in by viewers. Tuseday's recorded images were also broadcast at comparable times on Wednesday, so that night-time images were never broadcast during the day.

Many of the text messages sent in by viewers were aggressively in favour of the protests, such as "Come on brave Egyptians, get rid of this regime!" and "Get rid of this President." Moreover, the banner headlines on the news bar almost read like lessons in protesting, advising people on how to deal with police pressure, what to take on demonstrations, and the like. In later days, when the major demonstrations really got going, Al-Jazeera broadcast instructions on where people were congregating – which squares, which streets, in which towns, etc.

There are several reasons why Al-Jazeera took such a partisan stance. At this point, I must point out that this only relates to the Arabic language station. The coverage from their English language service, Al-Jazeera International, was exemplary. Since AJI began, they have always maintained a very professional and polished media service.

The Al-Jazeera Arabic service, however, is much closer to the Qatari government, their primary sponsors. In recent years, the leaders of Qatar and Egypt have eyed each other with suspicion and mistrust. Rashid Mohammed Rashid, the former Minister for Trade, was a good friend of the Emir of Qatar, arranging a meeting between him and Mubarak the previous November. It was an important meeting as relations between Qatar and Egypt had been strained. Rashid told me over dinner about a month later that everything went well and the Emir promised Mubarak his full support from then on; Al-Jazeera would take a less ambivalent line with the Egyptian government. I never really believed this, as some friends of mine in the Cairo bureau of Al-Jazeera told me that as soon as the crisis erupted in Egypt, a decision was made in Doha to support the protests unequivocally.

There is a reason for this.

The relationship between Qatar and Egypt was damaged some time ago. The current Emir of Qatar, Sheikh Hamad bin Khalifa Al-Thani, deposed his father back in 1995 while the older Emir was in Switzerland for the summer. The father tried to reclaim his throne a year later with a counter coup in 1996, and the Qataris were convinced it was with the support from Egypt and Saudi Arabia, due to their leaders' preference for the older Sheikh over his son.

The counter coup was a total failure, and the conspirators were promptly rounded up by the Qatari security services. Qatar captured some of the mercenaries who had taken part in the unsuccessful coup. It was claimed that some of them were Egyptian. The Qatari leadership did not forget the role Egypt played in trying to unseat them.

Sheikh Hamad's new regime in Doha pursued a policy of expanding their political influence in the region, seeking to be part of the new political equation of the Middle East. Their vast accumulated wealth, due to enormous oil and natural gas revenues, helped them realise their aspirations.

The media would be a tool to help them pursue this dream. The perfect opportunity arose when the experimental BBC Arabic channel fell apart due to clashes between the BBC's editorial policy and Saudi Arabian political sensibilities. The BBC Arabic television channel had been set up, with Saudi finance, in 1994. It was a well-built, professional news organisation that was forced to close when the Saudi funders withdrew their support for programming critical of the Saudi government that appeared on the channel. The body of it was transferred almost as it was to Qatar with many of its presenters, editors, managers and administrators becoming the foundation of Al-Jazeera. To achieve this goal, Qatar used Sheikh Hamad Bin Qasim Al-Thani, the Qatari Foreign Minister, who was well connected with BBC Arabic and Al-Jazeera. BBC Arabic closed on the 21st of April 1996, Al-Jazeera launched on the 1st of November 1996.

Al-Jazeera has always been antagonistic to the old dictatorships in the region as it blazed its own trail and gained a considerable reputation globally. They have also always been particularly critical of Saudi Arabia and Egypt. The channel has been criticised for being too supportive of Islamist movements, and has also picked up a reputation for anti-American populism. This contrasts with Qatar's pro-American political relations, including the Al-Udeid US air force base in Qatar, which was used to launch operations into Iraq during the US-led invasion.

In the last fifteen years, Qatar has sought a leading role in the region, a role that used to belong to Egypt. Qatar has stepped up its attempts at conflict mediation in the region. The small sheikhdom has also attempted to assert cultural dominance in the Middle East, as evidenced by recent developments such as the Qatari bid for the FIFA World Cup, the purchase of Harrods, and the like. Egypt, as the region's traditional economic powerhouse and most populous country could potentially undermine Qatar in its new role.

I called the manager of the Cairo Bureau of Al-Jazeera. He admitted to me that he was under pressure from Doha with regards to their coverage. "It's not me," he claimed, "Doha are the one who is controlling Al-Jazeera Live, they're controlling everything. Please, don't be upset, I will try to fix it, I'll get it on the right track." However, Al-Jazeera Arabic carried on as before.

Wednesday drew to a close. The demonstrations were ongoing throughout the country, but the new battleground was in the media. Meanwhile, meetings were going on all day in the central National Democratic Party building, just down the road from us, towering over the Nile.

Despite the widespread deployment of government ministers in the public eye, the Prime Minister, Ahmed Nazif, was strangely absent. He made a statement through his press secretary, saying that he was against attacking or spoiling the country, though he understood the needs of the people. The usual sort of thing.

I had never thought that he was up to the task of being a Prime Minister. He simply wasn't a statesman; he's not even a politician. The obvious question, then, is how could somebody like that become Prime Minister? Well, this is Egypt.

Sporting a thick crop of short white hair and a matching moustache, Ahmed Nazif's weary features made him seem older than his 58 years. His most striking feature, however, is his height. A huge man, he towers over all those around him. His first role in government was as a Communications Minister, having come from the Faculty of Engineering in Cairo University. He was a perfectly capable Minister of Communications, having a MSc from Cairo University and a PhD from McGill University in Canada. However, he didn't have the charisma or ability which the premiership required.

I think his appointment was an action indicative of Mubarak's personality. Mubarak liked to come out with surprises. It was like when Amr Moussa left the post of Foreign Minister to head the Arab League 10 years before. Mubarak, to everybody's surprise, didn't go with a serving minister, but appointed an ex-ambassador, a man who had been retired for a good few years.

I did an interview with Ahmed Nazif a couple of weeks before this all began, on the 6th of January. Apparently, he asked for me personally. I put my head round Anas's door after it was done.

Anas stopped me from leaving, with a look of concern tinged with the slightest hint of amusement.

"Look," he said, "You don't like the guy. It's obvious. You looked at him disdainfully throughout the whole interview."

"Yes," I admitted, "You're right." I didn't try to hide it, I couldn't stand the man. At one point during the interview, I asked him a difficult question. The same question I had asked him six years before when he took up his post, at a large meeting with various prominent writers and journalists: "There's a gap between you, as a government, and the people," I began, "and you will not succeed if you don't bridge this gap. You don't have the same language. You don't have the same feelings. The people don't consider their problems to be your responsibility, and they don't consider your problems to be theirs."

He could barely answer. He just gave off the impression that he would continue at his job simply by virtue of already being in it. He constantly talked in a way that made him seem out of touch, which made people angry. I even tried to ask him about the issue of reserve water and irrigation (there is a big problem with wasting water on needless lavish suburban projects in Egypt at the moment). When I asked about the lakes of wasted water siphoned off from suburban irrigation projects, he responded, "No, why are you saying that? I live in one of these compounds and it's a very nice place, there aren't any lakes."

"I've seen them!" I exclaimed, "I can send you to see them too!"

"No," he countered, "we even have good plants around there. We have a date tree. It's very nice – I'll send you some dates."

Like many in the highest ranks of government, he was arrogant. Certainly not the best man for such an important job.

Come to think of it, I don't think he liked me either.

Back in the office, we were running through our correspondents' reports before we started the nightly news cycles. Suez was still a flashpoint. I got wind from the palace that the Governor of Suez called the President, reporting on what was going on. He told Mubarak that everything was under control, and not to worry. I knew this wasn't true. This was completely at odds with all the reports of trouble we were getting from the ground.

We had heard that the protests in Suez had continued unabated throughout the day. Protesters had laid siege to the Al-Arbeen police station and repeatedly tried to enter it. There were constant reports of clashes between protesters and police, leading to injuries on both sides. The fire station, with its vehicles still inside had been engulfed in an arson attack.

I went into the control room to talk to my staff. We were facing a problem. The official presidential newswire had declared that the police had the situation in Suez under control. This was untrue. How were we to deal with it? We couldn't ignore it. As the state broadcaster, we had to broadcast presidential statements, though this one contradicted all our reports from the ground. We all agreed that since we were under pressure, we should start running with all our news. While we still read out the presidential statements, we would also have our reporters phone in to the studio to tell us what was going on.

We put through our Suez correspondent on a direct line to the studio and had the anchor ask simple questions which would yield unequivocal answers.

"Still problems there?" asked the anchor, after introducing the field reporter.

"Yes," replied the correspondent.

"Is there still fighting?"

"Yes."

"Did they burn the police station?"

"Yes." he reported. "Yes, they burned it."

We started getting reports from other places. News came in from El-Arish, in the north of Sinai, near the Israeli border. There had been tension between the local population there and the government for decades. The large Bedouin population and its proximity to Israel made it a critical area. Sinai was somewhere I was really interested in. I'd been there many times before and met with the people in the course of my work. I tried to convince the government, telling Anas, Rashid Mohammed Rashid and Gamal Mubarak to go there, warning them that Sinai was a bomb that could explode in their faces at any time. I wrote lots of articles and reports about Sinai. I tried to discuss it with Gamal and other officials to give it more attention, I even sent a copy to whoever might be interested on this issue, hoping they would take some kind of action. Trouble had always been bubbling away in these places. The uprising just brought the problems to the fore.

Much of the population of El-Arish, and Sinai in general, is Bedouin. As such, many of them are armed. This brings a dangerous dynamic to the area. Cars driving without number plates are commonplace. It's also a very tribal place. The government does not have control over the tribes. In El-Arish, people were firing guns in the air and congregating outside the local government buildings. They were demanding the same things they'd been demanding for years: for the government to respect their traditions, to release their family members from prison, to change the laws regarding land ownership (laws relating to the Bedouin and their land are very restrictive in Egypt), and to just be treated well, and have the police treat them with respect.

At El-Arish, the behaviour of the police was abysmal. They killed a young man with a bullet through his mouth. Quite an undignified way to die. People were infuriated.

It suddenly became apparent that this recent unrest wasn't just a Cairo phenomenon. Some of the most worrying developments were in towns spread out across the whole country.

It became clear that whatever it was that began the day before, we certainly hadn't seen the end of it.

JANUARY 27TH – THURSDAY

The day began with a major meeting just down the road from us in the party headquarters, at about 9am. It was a meeting of the "Big 6": Gamal Mubarak, Ahmed Ezz, Zakaria Azmi, Safwat El-Sherif, Moufid Shehab and Ali El-Din Helal, the political committee of the National Democratic Party, each one a senior official or minister. My contacts on the inside told me that they were throwing ideas into the air, trying to think of a way to calm down the protests. Tomorrow would be Friday, when everybody would be out on the streets for Friday prayers. In the Middle East, Friday has traditionally been the day for major protest. The whole country knew that something big was going to happen tomorrow.

One of the ideas was to sack the entire cabinet and get in some fresh blood. However, due to the pervading sense of power and entitlement, this idea was rejected out of hand. Another suggestion was to organise a mass series of counter demonstrations, marshalling NDP supporters across the country to show gratitude and support for Mubarak, the government and the party. The idea was to show that the opposition would not be the only active force on the ground in Egypt. The idea was later vetoed by Habib Al-Adly, as his police forces could not remotely hope to maintain order with two sets of opposing protesters in every city in the country.

The meeting went on for four hours. Gamal was supposed to give a press conference at the party HQ immediately afterwards, but he did not show up. No explanation was given, and Safwat El-Sherif gave the press conference instead, most likely because they were trying to keep the provocative personalities, of which Gamal was one, out of the public eye. I was watching it on the live feed coming through to my office.

Safwat was a more useful man to give the press conference as he was well known as a spokesman for the NDP. During the press conference, he was forced to bat away the persistent rumours that scores of wealthy Egyptians had fled the country. A well-known media entrepreneur, Emad El-Din Adib, had publicly claimed that these businessmen were joined by a number of top NDP officials who used their private jets to escape the country, shortly after transferring their assets to foreign bank accounts. Safwat had to deny further rumours that there would be an imminent cabinet reshuffle.

Using an Egyptian expression, he said that the party was *Al-Tawd Al-Shamikh*, it sort of means that the party is immovable, like a mountain. It was a remark that drew a great deal of criticism from the public.

I went back over to Anas's office.

"Gamal should be in this press conference," I announced as I walked in.

"We thought it better to keep him away now," came his response as he looked up from behind his desk.

Anas didn't have to explain the reasons; they were easy enough to figure out. They wanted to keep Gamal away from the public, so people wouldn't associate Gamal with the current unrest. If he wasn't thought to be running the country, he wouldn't be blamed for its troubles. Secondly, they wanted the next most senior man in the party (after the President) to speak, which was El-Sherif.

They would never use the President to speak to the public at this early stage. President Mubarak would be saved for the "final move". The people around Mubarak used to refer to him as the king in a game of Chess. The king should not move at the beginning of a game, but restrict his movement until the game is in its dying moments. Only when all other options have been exhausted, does the Mubarak family make its move.

Anas made this clear to me, "We will keep the President, we're not going to burn him. There are many people before him. There is a Prime Minister – he should take responsibility." Anas complained often about the Prime Minister. He was also unhappy with Nazif's inactivity during the period. Nazif wasn't calling on us or his ministerial colleagues, he wasn't appearing in public, he wasn't even phoning in to get briefings on what was happening.

I glanced around the office. It was a lovely place, the size of a small tennis court. Anas had a desk at the end, just next to a comfortable looking Lazyboy chair positioned to face the window. The window was broad and panoramic, providing spectacular views of the city. At the entrance was a conference table, overlooked by an abstract painting of Cairo, awash with splashes of colour and indistinct shapes. The middle of his room was taken up with luxurious armchairs, perfect for informal meetings and relaxing chats at the end of the day.

As I sat there, it became apparent that the government's response to the demands of the crowds in the cities was wholly inadequate. The public would not be assuaged by the vague promises of reform that they had been offered. Somehow, a statement that the Prime Minister was having a meeting with some senior minister to discuss the possibility of new economic and social policy was not quite enough.

Egyptians were in urgent need of change, a term that had become something of a rude word in Egyptian politics in recent years. I tried more than once, through my articles and television platforms, to explain that change and stability are not mutually exclusive. Sometimes change can breed stability. The continuity of any government depends to a great extent on its ability to adopt and live with a changing reality. Unfortunately, the Egyptian state was too out of touch to realise this.

Aside from putting forward my views on the issue of change in the media, I also tried to influence my contacts within the circle of power. I explained that their shortcomings were inflaming an already volatile situation and increasing the indifference average Egyptians have for their government. It was wrong to view people's demands as an attempt to pressure the government. The crisis managers were under the impression that any positive response would make them look weak.

I also thought it unwise but intentional, to keep the President out of the loop, especially in those early days. Keeping the old man uninformed would prevent him from taking any decisive action. The President was a canny politician, there was no way he could have stayed in power for as long as he did if he had not been. However, by surrounding himself with weak and divided ministers, he would be forced to manage serious national crises personally. At the age of 82, it was easier for those around him to allow him to remain detached as they attempted to resolve the situation by themselves.

Another problem of the day was the issue of what to do with the large numbers of youth who had been arrested that day. Just before I went up to Anas's office, I telephoned the Attorney General of Egypt, Abdel Mageed Mahmoud. I knew him quite well, and we got on well.

"Abdel Mageed Bey, I think it would be a good idea, to ease the tension, to release the youth now" I suggested over the phone.

"Actually, I was thinking the same thing" he answered, "it is good idea, isn't it?

"Yes," I replied. Obviously, as I had just phoned him to suggest it. I knew that it would upset Gamal and Zakaria Azmi, going behind their backs like this, but I wasn't too concerned about that. He was a very good man, Abdel Mageed. He was trying to do the right thing under pressure. He was trying to manoeuvre. As part of the judiciary, he also had a degree of protection from the government which was not available to government ministers and party officials. At the same time, the government was always leaning on him. We used to talk often about important matters, it was that kind of relationship. Before I clicked my phone back on the receiver, he told me he would be making arrangements to have these people released.

When I was in Anas's office, I sat down in the chair in front of his desk. I decided it might be a good time to bring up the issue.

"Look, I think it would be a good idea if Mubarak himself were seen to release these protesters. If he says that it was his decision, on television, that would be very helpful," I explained.

Anas looked perplexed. "It wouldn't be wise to do that. No. We don't have to do that. This will encourage more to go on the streets. If they get arrested, and people know about it, parents will prevent their children from going out on the streets. Even if we do make this decision, we should do it late in the evening, so the public won't find out about it. We should be tough."

When he finished reeling off the reasons not to take any action, the hotline phone rang on his desk. He went to pick it up. Almost simultaneously, my mobile phone rang. I saw Abdel Mageed's name flashing on the screen. I stood up to take the call. Without leaving the room, I wandered towards the other corner of the room, where the conference table was, idly looking out the window. Abdel Mageed told me that all the measures were in place, he was going to release over a hundred detainees, and his office would send the news to my office. They weren't releasing everybody, they were going to hold on to those on specific criminal charges, but those who weren't were free to go. "Great," I whispered into my phone.

When we'd finished I tucked my phone back into my pocket and walked casually back across Anas's cavernous office, sitting myself back down in front of him.

"That was Zakaria Azmi," he began, "and Habib. I told them about your idea. They have the same opinion. We shouldn't be releasing anybody at this time." Even though he rejected my suggestion as soon as I brought it up, he still must have thought it appropriate to mention it to Azmi and Adly. Anas was liberal by nature, though he had accepted the responsibilities that went with being in government. He did have ideas, but he would do what he was told.

I didn't interrupt him to tell him about my conversation.

A few minutes passed as we discussed other matters. Suddenly, his phone bleeped. It was an SMS news alert. He glanced at his phone, paused to examine the contents of the alert and announced with mock resignation, "Oh, OK, here it is. Your idea…the Attorney General just did it. Your friend released them."

I called Abdel Mageed later on to thank him and to compliment his initiative. I knew that the people around the President were not happy with what he had done. It was a shame, because they missed a golden opportunity for the President to be seen to take a liberal standpoint and support free expression.

I believe that if Mubarak had fired his cabinet, released those detainees and gone out to speak to people right then and there, then possibly the regime may still be standing today. But again, the government was far too implacable to take such a step.

I went back to Anas's office once more that evening. He was on the phone when I walked in. Without having to listen in on the conversation, I could tell that he was on the phone to Suzanne Mubarak. I signalled to him, gesticulating that I would leave and come back later. He waved his hand and pointed to the chair in front of his desk. "Stay," he mouthed.

Anas had an Arabic manuscript on his desk, and was making alterations to the script as dictated through the phone. The two of them were editing the text of Suzanne's new book by telephone. It was a book that she had written about reading with her grandson who had died tragically two years before at the age of 12. She had written it in English and had it translated into Arabic. This was one of the many 30-40 minute sessions she spent with Anas on the phone reviewing the text.

It was depressing, though not at all surprising, that even at a time of national crisis, the First Lady was still occupying a government minister with her own personal projects. Cairo was ready to burn and here they were. Obviously, I sympathised with the tragedy she had gone through. The whole country did, but it was ridiculous. They were going over the 26th draft. It was clear from which side of the family Gamal Mubarak inherited his relentless attention to detail. The man was just like his mother. They both took five or six drafts just to produce a written statement.

Anas and I went over preparations for the day before I returned to my desk. Friday would be a logistical nightmare. It's difficult enough trying to cover anti-government protests across a large country on state television. It would be made an awful lot harder without the use of mobile phones or the internet. Sitting in Anas's office, I overheard the phone calls he made with Adly and Tareq Kamel, the Minister of Communication. I understood that the telecom systems in Egypt were to be turned off.

In preparation for the expected troubles of the next day, Adly assumed presidential authority. He was using all the resources available to him as Interior Minister in an attempt to curtail the protests in any way possible. The move to cut telephone and internet services was led by him. I later found out about the telephone calls he was making to his fellow ministers, barking instructions at them. In one call, Tareq Kamel, the minister responsible for communications was unwilling to sever the country's telecom services. Habib told him in no uncertain terms that he was speaking with the voice of the President, and his orders were to be followed. He went on to remind him that there was an article in the statute that gave the government the right to cut communications when there was a threat to national security.

I didn't find out at the time, but it turned out that Omar Suleiman called Adly that day. Suleiman told him they needed to meet that day with Field Marshal Tantawi, head of the armed forces, to coordinate their response to the Friday demonstrations. Suleiman offered support for Adly, if he needed use of the army or intelligence service. Adly was reluctant to meet so soon, offering instead to meet on Saturday, explaining that he was busy dealing with the protests himself and he would only be free after he had dealt with them.

There was another reason, beside his busy schedule, why Adly refused their help.

There were two main power blocs in the Egyptian government. On one side were those around the President, or more accurately, his son –its main aim was to ensure that Gamal Mubarak succeeded his father as President of Egypt. I always believed that wouldn't have happened while Hosni Mubarak was alive. He would never have handed power to his son, he would have done the job until the day he died. All the rumours that he would give up power were just conjecture from people who didn't understand the man's character. The main player in this bloc was Suzanne Mubarak. Zakaria Azmi, the Chief of Staff, was strong, but Suzanne was the most active in ensuring her son's succession. Habib Al-Adly, the Interior Minister always gave this clique the impression that he was their tool to carry out this project, as if he was the only man in control of Egypt. There were others in this bloc; Anas was very close to them, and there were assistants as well, but the real "gang of five" was Suzanne, Adly, Azmi, Ahmed Ezz and Gamal.

The other power bloc was headed by Omar Suleiman and Field Marshal Tantawi. They saw, like many in the country, that Gamal's ascendency to the presidency could have dire consequences for Egypt. When Mubarak was undergoing surgery in Egypt, the two of them were meeting daily, planning what to do in case the President did not return. Mubarak, always careful to ensure there were no strong competitors for his position, would often try to keep the powers at the top of the government divided. These meetings brought the two men, Suleiman and Tantawi closer together, helping to forge a new power bloc.

Suzanne Mubarak loathed the two army men. Anas told me often that Suzanne saw Suleiman and Tantawi as a threat to her family, and we spoke of her fears on several occasions. Most of us in Egypt expected Omar Suleiman to be appointed Vice President four or five years before he actually was. While the post of Vice President was still empty, in 2007 the Gamal bloc altered the constitution, giving emergency powers to the Prime Minister not the Vice President, should the President be incapacitated. There was also an ongoing movement to have Omar Suleiman become Prime Minister, a move also blocked by the First Lady.

Walking back to my office at the end of the day, I ran through the plans for tomorrow in my head. I was confident that my staff would be able to conduct themselves professionally. Conversely, the government didn't seem to know what they were doing. Adly was making his preparations, though I don't think he handled Tuesday's unrest particularly well. What made it worse was the posturing and manoeuvring for power at the top of government, in spite of (or perhaps because of) the impending crisis.

Memories of my career at the ERTU began to flash through my mind. It all began in 2005 when I started working for state TV. My appointment as head of the News Sector was meant to be part of a broader programme of change across the government. President Mubarak pushed for constitutional amendments, changing the process of presidential selection from a referendum system (Keep the president? Yes or No) to a direct multi-candidate election for the first time in Egypt's history. It was to be a very important step towards democracy. Though significant, these reforms were ultimately diminished after the usual laborious legislative procedures.

It was my first year, and I believed I was capable of doing something different with state TV. My plan was to achieve a professional level of television journalism that would match the needs of a changing society. Though I had a reputation of special interest in public issues, I never sought a government position. It was the first time I assumed public office. Even now, I have no idea who put my name forward.

At the time, I wondered if it was actually possible to change the corrupt mindset that had for so long permeated Egyptian public life. I asked Rashid Mohammed Rashid, who was considered one of the reformers in the Egyptian government, if such reform was possible. I will never forget his answer: he said that the percentage of people pushing for change within the regime itself, back in 2005, was no more than 10%. As hard as it seemed, Rashid and I agreed that meaningful change would have to come from the regime itself.

I thought about the subsequent years I spent working there. I almost resigned in 2007 during the Shura Council election (for the Upper House of Egypt's parliament). The candidates being appointed were worse than useless, the only selection criteria being their loyalty to the party. I was feeling dejected, certain that there was no chance to repair the country. It was clear to me that the only political project with any momentum was the plan to prepare Gamal to succeed his father as president, later nicknamed the "inheritance project". Though never discussed openly, the signs were frequent and obvious.

I practically stopped working until a conversation I had one day with Anas. I was complaining about how the government was backing down on all the promises of reform it had made. When I accepted this position I was not looking for authority or power – I wanted to be part of the process of change. I felt then that it would be positive to be part of the country's regeneration, even if I wouldn't have a large role.

My idea was to turn state television into public television. We could give the public direct ownership of the media rather than have it controlled through their government. During our long debate I accused them of trying to con the public and of making countless empty promises. The Shura Council were the latest in a long line of disappointing public acts by the government, which ignored the public's best interest. We discussed the deep divisions tearing the state apart. Each minister and official was operating their own private fiefdom, jostling for position within the circle of power.

Eventually, I chose to continue. It was a difficult choice to make. I reasoned that if I could stay within the state system I could at least exercise what little power I had to make small steps towards some kind of reform in Egypt.

As the crisis unfolded, and I saw the measures taken by those in power to keep hold of their jobs, I kept wondering, "should I have quit back then?"

The demonstrators out on the streets were also making their own preparations. I was running through the office, organising my crews, making last minute calls and generally trying to get us ready for broadcast. I sent crews to Suez and Alexandria and checked that we had our correspondents in the other governorates of Egypt.

I left the office late that night. Very late.

JANUARY 28TH – FRIDAY
"THE DAY OF RAGE"

I left home early in the morning on Friday, around 7.30am. I asked the driver to take a round-about route to the office, to let me see the city. Cairo is usually a quiet city on Fridays, especially in the morning, before prayers at midday. Friday prayers are very important in Egypt, even if people don't pray on other days, they still pray on the Friday.

It was a sunny day. The city was tense once again, more so than before. There was expectation in the air; something was going to happen today. I could see police cars parked on the city streets. Starting in Mohandiseen, in the west of the city, we crossed the Nile over the 26th July Bridge. The bridge merges seamlessly into a viaduct that spans the fashionable island of Zamalek. From one's car, you can peak into the second stories of the ornate 19th century apartment blocks. Once over the other side of the Nile, rather than turning right towards the Maspero building, which stands less than a hundred metres away from the bridge, we ventured further into downtown Cairo.

I wanted to take in the city that morning. I'd lived in Cairo for years and seen it all, but I wanted to have a sense of the situation on the ground. Through the window of my car I watched the police organising themselves, setting up barricades and parking their police cars beside every corner. Despite the huge show of force intended to defend the regime, it always seemed to me that in times of crisis, no one would stand by the regime in public. Since I started working in state television, I noticed that major figures in government would always disappear at the first sign of trouble. When a controversy erupted, it would become very hard to find even one member of the National Democratic Party to agree to put the regime's stance to the public. This was a recurring problem. If the government was under attack for a contentious new decision, which was often the case whenever a new law was enacted, the government's ministers would be unavailable. The only way to get someone to explain an unpopular government declaration was by direct orders from Gamal Mubarak in person or through one of President Mubarak's assistants, acting on the orders of the President himself.

The problems didn't stop there. If we finally managed to get hold of somebody to come and speak on air, we would find that they had no idea what to say; they were poorly briefed and would often have no knowledge at all of the subject at hand. It drove me mad. The government repeatedly picked spokesmen who had no charisma or media training at all. It seemed to the public that those in power were simply out to make money for themselves, and never held accountable to the Egyptian people. They would then toss out a stream of ineffective and inarticulate politicians or technocrats to act as the public face of the government.

The government was without a voice.

The heavy police presence on the streets was decided upon the day before at a meeting in the Interior Ministry between Adly and a few of his top officials. It was the same meeting that gave Adly the excuse to avoid dealing with Omar Suleiman and Field Marshal Tantawi. When it came to the police presence, the Interior Ministry decided upon a tactic of confrontation, but with no clashes. They were going to try dispersing the crowds, and prevent any large gatherings at central focal points. Entrances into Tahrir Square would be blocked off.

Meanwhile, the youth movements and opposition parties were making their own plans. Al-Jazeera Live proved to be a vital communication link for the protesters. Other news websites such as Al-Dustour, leftist Al-Badeel, and the conservative Shrouk news service began posting minute by minute updates of protests and clashes in Cairo, listing time and location. They posted instant updates of gathering points, marches and the reactions of the police. The Facebook group, "Rassd News Network" posted videos of the status on the ground using mobile phones. Rassd is closely associated with the Muslim Brotherhood, created during parliamentary elections in 2010, and had gained around a quarter of a million Facebook "likes" (today that figure is over one million). Protesters also mobilised themselves through other Facebook pages such as "*Gomaat El-Ghadab*" (Friday of Rage) and "*Kuluna Khalid Saeed*" (We are all Khalid Saeed).

Blocking websites was futile as users could access the forbidden websites through proxy servers. It didn't matter as the internet was now dead. The opposition websites and Facebook pages had been used the previous three days to pass on protest techniques, gathering points, means of police confrontation and codes for communication between groups.

We drove through Al-Galaa St and Ramses Square before finishing our brief tour by crossing Tahrir Square. We went back to the Maspero building along the Corniche, beside the Nile. Just before we finished, we passed by the NDP building, an ugly great edifice I passed everyday. It had just been refurbished, (Ahmed Ezz footed the bill) and it was looking modern and clean. That was the last time I saw it intact.

The last time I was actually inside was at a grand meeting a few weeks beforehand. The meeting was ostensibly Ahmed Ezz justifying his management of the recent election. It had been called by Gamal Mubarak, and featured all the major editors and writers from the state media outlets. The meeting went on for three hours. Part way through one of Ezz's monologues, I felt my phone vibrate. It was a text message in English from Anas, seated on the stage on the other side of the room.

ANAS: U want to go?

ME (joking): No, I'm trying to learn.

ANAS: This is a lesson U will never use in your life: To be stupid, dumb.

A lot of people really hated Ahmed Ezz.

He explained, over the course of several hours, how he secured the recent election victory for the NDP. He also brought his assistants, who had data with them to help in the lecture. The assistants, each one working in a specific electoral district, stood up one by one and described how they sidelined the popular characters, determining where support lay and dividing up districts which supported opposition candidates. In Egypt, elections were determined by those with the power and the money. In 2010, all the power and money lay with the NDP, and specifically with Ahmed Ezz. Ezz was a very organised person, he knew how to manipulate systems and data. The old men in the party did not have his abilities. Ezz had access to the voters' lists, and analysts working on them. But for all his organisational abilities, he had no political sense whatsoever.

I told them at the time, "You've been using fraudulent elections for the past 30 years to gain the NDP a majority. Now is the time to change. Even if you must have false elections, at least have seats for 150 or so opposition MPs, to save face."

The election in 2010 was the most restrictive in Egypt's history. A decision was made at the higher levels of the NDP to comprehensively remove the Muslim Brotherhood from parliament. The Muslim Brotherhood, or *Ikhwan* as we call them in Egypt, were officially an illegal organisation. In spite of this, they were tolerated and ran in elections as independents. In 2005, they, as independent candidates, won 88 seats in parliament (out of 450), making them the largest opposition bloc.

They finished the 2010 election with one seat. The NDP won 81% of the seats, which, together with the 10% of independents allied to the NDP gave them a majority of 91% in parliament. A needlessly vast majority. It was stupid; if they were going to get rid of the Brotherhood, they should have at least replaced them with someone else if they hoped to maintain even a semblance of democratic legitimacy.

Even Mubarak himself was unhappy at the result of the elections. Though he had no intention of relinquishing power, he was wise enough to realise that such a patently false result would ultimately be damaging to the NDP. In the first run of the elections, the police rounded up Muslim Brotherhood politicians and threw them in prison, to ensure that they would not be able to pose any credible challenge. In the majority of the seats, the NDP candidates were simply running against themselves. Mubarak was shocked and angry after the first round. They tried to undo some of the damage in the second round by running opposition candidates against NDP candidates, so a few opposition politicians made it through. However, this had the effect of alienating their own candidates. The election ended up upsetting everybody, even on their own side. It was a joke.

In Muslim culture, there is a concept of *Diyya* (blood money). When one has killed, by intention or not, there is a prescription to pay *Diyya* in order to atone and avoid execution. I said to Anas and Rashid Mohammed Rashid (the Minister for Trade and Industry) at the time that giving these cursory seats to the opposition was like paying *Diyya*, though no matter how much blood money the NDP paid, they would not bring the dead back to life.

On the Friday itself, rumours abounded that Ahmed Ezz had been prowling around the NDP building the day before, emptying everything from his office. In reality, Ezz was removing data, files and computer disks, which he drove away in a small van. He was clearly concerned that the building would be invaded, a legitimate concern, given its proximity to Tahrir Square.

When I got into my office, I checked all the screens and live feeds to the streets. As yet, everything was calm. I was early, so my staff started arriving around half an hour later. Everybody knew their place and what their job would be that day. My office was open to my staff: people would often come in and out. I had 3,000 staff, but in terms of those I really worked with, I had less than a hundred. Most of them were young. They understood journalism. They loved to work, and they understood my ethic. It's not that I preferred to work with young people exactly, it's that I preferred to work with people who love their work, many of whom happened to be young.

Anas arrived a little bit later, at about half past eight. I walked up to the office shortly after he got in. I heard him talking on the phone, I assumed it was someone at the palace, later I found out that it was Zakaria Azmi. He was saying that the Republican Guard would be the first units deployed to protect the Maspero building until Unit 777, the counter terror special forces unit of the army, arrived. They were the elite forces of the army, who were also tasked with protecting the President.

After he put the phone down, he laughed when he saw the concern drawn on my face.

"Why are you panicking?" he chuckled.

"What were you talking about on the phone?" I questioned him back.

"No," he reassured me, "this is just the worst case scenario. It won't come to that, Insha'alla. It won't happen because Habib Bey is confident that everything will be fine. Maybe it will be a bit harder than before, but it will pass."

Anas was a very trusting man. He tried to calm me down. He explained that we might need some additional means of keeping in touch. He produced a walkie-talkie and handed it to me. We had ten, one each for me and Anas and the rest distributed to our assistants, building security and maintenance department. "Just to be connected with each other," he assured me. I knew then that the mobile phone networks would be shut down – this was the proof.

At around 9.30 in the morning, our mobile phones began to die as the service was cut. At around the same time, the internet also shut down. We were back to landlines. One of my colleagues had a phone that remained working for a few minutes after all of ours had lost signal. She was showing off her phone, the only working one in the building, before that too passed out of service.

There are only three mobile phone companies in Egypt; Vodafone, Etisalat and Mobinil. Each had been given instructions from the Ministry of Communication to cut their services that morning. Likewise, the big internet companies had already cut their services. The telecoms companies had no choice but to switch off their services.

One of the channels I was responsible for is Nile TV, it broadcasts five to six hours a day in French and the rest of the time in English. A couple of years before, it was a multi-programme channel, but the heads of the ERTU were considering shutting it down. When I spoke in the channel's defence, it suddenly became my responsibility, so I changed its remit to news and current affairs.

I had young reporters working on the channel. They came to my office in the morning asking me how they should cover the demonstrations. All the reporters on that station were young and enthusiastic. They exuded idealism, honesty and objectivity. I told them our policy should be simply to say what they see.

"Really?" one of them asked.

"Yes." I replied.

They came back a little while later, telling me that their boss at the channel had different ideas and would be controlling their coverage.

"I'm the head of this place," I responded, "and I'm telling you that this is our policy. Say what you see."

Unfortunately, out on the streets, our cameras would sometimes be broken by the crowds, due to the general suspicion and distrust of the TV. My instructions to all my staff, and my reporters on the ground were direct. They were to report objectively, but they were to keep themselves safe. Violence was expected that day, and I reminded them of the old journalistic credo, "No story is worth a life".

Everything was calm until it came time for Friday prayers. There was a mosque on the seventh floor of the Maspero building. Just a small room. They had to use the corridors as it was often too small to fit everyone in. I went up for prayers at noon. As usual, the sheikh was giving his sermon.

When we finished, everything was calm. I got a call from Anas on my desk phone.

"Habib Bey is very happy," he declared, "everything is going smoothly. The communications are fine. He knows where they are, how they move. They have no connection, no communication. It's like a video game. It's easy."

Our reporters called us from all around the city. The general consensus was that there was nothing big happening yet, though people were massing.

Suddenly, as if by magic, all these little demonstrations scattered around Cairo began to move as one. All of them were heading towards Tahrir Square. Much of the initial demonstrations were focused on the area around Al-Azhar mosque, which has a long history of political activism. It was there that Egyptians protested against the invasion of Iraq and Israeli aggression against the Palestinians. Protesters usually gather at the main hall of the mosque after prayers. As such, many police were deployed in the area, which is also close to the large Al-Hussein mosque. It's a densely populated part of Cairo, an ideal spot for the protests to gain momentum before moving off.

Another large group came from the Al-Nour Mosque and the Al-Abassiya cathedral in north east Cairo. Others came from Giza, in the west, marching through the streets to the Nile.

Everyone from the north and east of Cairo funnelled through Ramses Square, a big square just northeast of downtown, which surrounds Cairo central station. There, the police made a stand against the protesters, desperately trying to stop them from breaking through on their way to Tahrir Square. The police had hastily erected roadblocks and barricades in an attempt to control the marchers.

Instructions were circulating through the crowds. The marchers were to start from mosques and churches after prayers, where they would then head to Tahrir Square or the NDP headquarters in whatever city they were in. The instructions emphasised the need for every person to bring 3 to 4 friends or relatives. Demonstrators should hold aloft the flag of Egypt and refrain from chanting ethnic, religious or ideological slogans. The instructions stressed the peacefulness of the protests and warned against vandalism or violence against police recruits, as "the poor are not the enemy". Other instructions included ignoring sheikhs who condemned the protests and stressed keeping together in the face of police attempts at dispersal. Protesters were advised to wear sports clothing and to bring a scarf or towel to protect against tear gas.

We started broadcasting at 2pm, announcing that there were protests across the city. We tried to simply explain what was going on: there were demonstrations, and there were police trying to curtail the demonstrations, and the demonstrators were moving towards Tahrir.

Many of the police had been on duty since Tuesday morning. They were tired. They were armed but they were not issued with any ammunition. They were tense, exhausted and had instructions not to fire on anybody that Friday. They were armed with their batons, some had teargas launchers. A few more had blanks to load their guns with, to be used as a warning. Many of them were kitted out in their riot gear, shields and helmets.

The police behind the Maspero building started firing blanks in the air when they got into clashes with protesters near the

Ramses Hilton, just off Tahrir Square. By 3pm, I started to see the first teargas cannisters launched and the first wisps of smoke started spewing from the streets, as some protesters set alight car tyres.

The vast majority of protesters were still heading to Tahrir Square. The police, too exhausted to hold out, started falling back, and the masses of people hitherto held back by police blockades poured forth towards Tahrir Square.

At this point, there were only small groups converging in Tahrir Square; it was yet to become the heaving mass of people familiar to those who watched the scenes of protest on television. However, that would soon change as people started streaming into the square from every direction.

Tahrir Square is bordered by some of the most important buildings in Cairo. On the south side is the Mogamma, one of the densest governmental buildings in the world, usually filled with thousands of government employees and citizens using its services. A gift from the Soviet Union, the giant Stalinist construction dominates the square. On either side are two of Cairo's most important cultural landmarks, the Egyptian Museum and the original American University in Cairo campus. Behind the museum stands the NDP headquarters, which overlooks the Nile, adjacent to the towering Nile Hilton Hotel (Now the Crown Plaza). The square is served by the Sadat Metro station. The central roundabout lies at the heart of downtown Cairo's congested traffic system, and is usually surrounded by herds of cars honking their horns as they try to push through the square. The north side of the square is bordered by cafés, tourist offices, hotels and fast food outlets. Very close to the square are the upper and lower houses of parliament buildings, cabinet headquarters and several major government ministries.

I examined the scenes from our cameras in the control room. I didn't bother checking in with Anas, I was too concerned with what was unfolding before us and working out how we should handle it. Most of the commercial TV channels were broadcasting their normal programming. I remember one was showing a comedy film. By that point, we were the only domestic channel actually broadcasting what was going on in Cairo.

The plumes of smoke rising from the streets gradually became stronger as the fires burned, and new fires were ignited. The smoke mixed with the stinging tear gas in the air, and before long the acrid smell permeated the Maspero building. Some of my staff were affected by the stinging gas. In my office, I tended to close the windows and keep on the air conditioning even during the winter. My office became something of an oasis, (almost) free of the tear gas. My staff poured into my office for some respite from the gas, and to watch the burgeoning chaos on the screens I had set up.

It became clear that the police on the ground had lost contact between themselves. I'm not sure why, but they too were suffering communication problems, and were obviously unable to use their mobile phones as backup.

The CCTV feed I had centred on Qasr El-Nil Bridge. As we watched the screen, we caught a running battle develop over the Nile between protesters and police. We started broadcasting it. The bridge connects the centre of Cairo, on its west side, with the district of Dokki on the east side of the river, cutting through the island of Zamalek. The bridge flows right into Tahrir Square.

The police on the east side of the bridge were trying to push the protesters across the Nile back towards Dokki, away from Tahrir. At around 3.10pm, it was time to pray again, and the demonstrators suddenly halted their advance and knelt down to pray. The protesters on the bridge were soaked, as the police were using a mounted water cannon as their main weapon to hold them back. When their targets stopped their advance and began to pray, their sodden clothes sticking to their skin, the officers eased off the water cannon, allowing them to make their prayers without being assaulted. As soon as the prayers were over, the scores of protesters got up and once more charged the police, only to be beaten back to the other side of the bridge by jets of water. However, being pushed back only served to strengthen the resolve of the protesters, who consequently charged forward again before being hosed back once more. This game of cat and mouse continued for around 40 minutes, with neither side able to break the impasse.

Suddenly, the police on the bridge lost control or concentration. They may have run out of tear gas or blank ammunition. Whatever it was, the police fled the bridge – hundreds of riot police, just running away. A river of people flowed across the bridge and poured into Tahrir Square: thousands, carrying road barriers, fencing and homemade banners. It was incredible.

It was around this time that the police van careened across the road, hitting protesters, clips of which were subsequently uploaded onto YouTube and broadcast around the world. Though seen as a malicious act of wanton brutality on the part of the police, I'm not so sure this is the case. I believe that it's far more likely that these police drivers were actually inept at driving their vans. Here in Egypt, the standard of driving is very poor, and it's not unusual to see accidents on the drive into work. The men who drive these vans are some of the worst drivers around. Some of the protesters were targeting the police vans, pelting them with rocks and even trying to mount them or push them over. Many protesters brought spray paint to the protests, with the aim of spraypainting the windscreens of police vehicles, further hampering their visibility. These drivers, terrified and poorly trained, slammed on the accelerator to get away from the protesters, with little regard for the rules of the road.

Around 4pm, protesters started coming across the 6th of October bridge, which meets the east bank of the Nile close to the Maspero building.

After seeing the scenes of protest envelop Cairo, I marched up to Anas's office. Bursting in through his door, I demanded, "Can you see what's happening? Can you explain?"

He looked perplexed, shrugging his shoulders, he responded, "I don't know. Nothing." He was clearly in shock. Throughout the day he was on the hotline to the President, Gamal and Zakaria Azmi. He was just telling them what was going on, not giving them an opinion, just informing them of developments.

"Where are the police?" I asked.

"I called Habib many times," he replied, "He's not answering."

Anas had little to say, the man was in shock, and he was powerless to do anything. While I was sitting opposite him, the phone rang again. It was the President. After a brief exchange, he put the phone down, paused for a moment, and looked up at me. "The army is coming."

At that moment, I suddenly remembered coming in to see him that morning, when he was talking about the Republican Guard and Unit 777, something that he said wouldn't happen. It was happening now.

He told me that shortly beforehand, Adly had called the President and told him that the police could no longer handle the protests. The President told him to call Field Marshal Tantawi and tell him the President ordered the army to be deployed.

The Republican Guard were readied to protect the strategically vital areas in Cairo, the state TV building being one of the most important. The Republican Guard had a base on the southern side of Zamalek, in the centre of Cairo, on the Nile.

At 5.05pm I saw the first Republican Guard vehicle on the Corniche heading to the Maspero building. Within minutes, the army forces had secured the area and surrounded us.

Far from being intimidated, the demonstrators greeted the army with cheers. Some stood up, saluting them as they drove along the roads. Those out on the streets began to chant, "The army and the people are one hand!"

An army officer came to my office, to let me know that they were now in control. It was a terribly shocking moment for my staff. Many of them were professional journalists who lived with their pens as their swords, suddenly they found themselves guarded by men with guns. For the most part, they had no idea what was going on, or why these soldiers were there.

At 5.30pm, the President declared martial law. It was announced that a curfew would be imposed across Cairo at 6pm. The President, in his position as Commander-in-Chief of the Egyptian military, issued a statement stating that the imposition of martial law was made in response to widespread civil unrest, looting and vandalism. The curfew would be in place from 6pm that evening until 7am the next morning. He also gave orders for the army to cooperate with police in order to protect and secure private properties and public services.

Looking at the statement that we were about to broadcast, I thought it questionable to include the line about the army cooperating with the police. There were no police. A couple of hours later, an army general called me and asked to edit the wording of the statement in subsequent broadcasts, removing any mention of the police. From now on, only the army was in charge.

For the Egyptian people, the army commands far more respect than the police. Most people in Egypt, a country which still has conscription, will have a family member who has served in the army. In recent decades, the army has fought in four wars against Israel, and is seen by many as committed to the protection of Egypt.

The army organised themselves rapidly, setting up positions around several major points, securing the perimeter of the building. The Republican Guard filtered into the building and set up secure points, guarding the studios and other vital access points within the building.

The imposition of a curfew was a worrying development, bringing back memories of 1977 and 1984. Back in 1977, the army hit the streets to quell riots sparked by high food prices. In 1984, they were back to confront a rebellion of the police central security forces in Cairo. We thought those days were long behind us in 2011.

When the army arrived on the streets, the police just disappeared completely. They just melted away. There were a lot of stories about the police withdrawal. Some police officers who were involved in the direct confrontations with protesters claimed they were too fatigued after being on duty for days. The protesters were too numerous and many police believed the protesters were too well-organised for them to handle. The police also claimed they had strict orders not to use firearms. Once they ran out of rubber bullets, blanks and tear gas, they had nothing to use in confrontations with the crowds. The protesters pelted the police with rocks and debris, as well as with other improvised weapons.

With communications down, and no way of reaching their command centres, many police simply opted to run rather than face the possibility of injury or death in any resultant clashes on the street. The police took off their uniforms and disappeared.

Another story says that the police had instructions from the Interior Ministry to withdraw all forces after they saw the Army deploy on the streets. This would have been an abdication of responsibility for the Ministry of the Interior, passing total control of the streets to the military. This could have been an arrangement made beforehand between the Interior Ministry and the Army or it could have been a cynical ploy to vindicate police claims of non-complicity in a potential crackdown in case of further bloodshed.

When I think back to what I witnessed through the CCTV cameras, taking in a bird's-eye view of the demonstrations, especially the running battle on Qasr El-Nil Bridge, it looked far more like a sudden collapse than a tactical withdrawal. It's difficult to believe they could have been that far-sighted or organised.

At around the same time as the army were deployed on the streets, the headquarters of the National Democratic Party began to burn. A symbol of everything hated in the Egyptian government, people had gathered outside throughout the day, chanting slogans at it, then throwing stones and improvised projectiles at it. It must have been around 5pm when people managed to get inside it, raiding the offices of the most senior officials.

Thanks to Ahmed Ezz's renovation work, the building sported a new coat of paint on the outside, new halls inside, a modern computer network and brand new special offices for party officials. Gamal Mubarak had an office there on the second floor right next to Safwat El-Sherif.

Once inside, the protesters threw computers and furniture out of the windows. There were some opportunists who just took advantage of the chaos and looted the offices. A bizarre scene played out, as some looters threw cushions from the windows, caught by their friends waiting outside. Before long, a group of those who seemed familiar with the internal building plans headed for the central offices, grabbing computers, official records and documents before running away.

It turned out that Ezz was wise after all to clear the building of sensitive material and move it somewhere else. The building was later subject to an arson attack, a fire started inside the building, gradually growing to engulf the whole place. No one bothered to intervene, the fire brigade was not called, and the building burned all night, lighting the night sky red. It burned for two days.

At half past six, I got the first call for help from one of my friends. She was a journalist at Al-Ahram, and her name is Fotoh. She lived alone in an apartment beside Al-Azbakia police station, very close to Ramses Square. She was screaming down the phone.

"Please help," she cried, "they're trying…they're invading. They're chasing the police, they're trying to kill…they're trying to get into our building. Please do something…help us."

Some of the demonstrations, such as this one, had turned to riots. The police station next to Fotoh's apartment building had been set alight and the police inside attempted to flee into her building. I tried to call the ministry, to help my friend.

I told the Republican Guard Commander in the building that something bad was happening out near Ramses Square. I didn't realise until later that this is what happened to 99 police stations, 19 in Cairo, across the country that night and the following, which had become targets of arson in the tumult which followed the demonstrations. This was a worrying development: prisoners escaped, and many police stations were looted of their weaponry before being burned down. The attacks were highly organised, coordinated and synchronised. This suggests that the attacks were not a spontaneous act of public aggression, but something that was planned. The attacks tended to pan out in the same way and at roughly synchronised times. The attackers would start by gathering around a police station, then the ones who were armed would shoot at it, before the crowd would break in and try to burn it down. Because most of the police were busy policing the demonstrations, most stations lacked the appropriate forces to protect them. What happened inside those stations was similar to what would happen with the NDP building: the burning of documents and records, then the seizure of all weaponry. The police, and in some cases soldiers, would try and defend the stations, leading to casualties among the attackers.

There was still a small group of police protecting the Maspero building, as there was a small police station inside. At 7.30pm, vicious fighting broke out between the remaining police and the protesters outside. The army did not intervene; the soldiers just sat and watched as the police and protesters traded blows.

Overwhelmed, the police retreated back into the building, changed out of their uniforms and quietly sneaked out.

The protesters tried to get inside the Maspero building many times throughout the evening, trashing some of the entrances, though each time, the army and the building's internal security team managed to stop them from actually getting inside.

The protesters and the army didn't quite know what to make of each other at first. The troops had deliberately not intervened with or attacked the protesters. I watched one of the protesters, in what appeared to be a test, scrawl "Down with Mubarak" on one of the tanks out on the street below. The soldiers stood by, and did not attempt to apprehend the man. What's more, they didn't even try to scrub out the graffiti, instead they just left it there.

Later, when people were gathering around the tanks, one adventurous protester began to cautiously haul himself up over the side, climbing onto the tank. The soldier remained motionless, standing in the hatch, watching the protester as he climbed towards him. Slowly, the protester offered his hand to the soldier. The soldier, returned the gesture, and grasping the hand in front of him, the two shook hands, before finally embracing one another. At that, the surrounding protesters jumped up onto the tanks, cheering, raising their arms and celebrating together.

Meanwhile, the city was burning, buildings were on fire and cars were being torched in the middle of the street. I had never seen anything like it. Some opportunists stormed Arcadia Mall, the large shopping centre in downtown Cairo, and looted the shops and apartments within, before setting the building alight.

Aside from the army units protecting the vital organs of the state, the rest of Cairo was devoid of any kind of authority. There were no police, the curfew was totally ignored, the city was lawless.

At around 8pm, I received a closed envelope from the minister's office. It was the text of the President's speech that he was to make on the protests; written on the top of the first page was the date of the 29th of January. There was intense discussion as to whether he should speak that night or the next day. It was decided, in order to quell the unrest as soon as possible, he would speak that night. The King was to make his move on the chessboard.

However, I discovered that the statement that he had prepared was exactly the same, almost word for word as one he gave 10 days earlier to parliament. It had nothing about the protests, and only mentioned a few vague references to economic or political reform. There was no reference to dismissing the cabinet.

After I had looked through it, I phoned Anas and asked him "What have you sent me?"

"This is the statement which the President will be reading out. Did you read it?"

"Yes," I answered, "this is an old speech."

"How come?"

"This is exactly what he said at the opening of parliament and the NDP conference! Nothing new," I pointed out, "this will just make the people more angry!"

"OK," Anas conceded, "I'll tell them."

At around 9.30pm a group of youths succeeded in breaking down one of the gates outside our building. Once they got inside, they ran around smashing furniture and computers, trying to destroy whatever files and documents they could. They wrenched plasma screens off the walls both inside and outside one of the main studios on the ground floor. Once they got upstairs, they started a fire on the first floor, at the foreign press office. The invaders managed to get up to the third floor. They were vindictive and violent. One could not help noticing that some of them were just kids, no more than 11 or 12 years old. The encroachment was only stopped when the building's internal security guards, army men, snapped into action. They ordered a curfew in all corridors before locking staff inside their offices and studios for their own safety, positioning armed guards in front of doors. They then launched tear gas canisters within the building, far more effective in the confined space inside than outside. At the same time, the soldiers stationed outside moved to secure that entrance. We were all watching in terror through the banks of monitors relaying the havoc seen through the building's security cameras. At that time, the soldiers were ordered not to engage the protesters. The soldiers inside were positioned in front of the studios, but we couldn't see them moving through the corridors. It seemed they were ordered to stay put – only the commanding officers were to move through the building and they would only react to direct attacks on the studios.

The attackers did not stop there. They headed for Gate 7, smashing its glass doors. Internal security stopped them from entering using fire extinguishers, blasting them as they arranged their own bodies to block the way. Gate 7 is the only access point in a fence which surrounds a small parking area where employees park their cars, both inside and outside the gate. A lot of cars were smashed that day. My secretary's office windows, which overlook the whole street area, was regularly checked by employees looking to see if their cars had been destroyed.

A group of protesters gathered around an army armoured vehicle parked outside the fence. They sat around and on top of it, chanting and cheering on the attackers. Some of my colleagues' cars were destroyed.

After the brief assault on our building, my nerves shattered, I went back to my office to wait for the President. I had been waiting for Mubarak to come out and speak since 8pm. There was a direct link in my office to the studio in the Presidential Palace, which I was staring at. My office had turned into something resembling a busy market place. All the managers were sitting inside watching CCTV feeds on the banks of screens, though they were also there for protection. People were still scared, as the corridors were filled with soldiers. Staff had been vacating the building all day, leaving us with a minimum working crew.

The phone calls started coming in at 9pm. Every phone in the building was ringing with people asking for help. We were taking the calls on air and informing the army what to do. I had no idea that these calls would keep coming in for as long as they did.

By 11pm, even my staff inside the building were worried as to why Mubarak had not shown up yet. They kept coming into my office, asking where on earth he was. Someone said people will go to sleep before he starts speaking. I replied with a question, "Will you go to sleep with the country in such a mess or wait to hear what your President will say about it?"

A few minutes before midnight, the President appeared. I asked Anas over the phone whether we would be broadcasting live.

"No," he replied, "we will record it and broadcast it as soon as he is finished."

On the screen in front of me, Mubarak came in. The presidential studio had a formal, standard set up. A wide podium, decorated with the national emblem of Saladin's Eagle in the front, set against a blue background, which was again adorned with a much larger golden version of the national emblem. An Egyptian flag stood beside the podium. Mubarak shook hands with the team stationed there. He came in flanked by his son Gamal and Suleiman Awad, his press secretary. He asked one of the producers in the room if it would be going out live or be pre-recorded. The producer politely informed him that it would be pre-recorded.

He started reading out the speech. I was following with the hard copy I had in the office, to check if anything had been changed. It was five pages long. The time it took to read it, as it was written, was roughly 10 minutes. The first page he read was identical to what I had and my shoulders sank. The second page, again identical. A few words were changed in the last paragraph on the second page. Small words. Instead of saying that he would make better efforts to combat poverty, he said that they would make extra efforts to increase employment. Just little things like that. They added one sentence: "We will firmly fight corruption."

The only important thing they added was that he had asked the government to resign and he would start putting together a new government.

The speech ended: nothing new, no concrete commitments, just vague promises and a plan to dismiss his cabinet.

He had fluffed one of his lines and corrected himself as he did so half way through. We made a quick jump cut, but it was a good edit, nobody noticed.

The speech was broadcast at 12.12am. It took fifteen minutes to broadcast, rather than ten. Most importantly, it didn't live up to the people's expectations. It was no King's move.

Just before the President left the studio, after his speech had been recorded, he asked the team, "do you want anything else from me?"

In light of what had gone on that day, one could read that as a loaded question, and it needed a better answer than the one it got.

"No, Mr President, nothing else."

JANUARY 29TH – SATURDAY

Friday night flowed into Saturday morning. From then onwards, every day felt the same. All the different days blurred into one, so long and straining that it seemed endless, as if they had begun abruptly at a moment of which we were never aware. There was no clear division between day and night: our sense of time had become vague and indistinct.

That night, smoke filled the capital's skies, mixed with the tear gas that lingered in the air. The blazes that lit up the sky stretched across several districts of Cairo. The fires, the result of numerous arson attacks were around every street corner. Police stations, government buildings, offices, shopping malls, cars. They were all burning.

There was, supposedly, a curfew going on, from 6pm until 8am in the morning. It was put in place in Greater Cairo, Suez and Alexandria, subsequently amended to include all the governorates of the Republic. All the curfews were comprehensively ignored. When talk of a curfew first started, people initially remembered the curfews of the past that were rigorously enforced. It was not the case this time.

The explosion of crime which occurred that night poses some deep questions for Egypt. Thousands of prisoners escaped as their jails were broken open across the country. Meanwhile, as criminals were on the loose, the police disappeared. There was nobody to keep law and order. That's why people were calling the state TV. There was nobody else to call.

The prisoners escaped not because they rioted and overpowered the guards, neither did they break out because the guards had fled. The prisons were broken into from outside.

The reports that I heard, many of which came from the prisoners themselves, followed the same general pattern. In the middle of the night, the inmates suddenly heard the crack of gunfire close by. Within moments, bulldozers were driven into the prison walls, as the prisons were raided by gunmen, killing guards in the process. The raiders had their faces covered by their Keffayahs, or were wearing Bedouin dress. The same course of events was repeated in the main prisons of central Egypt (the region encompassing Cairo, Feyyoum and Burg Al-Arab). I believe that these attacks, and the systematic nationwide assaults on Egypt's police stations, were no coincidence.

At the time that these attacks happened, conspiracy theories materialised immediately. Many believed that this was the government's doing, that they had emptied the prisons in the hope of somehow marshalling these escaped convicts to harass the protesters. Indeed, this is one of the charges that Habib Al-Adly faced in his trial for human rights abuses. It's certainly possible, but I'm not convinced. Extraordinary claims require extraordinary evidence, and there is simply no proof that the Interior Ministry did this.

I have pointed out many times how stupid the government were in their handling of the situation; however, I do not think that they were so foolish as to unleash such an unpredictable element into the fray. Indeed, it would have to have been a fairly elaborate double bluff, as the Interior Ministry itself was also attacked in the chaos. In addition, it would have had to have been carried out with inordinate skill, as the police had problems with their own communication system, leaving them in disarray.

There are other stories as to why this occurred. Many of the prisons that were attacked held committed opponents of the government, not only Muslim Brothers but also members of more aggressive organisations, such as Al-Jihad, Hamas and Hezbollah.

One member of Hezbollah had managed to make it back to Lebanon to give a press conference within hours of his jail break. There have been other reports of Hamas members making it back to Gaza within days of their escape. These men would have to have been aided and protected to get back so easily. Their escapes must have been planned.

Egypt has had its fair share of terrorist attacks in recent decades. There are many who would wish to bring down the entire edifice of the state and replace it with an Islamist regime. Many of these groups are related to other terror groups in the region, and have been oppressed by the government for many years, since the assassination of Sadat. Opportunities to break their men out of prison, perhaps even make a bid for power, do not come along very often, and they will take them when they present themselves.

I do not suggest for a moment that these attacks were connected with the majority of peaceful demonstrators in the cities. Indeed, many of those demonstrators were liberals and secularists who also did not want to see a violent Islamist government take power. However, it must be understood that Egypt is a large country, with many different streams of opposition, some more fundamentalist than others. With such a breakdown in law and order, it is inevitable that opportunists will emerge to take their chances. Some of the blame does ultimately lie with the government and Interior Ministry. By blaming all the unrest on the Muslim Brotherhood and other Islamist groups, they pushed their backs against the wall, forcing the Islamists to take larger risks and make bold moves against the government.

There were also the criminal opportunists who came out that night: thugs who looted shops or tried to extort money from helpless citizens. The word in Egyptian Arabic is *Baltagiyya*, and it is a word that gets used a lot in Egypt. Unfortunately, Egypt has an abundance of criminals. With no police on the streets, there was nobody to stop these thugs heading out and stealing from businesses and neighbourhoods.

At the TV station, one of the first calls for help we put on air was from one of our best-known light entertainment presenters, Tareq Alam, famous for his gameshow, "Gold". When he was talking to us on air, he collapsed on the phone: "This is not Egypt," he wept, "the thugs are threatening people, they are raping women, please do something, turn on the phones! Please!"

We got blamed by anti-government activists for scaring people and terrifying the populace. However, people were already scared, it didn't matter what they saw on television. With the collapse of communications and the police at the same time, they had no one to turn to. We were the only line of communication left to connect them to a government that had disappeared and a security system that was not there. Al-Jazeera posted a number on screen, urging viewers to call in if they had trouble with thugs in their homes. Though, as it was a Qatari number, I'm not sure how helpful the operator would have been over in Doha. I considered it another tool they used to wield some influence over events in Egypt.

I decided that we too should have a number on screen for people to call. It wasn't our job to provide such a service, but I believed it was a role we should take on; we would report what the callers had told us, and pass the details on to the army.

The evening before, we had started receiving panicked phone calls on the office phones from all over the country. These calls continued throughout the night. My phone started ringing ceaselessly. I didn't even know most of the people calling. I've still no idea how they got my number. The tenor of the calls was always the same: people screaming and crying, desperate for some help. Callers told of armed men wandering the streets, brandishing guns and knives. Others complained of thugs trying to get into their homes and intimidating them. Some of the more enterprising criminals came out in front of people's homes with megaphones and demanded protection money from the terrified residents. There were also numerous reports of serious sexual assaults on women and girls. People wanted any kind of help, they were even asking for tanks to be sent to defend their neighbourhoods.

A friend of mine, Youssef Qaeed, a famous writer in Egypt, called my office. "My daughter is trapped in her flat, she's surrounded by thugs! You must do something!" he begged. Another colleague of mine, Azza Mustafa, the head of Channel One, called in from Agouza (central Cairo), desperate for help. She called on Omar Suleiman and Hussein Tantawi directly to send units to help her. Others called me from all around Cairo, from all the main districts, all with the same pleas for help. Some admitted on the phone that they didn't know me, but explained they had been told that I was senior in the TV station and could help. One of the callers even asked, "Is this the phone of the Egyptian television?" before asking for aid.

This went on for about 72 hours, at all hours of the day and night. I could never bring myself to turn off my phone. Instead, I patiently took the calls to see if I could help.

At one point on Saturday evening, I walked into the main office near the TV studios. I could see everyone in my office: journalists, editors, even the office boy diligently taking calls and writing down details, before faxing or calling the army headquarters. I was so proud of my staff. In Britain, they call it the "Blitz mentality," everybody buckling down together, doing their best to help in any way they could. Keeping calm and carrying on. Everybody worked together, doing the noble thing and providing a helping hand for people they didn't even know.

The chaos had ensued in part because a decision was made early on that the army would not engage with anybody, and no shots would be fired. Whilst this prevented any bloody clashes from taking place that night between army and demonstrators, it also meant that when it came to the looting and the arson, the army stood by and let it happen.

At first, the only thing that the army did, that we saw, was prevent anybody from invading the TV building. Banks were robbed and El-Qasr Al-Ainy, the big hospital in Cairo was raided by thugs. The children's hospital was raided too, but the parents of the children there bravely stood up to the attackers. Later, the army started following our broadcasts, and sent forces to protect addresses that we had given them, though still without actively engaging anybody.

Some people in Burg Al-Arab, near Alexandria, called the TV station. There is a train line between Burg Al-Arab and Cairo. A train was running on the track, transporting over a hundred prisoners. The call we got was from a village near the line. The caller explained that train only had two guards. The relatives of the prisoners knew the train had stopped and were coming to free the prisoners. The caller was asking, on behalf of the village, for help. We notified the military at once. The army sent a unit there, and managed to take back control of the train.

There was another worrying call that day, this time from a young police officer. He called my office phone. He explained to me that there were three of them left guarding the central police armoury, protecting literally thousands of weapons, assault rifles and handguns. There was no one else there, and if the public knew, the stores would be raided and the weapons would be on the streets. The young man also explained that his colleagues over at the Interior Ministry had just told them to flee and protect themselves. They refused. "We're not leaving here," the officer declared, "and we'll protect it with our bodies to the end. We have thousands of guns here, if they are taken, it will be a big problem, so we will protect them." Fortunately, we managed to make some well placed phone calls and got those officers some additional protection.

We also got some strange calls at the station from prisoners who had been broken out of prison. One prisoner explained, "They freed us from prison, but we want to go back. I've only got a couple of weeks left on my sentence. I want to go back." Any prisoner caught after escape would surely receive a much tougher sentence as punishment. We called the army and asked about their predicament. All we could do was advise them to present themselves to the military police at any opportunity.

Late that night, we started seeing escaped prisoners, still in their uniforms from the windows of the Maspero building. I called the armed forces, and decided we should at least do something to bring relief to the viewing public, and show that there was still a semblance of law and order in the country. I got the army to allow us to send out a camera crew to follow an army squad, and try to capture on film criminals and convicts actually being arrested. The army had already begun rounding up criminals in different districts, and now they were hunting them just outside the building – it wouldn't be difficult to get some footage.

We managed to capture the army rounding up some looters on camera. They were caught red-handed, live on television. Many of them were young boys, some were thugs, and others were bearded. It sent a message to the public, that the army, if not the police, were still out there trying to protect them.

The news broke in the bulletins that the army had arrested thugs across Alexandria and Cairo. It was a small victory in the fight against theft, looting and intimidation. We were sent a list of those who were arrested nearby, while the army turned part of the ground floor of the building into a holding area for those they arrested, as there were no prisons or police stations into which they could put them.

One of the most significant attacks that we heard about that day took place on the night before in Mohandiseen, against the headquarters of Ahmed Ezz's company. Like the NDP building, it was set alight and left to burn. Across town, the fire at the NDP building had been going all night. No effort was ever made to put it out. This was a concern, as the Egyptian Museum, which houses Egypt's most precious ancient artefacts was directly behind the inferno. The museum had already sustained damage during the unrest. The day before, amid the chaos, some looters had broken into the museum, stealing some priceless treasures and damaging many more. In the rampage, two of the mummies were decapitated.

Khaled Youssef, a film director, famous for his films about Egypt's social problems, and a prominent supporter of the protests, came up to my office. He demanded that we do something to save the museum. I was angry at the time, "Look Khaled," I snapped, "you called on the people to come out on the streets, now look at what is happening! Those people are the ones who are looting." I relented though, and let him on air to call upon the people to protect the museum. I called the army once more to get them to protect the museum, and stop it from catching the flames from its blazing neighbour. Sure enough, protesters, determined to protect their heritage rallied to Khaled's call and formed a human chain around the museum, until the army arrived to take over. A number of TV officials were present when we had that conversation. They were all against him.

The whole state was dead. No government, no police, no ministries, no ministers, there was no one. All that was left were the people on the streets, the army and my three offices in the Maspero building. Had we announced that fact to the country's citizens on air, it would have been terrifying for the populace. The least we could do was take people's calls and connect them to the army. That night, and the night before, around 20,000 prisoners escaped, thousands of firearms were stolen, 99 police stations were set on fire. 2,000 police vehicles, of all shapes and sizes, were torched.

When people knew that messages were effective, some other more ominous calls started coming in. One of my colleagues grabbed me, saying that someone was calling to tell him there was an armoury somewhere left unguarded. He gave us the address. We asked the caller if there was any threat. He said no, but he asked if he could go on air to announce that there was a loaded armoury lying unprotected somewhere in Cairo. I told my colleague to ask for his number and to tell him that we would call him back. When asked his name, the caller hung up. As far as I could tell the caller was trying to stir up trouble and get people to raid this arsenal for its weapons.

Another call told us that people were cutting down trees in Maadi. Maadi is a nice suburban area to the south of central Cairo. I have no idea why people would want to cut down a tree. Whether they just wanted the wood, wanted to start a fire, or whether they just wanted to see them fall, I can't begin to understand.

Two different attitudes arose among the citizens of Cairo that night. For some, the crisis brought out the noble, caring aspects in people, roused to help their neighbours in a time of need. For others, it caused them to commit opportunistic, selfish and violent acts of thuggery.

In a way, it encapsulates the division in Egyptian society. There are two Egypts. On the one hand, we have seen an explosion in young educated, interested, and tech-savvy youths. There is a vibrant cultural scene in Cairo, it's an exciting place to be young. On the other hand, there are hooligans and thugs. We have severe problems with petty crime, sexual harassment, conmen and threatening behaviour on the streets. In a way, there are far more than two Egypts. There are many different societies living on top of each other, some secular, some religious, some Muslim, some Christian, some subservient to others and some superior. Many of them are in conflict with each other. I think we saw some of that conflict spill out that night.

In order to protect themselves, residents took the law into their own hands and formed "popular committees" to defend their neighbourhoods. Residents banded together, setting up checkpoints and patrols to protect their homes from thugs, looters and criminals. The idea quickly spread throughout Cairo. This idea was called for on Egypt News by one of the citizens. Channel One news kept campaigning for it all day until by night they were everywhere.

Back in the office, we had hardly any food. All the food in the small kiosk in the corridor was gone and the building cafeteria was locked up. There were some boxes of dates in my office, and a few bits and pieces tucked away around the studios. We were forced to nibble on what we could find. We sent out the office boy in the morning to get some food. He had to walk for some time until he finally found an open shop, and he just bought whatever was left. When he came back a couple of hours later, we could have kissed him. He was carrying sandwiches, ful (a popular Arab dish made from beans), bread, juice and some sweets. A feast.

Anas had spent the whole night at the office. I went up to see him late morning. He was standing at his window, looking out over the Nile and the rest of the city. I went to stand with him. He pointed at a small moped riding along the Corniche, "Look, look at this one…where's he going?" he wondered aloud. Then he pointed out another motorbike: "Look, do you see the man with the beard, on the bike…he's one of them…this is the third time he's come round now!" He was obsessing over the comings and goings of the little motors down on the street below. The demonstrators were using a new form of communication. In lieu of mobile phones, motorbikes and mopeds were busy zipping across the roads and bridges, relaying messages between the groups of protesters.

In the morning, we had a visit from one of the commanders of the central area armed forces. Anas knew about it and asked the head of security if he could show the visiting general to his office.

The general came up and shook hands with Anas. He was very polite, but he gave the impression that he was in charge, not Anas, and he wouldn't take any orders from him. He was smiling, but strict. He had given orders for his men not to concede authority or let themselves be ordered around by any civilians, even if they were ministers.

After he left the meeting, the general told the head of security, "Tell your minister I'm not with him. I have orders from my superiors, I don't take orders from your minister."

In a time of crisis, you can really see the true mettle of your colleagues. As the crisis dragged on, people started fleeing the building. It was like a sinking ship, and people were jumping overboard. Only a few stayed. Some of my staff suddenly came out with severe back pain or other more embarrassing medical problems. Though they were coming up to me with medical complaints and doctor's notes, I didn't bother checking. If they wanted to go, they could go. I wouldn't stop them.

I reminded those who stayed that we had a job to do, and we were working for the country, not for any one person. We would try our best to report what was happening. Of course, we tried to go to Tahrir Square to report on the largest demonstration, but it was just too dangerous. On the first day we lost three cameras and our reporters were physically attacked. From the beginning, the protesters targeted the state TV, labelling it as just another one of the government's tools of control. The demonstrators saw the TV station as against people and more importantly, against Tahrir Square. Some of our journalists were also attacked by police and some were even almost arrested.

Meanwhile, at the Presidential Palace, Mubarak started getting calls of support from other world leaders. The first call he got was from Muammar Gaddafi. I didn't think that it would be wise to run with Mubarak receiving a message of support from Gaddafi at the top of the news order. Anas overruled me, telling me that this was presidential news and it must be run first. Later, he got calls from King Abdullah of Saudi Arabia and King Hamad of Bahrain. Mubarak also got a call that day from President Obama, during which the American President urged restraint and respect for the human rights of the protesters. Anas phoned up Gamal, they talked for a while and it was announced that they would put Obama's call at the end of the running order. Of course, this is the complete opposite of what would have normally happened. We would always have run with Obama first, but after what he had told the President, we wouldn't be doing so today.

There was also a meeting of the cabinet, ostensibly called to give them the opportunity to resign. Anas, Habib, Ahmed Aboul Gheit (the Foreign Minister) and Field Marshal Tantawi did not attend. The meeting was not held in the cabinet building near Tahrir, but in Smart village, a modern business park on the desert road to Alexandria, to the west of Cairo. I called our reporter there to find out what was going on.

"They've all arrived" he informed me, "most of them have come in old cars." A cabinet minister travelling in an old car is highly out of character. They would usually travel in the latest models, shiny new Mercedes or BMWs, though not today. The reporter also mentioned how sombre they all looked.

The four who didn't turn up all considered themselves too busy to attend. Tantawi was busy running the army, Anas was busy with the media and Adly was under intense pressure at the Interior Ministry. Ahmed Aboul Gheit was still abroad. It didn't mean they were against resigning in principle, they were just busy.

By the end of the meeting, the cabinet had all handed in their resignations. We reported the news when it came on: breaking news, the cabinet had quit.

At the same time, around early afternoon, the demonstrations began to grow. With no police, there was a total security vacuum, leaving a space that would soon be filled by chanting protesters.

Simultaneously, our correspondents reported that other areas of Cairo such as Helwan, Giza and Haram witnessed the formation of crowds in their side-streets and squares. The gatherings were preparing to head to Tahrir Square. It was starting again. At around 1pm, a message came from the palace to put back the start of the curfew from 6pm to 4pm. It was a sign that they were losing control. It was a joke. Nobody respected the curfew the previous night, there was no reason why they should again.

I went to my staff and announced that we needed to have a slogan. It's common for a news channel during hectic or important times to adopt a slogan. We agreed on "Protect Egypt". From that Saturday, we had it on screen everyday. It was our mission, our aim. We used the flag as well. The flag has intense symbolic importance for Egyptians. It represents the independent spirit of Egypt, and is something that commands tremendous respect.

At exactly 1.45pm, we received the footage of the cabinet meeting with all those grim faces presenting their resignations. They would not be leaving immediately, for a presidential mandate assigned them to manage the ministries' affairs until a new government was appointed.

There was no clear information as to who would form the new cabinet. I asked Anas whether he had talked the matter over with the President. He told me that he hadn't spoken to the President all day, and that there were meetings and consultations going on that were not yet resolved. A little while afterwards, I learned from other sources that the candidate for premiership was Ahmed Shafik, the former Commander of the Air Force, and Minister of Aviation in the resigning government. My sources guessed he would be getting the Prime Minister's job as he was the only minister summoned to the presidential headquarters immediately after that cabinet meeting.

Gamal and his clique in the palace started making their moves. They held hurried meetings and clandestine discussions to search for a way to try to ease people's anger and frustration. The first person sacrificed to appease the public would be Ahmed Ezz. The resignation was announced by Safwat Al-Sharif, the Secretary General of the Party, a little after 4pm. Ezz was one of the names most often heard chanted in the demonstrations, and they thought that his resignation might be enough to persuade the protesters to start leaving. Sharif managed to get Ezz to resign by telling him that all the leaders of the party would resign. Ezz, unwittingly, resigned while the other leaders kept their positions.

Even though the protesters did not care much about the restructuring of the government, this move preoccupied many of the traditional political forces, such as the Wafd Party which called for a government of national unity. The Nasserite Party also demanded a national unity government, which would not be made up of members of the NDP. They wanted the government to be transitional, having a provisional duty until they handed over power in the upcoming presidential elections.

At the same time, there was talk in different political circles on the nature of the new ministers who would form the government. It was seemingly a subject of heated discussion amongst those in power, who insisted on holding on to some of the old ministers. At the same time, there was stubborn resistance to the introduction of any opposition politicians to the cabinet. Once again, both sides were at an impasse, each unwilling to make any concessions.

In a further effort to assuage the protesters, it was announced that there would be a new Vice President. The position had remained vacant since 1981, when Mubarak himself left it to assume the presidency in the wake of Sadat's assassination. Since the middle of the day, there had been numerous leaks and rumours suggesting that the new Vice President was to be Omar Suleiman.

Omar Suleiman commanded a great deal of respect in Egypt. People believed that he would solve many of the country's problems. He was a strong character; if there was a problem with politics, people really thought that he would fix it when he became Prime Minister or Vice President. He had been a man waiting in the shadows for many years, perhaps that's what contributed to his aura of political prowess. A career soldier, who holds two degrees, Suleiman was transferred to military intelligence in the 1980s, rising to become the director of the General Intelligence Service in 1993. He had long been known to the public, though he was not a public figure, and did not give interviews to the media. It was a wonder to the Egyptian people why he hadn't been given such a high profile role until now. He had charisma, he was seen as a hard worker, and most importantly was not corrupt, unlike the rest of Egypt's modern political class. Some even thought that he would be president before Gamal.

The choice of Omar Suleiman was welcomed by various political forces; he was, to a large extent, accepted, as I have already mentioned. Yet, for the demonstrators, this news wasn't want they wanted to hear. For one thing, it wasn't the prospect of a new Vice President that brought them out onto the street. Although many among the demonstrators had welcomed the appointment, the majority were against it, as they perceived him to be part of an already broken system.

At around 5pm news came in of Omar Suleiman's confirmation as Vice President. President Mubarak left his villa and came to his office in the presidential compound. We had a camera crew over there ready to record it all. I was watching developments live through the direct feed in my office. He was standing in front of Mubarak, making his oath. It looked rushed. The crew had also missed the beginning of it. They took the tape to the presidential studio and fed it through to us. After he had finished, Suleiman saluted the President. Mubarak shook hands with him saying *Shed Hailak ya Omar* – be strong Omar.

At around 5.55pm I got the other news, that Ahmed Shafik was the Prime Minister. He was an air marshal, and had hitherto been referred to as Marshal Ahmed Shafik. I got the news that a *Dr* Ahmed Shafik had been made Prime Minister. He was a doctor (with a PhD rather than an M.D.), but it was still unusual, and he was never addressed as such. Zakaria Azmi called me to confirm that this was how he should be described.

"Why?" I asked.

"We want him to have a civilian image," he replied.

I understood later they wanted to play down his military background and didn't want to suggest to the public that the military was slowly taking control of Egypt. Especially not now, as the military represented a threat to the dominance of the Presidential Palace.

Mubarak had a few meetings that day, one of which was with his Defence Minister, Field Marshal Tantawi. He offered Tantawi the position of Vice President. Tantawi refused. He offered him the role of Prime Minister. Tantawi refused. Tantawi was insistent he would not leave the army.

The Field Marshal's intransigence angered Mubarak. In a moment of rage, the President told him he could either take up one of the appointments, or go home. The Arabic word he used *emshy* is something of a derogatory imperative, almost like saying *get lost* in English.

Tantawi left the palace, but he didn't go home. He instead headed straight for Group 66. Mubarak was convinced that he had lost control of the army. It seemed Omar Suleiman had attempted to reconcile the two sides by accepting the role of Vice President. He accepted it out of loyalty to the country and the President, potentially damaging his own career in the process.

I heard later that after the meeting, the President instructed the Interior Ministry to bug the telephone lines of all the army leaders in the SCAF (Supreme Council of the Armed Forces). The government was cracking.

Field Marshal Tantawi felt that his place was with the army. If he left the army, then it may have fallen back into the control of the Presidential Palace and could potentially be used against the general public, if the protests were to drag on.

At the time I didn't know all the details, but I knew that there was tension between the President and the army, specifically between Mubarak and Tantawi. Rumours started spreading that General Sami Anan, the Chief of Staff (the second in command of the army) would be the new Defence Minister. Anan had been out of the country since the start of the unrest, but was on his way back from the United States that Saturday evening. These rumours were coming from the palace. Anas confirmed the rumours to me when he mentioned that he believed that Tantawi would not be part of the new government, but would be replaced by Sami Anan.

I received a strange statement that night. It was on tape, read by General Etman, the army spokesman. It consisted of one sentence: "The Defence Minister and General Commander of the Armed Forces, Field Marshal Mohammed Hussein Tantawi thanks the Egyptian youth for what they are doing and asks them to deliver any criminals to the military police."

It was completely out of the blue, and used Tantawi's full title. They never even used to attach his name to any of the army statements. It was also a rather unnecessary statement to give the general public at that time. It wasn't for the public though.

It was a message to the palace. Tantawi wasn't going anywhere.

The author interviews President Hosni Mubarak at the High Dam in Aswan on the 11th of June 2009, shortly after the death of his grandson.

The author interviews Omar Suleiman on the 3rd of February 2011, five days into his short term as Vice President.

The author interviews Prime Minister Ahmed Nazif on the 6th of January 2011.

Gamal Mubarak during one of his meetings with Egyptian youth in August 2010.

The author interviews Pope Shnouda III on the 4th of January 2011, shortly after the bombing of Alqedseen church.

A chat with the then Governor of Sinai, General Mourad Mowafy, who preceded Omar Suleiman in presiding over the Egyptian General Intelligence Service (GIS)

An arial photograph of Tahrir Square on the 6th of February.

Tanks and barbed wire protect the Maspero Building from protesters.

JANUARY 30TH – SUNDAY

In the morning, I was sitting with Anas in his office. He was talking with admiration about Mubarak's response to the unrest. "You see…" he went on, "Mubarak now, is at the headquarters of the army, he's that kind of man…he wants to control everything from there."

Anas was unaware of the power struggle between the President and the army that had occurred the night before. I asked him if he had heard about any conflict between Field Marshal Tantawi and President Mubarak.

"No," he replied, "but I think the President would prefer Sami Anan. He was complaining that Tantawi hadn't deployed the army fast enough. They were very slow, they still don't control everything. They don't interfere in everything."

This was a strange turnaround. Tantawi had worked with Mubarak for decades, having been his Defence Minister since 1991. The two men were close. To Mubarak, Tantawi was a useful tool to check the influence of Gamal and his inner circle. The Field Marshal even obstructed various business projects undertaken by Gamal and his associates, citing interference with military operations. In Egypt, large business projects may be vetoed by the army on any vague grounds relating to "military purposes". This hindrance of the group's business affairs was actually coordinated with President Mubarak. Mubarak also used his Justice Minister, Mamdouh Marei, to cancel some of the business contracts his son's people had been putting together. Marei, a man from the older generation famously said, "In the cabinet meetings, when they start opening their laptops and talking in English, I just ask them if they want anything from me, then leave." Mubarak would have

Marei personally inspect the building sites of projects invested in by his own cabinet in an effort to keep the rampant corruption in check, and have them shut down for the slightest legal violation. The two of them hated this young clique of businessman who had infected government, particularly the ageing Field Marshal, who, in one cabinet session, banged his hand against the table, shouting "You are sinning against Egypt!" when the cabinet began to discuss a business deal.

Anas was notified that we would shortly be receiving a tape of Mubarak's visit to military HQ, and we were to broadcast it as soon as it arrived. While I was waiting, one of the military commanders at the station informed me that Tantawi himself would be visiting the building, to check on the troops guarding it. As I was on the phone to Anas, telling him to expect Tantawi to come by, my walkie-talkie crackled with the sound of the head of security announcing his arrival.

Anas left the building straight away to go down to receive Tantawi out on the street. After saluting the Field Marshal, he invited him up to his office.

"No," came the refusal, "I'm here to see my men. Just go back to your office and carry on with your work."

As Anas humbly walked back into the building, Tantawi walked among his soldiers. The men were standing to attention, bolt upright. Their eyes betrayed their nerves. These men would hardly expect to come across a colonel during their duties, let alone a field marshal. Tantawi asked them their names and units before reassuring them, telling them to be strong and patting them on the shoulder.

There weren't any protesters outside the building that morning, but a few passers by noticed the Field Marshal there on the street. They began to gather and chant slogans in support of the army, still popular with the general public. Tantawi even shook hands with a few of them. I don't think people cheered specifically because they loved the Field Marshal, a lot of people wouldn't have known who he was, but he was clearly a senior general, someone the public would respect.

I sent out a camera crew to record the incident. The army had a camera crew out there as well, recording it for their own purposes. Tantawi was only out there for about fifteen minutes, and after he had left, the crew came back inside to edit the footage.

When Tantawi was gone, I went up to Anas's office and asked him why the Field Marshal had come to visit.

"Oh nothing," he sighed, "he's just here to check on his forces."

"Is he coming in?" I asked.

"No."

"Why didn't you stay with him?" I persisted.

"He asked me to carry on up here. He wants to carry on with what he's doing."

Anas asked me to include the bit where he received the Field Marshal in our report of the visit. Shortly afterwards, back in my office. I got a call from one of the generals.

"Did you see what Field Marshal Tantawi did? He came to visit you today, did you tape it?"

"Of course" I replied. "What do you want me to do? I've got some shots of him with the soldiers and I've got him meeting Anas."

"Can you wait a few minutes?" came the reply, "We'll get back to you."

After I hung up, I looked at the clock. I couldn't wait as the bulletins would be going out soon, so I had my editor make a quick cut of the rough material we had. It was just the Field Marshal visiting the TV building and the Minister of Information meeting him, a brief filler of news. After a few minutes my phone rang again. It was the military.

"Can you only have Anas in one or two shots? Don't feature him too much. Broadcast what you have for now, but in a while, we'll send you a tape."

Later on, the military sent me a tape. It was essentially the same footage of Tantawi wandering around in front of the TV building, but Anas was only seen for a couple of seconds at the end. They called me again at the end of the day, and asked for Anas to be removed entirely from the piece.

Tantawi's impromptu inspection of his troops outside the TV building, following on from the statement the night before was a confirmation to the country that Field Marshal Tantawi was exercising his authority as Minister of Defence. If President Mubarak had thought of, decided, or even begun to take steps towards removing the Field Marshal, then he would have to stop. The Presidential Palace had fought a small battle with the military, and the military had won. They were not going to look weak in front of the public. They would not be reorganising themselves, unlike the cabinet and the NDP.

Something similar happened with the tape of Mubarak's visit to the military HQ. When I sat in Anas's office that morning, he handed me a tape recorded while Mubarak had been with the military. Mubarak had brought Gamal with him, and according to the generals, Tantawi wasn't comfortable having the President's son there. In fact, the army man was very angry at having to accommodate him, going so far as to tell Mubarak that Gamal shouldn't have come.

The tape that Anas handed me had no footage of Gamal at all. Even though he came with his father, anyone watching the tape wouldn't have known he was there. They even called Anas later on to confirm that Gamal would not feature in the report.

My contacts in the palace told me that Gamal was livid when he found out, but after being told it was done with his father's consent, he went silent.

While we were putting together the news bulletin, Anas called me again.

"There's going to be another story coming," he stated blandly.

"What's that?" I enquired.

"Habib Al-Adly is at the army HQ with the President, Omar Suleiman and Field Marshal Tantawi."

"Really?"

"Yes," he confirmed.

I put the phone down on the receiver, thought for a moment, picked it up again and dialled my contacts in the military. My source on the other side confirmed that Adly had indeed been there, though he had arrived at the moment the President was leaving. I did not think the timing an accident. They would have had instructions to keep the visits separate; the army delayed Adly, making sure he wouldn't join the meeting while the President was still there. Adly's meeting was only with Suleiman and Tantawi, and my source also informed me that this visit was not filmed for the media – the army didn't want to record it, an indication that the meeting was actually of genuine importance.

We didn't know at the time who would be in the new cabinet, though we knew that all the businessmen, the politicians with small (or in some cases quite large) commercial empires would be gone. The only one I expected to survive was the Minister of Trade and Industry, Rashid Mohammed Rashid. Despite being one of the wealthiest businessmen of them all, Rashid was generally well liked by the public because people saw him as the most honest member of the cabinet. Perhaps it was also because of the trusting face which framed his soft features. However, despite his relatively impressive track record, he too lost his job in the cabinet.

Conversely, I was certain that Habib Al-Adly would lose his job. He was incredibly unpopular in Egypt, and his handling of the recent crisis had been abysmal.

When I sat that morning talking to Anas, our conversation inevitably turned to the coming sacking of the cabinet. I mentioned to him that Adly would have to go.

"No," came the terse response, somewhat surprised, "he's a very good man. He's a real man, he was the one trying bravely to do his job. I think he's the best man for the job. He should continue." I was surprised at Anas's genuine affection for the man.

"Anas," I explained, "my opinion is this. Even if Habib Al-Adly was the angel Gabriel, he should not stay. Even if he was the best of the best, there is something called political necessity. Political necessity means we should get rid of him."

"No!" Anas interjected, "he is a good man!"

OK, I thought, I'll just leave it there. It was a difficult discussion to have, and not worth continuing. I got up from the chair, walked out of his vast office, and headed down to mine.

I hadn't been sitting down more than a few minutes when Anas phoned me. The call was brief. "Expect some news from the Interior Ministry," he informed me. It was almost a command.

Not long afterwards, my fax machine buzzed into life, spilling out two pages. I picked them up from my tray, flicked them onto my desk and sat down to read. After I read had them, I felt as if I would faint. After the shock had subsided, I picked up the phone and dialled Anas.

"Did you know that Habib went to check on his police forces?" I demanded.

"Yes," he responded with excitement, "this is the news I told you about!"

I couldn't see why he was so excited. "But I don't think this is the right thing to do now."

"No, just prepare the statement, they'll send you the tape." He ended the conversation.

The fax said that Habib Al-Adly, Interior Minister, had gone to inspect his police forces and had given a speech to them. The content of the speech was essentially the same as what he had been saying for the last few months. In fact, it wasn't hugely different from the interview he gave back on the 25th, when this whole crisis had just started. He was blaming the Muslim Brotherhood for any unrest, going on about how the police were a national body working for the sake of the country. He reiterated how everything was under his control, and how the army was there to help the police take over again.

I phoned a contact in the Interior Ministry.

"Did you send this?" I asked.

"Yes."

"Are you sure you want it broadcast?" I persisted.

"Yes. It's very important for us. We need to show the people that we're still here, that we haven't disappeared."

"Are you sure you want to keep these words, that you are still in 'control' and the mention of the Muslim Brotherhood?"

"Yes. Yes we do."

"OK. Fine." I didn't feel the need to discuss it any further.

When I put the phone down, I briefly wondered what to do. To put out such a statement at this time would not only be misleading, it would be inflammatory and potentially very dangerous. People were waiting to hear an announcement of those who had lost their ministerial posts, and Habib Al-Adly should be top of the list. I called my contacts in the army, intelligence services and Presidential Palace. I told them all the same thing: that I had a potential disaster on my hands and was not willing to broadcast a ten-minute segment dictated by one of the most hated men in Egypt. I told them that I could delay, but eventually I would have to concede, as I was under orders from my superior here in the building. I told them that if they had the authority, they should stop it and prevent the country sliding into catastrophe.

My phone was ringing every couple of minutes. Every time, it was Anas, asking me if they had sent me the tape. Each time I denied that I'd received it. Eventually, he said to me, "Look, I'm pushing you because I've got Habib pressuring me on the other line! He's calling me every minute."

"What can I do? The tape hasn't arrived yet!" I lied.

"I know that tape has arrived already!" he came back at me.

"Yes," I admitted, "but I need time to get it ready for broadcast."

"Just play it!"

"Alright, alright," I relented, "I'll put it on."

Barely a minute after I put the phone down on him, it rang again. It was Anas once more, but this time he told me to hold it.

"Why?" I asked, "we're ready to broadcast it now."

"No, just hold it," he ordered.

My contact in the army called me and checked that I had received instructions to sit on the statement. Before he hung up, he told me to expect another statement from the Interior Ministry. The new statement buzzed though the fax machine, though not from the Interior Ministry itself, but the Presidential Palace. I assumed it had been penned by Suleiman Awad, the President's press secretary. The statement was two and half lines long, simply saying "The Interior Minister of the caretaker government visited some police forces to inspect them and confirm that they would be cooperating with the army to regain control of the government." No names, no speeches. It was also the first time that the palace used the expression "caretaker" in reference to the government.

My army contact called again, "you've got the news now?" he asked.

"Yes."

"And don't broadcast any footage with the news," he ordered.

I thanked him, sincerely, and returned to my other work. Anas called to check that I'd got the news. I read him the two lines and cheerfully confirmed that I'd be broadcasting it straight away.

"Can you have some footage of him?" he asked.

"No." I answered, "no I can't."

"Any little bit? Just a small clip."

"No, I can't. They don't want it," I declared.

"Who doesn't?"

"The army." I responded.

"Just one photo?" Anas was never one for giving up easily. "He's harassing me!"

"NO!"

Apparently, Anas told Adly in their last phone conversation, just before the broadcast of his statement, that the palace was reviewing his footage before broadcast. The Interior Minister thanked him and hung up the phone. Anas never got a call from Adly again.

I let the statement run on a couple of news cycles, before quietly discarding it. I understood then that there was a great deal of pressure from somewhere to keep Adly in the cabinet. At the same time, other parts of the government, namely the army, knew what a liability he was. The pressure to keep him, it became evident, was coming from the palace. From Gamal. Adly was part of the group around the President's son, and one of their most powerful allies in the cabinet.

On another front, Al-Jazeera continued to conduct its media campaign, following the same pace it started with, bringing live broadcasts of the events, and sensationalising any developments. When the demonstrations slowed down slightly, it would push, encourage and fuel the enthusiasm so that people would rush back to demonstrate on a larger scale.

The previous evening, after midnight, minutes after President Mubarak's speech, they stressed that the Egyptians had comprehensively rejected it. The protesters refused what he had to offer.

That morning, I got a phone call from Naguib Sawiris, the well-known Egyptian businessman. He was calling from El-Gouna, Hurghada, on the Red Sea, asking me to go live on air, to refute the allegation made by Al-Jazeera, that he had fled the country along with his family. He went live on air and talked about the accusation, stressing that he and his family were still in Egypt. He suggested that the reason they broadcast the story was because of his attack on the channel the previous day, when he accused it of intimidation and incitement, and questioned its impartiality.

Throughout the previous day, Al-Jazeera reported the presence of demonstrations in certain places; for example, it stated that there were protesters moving towards the Maspero building and surrounding it, when this wasn't true! However, these reports would become self-fulfilling prophecies, as shortly after the reports were aired, we would find demonstrators moving towards the Maspero building to surround us! I mention the Maspero because it was where we were, so I had direct experience of it, though their reports mentioned protests in several other locations I wasn't so sure about. Overnight, the channel would confirm the presence of tens of thousands of protesters in Tahrir Square, while the reality was, according to other estimates, there weren't more than five thousand people camping out there. The numbers would not reach tens of thousands until daytime.

That morning, I received a sealed envelope from Anas's office. I opened it, and learned that the government would be shutting down Al-Jazeera. The news read; "The Minister of Information issued a decree shutting down the Al-Jazeera channel, and gave his instructions to the State Information Service to decommission all the permits and devices and prevent its correspondents from working in Egypt." I talked to Anas on the phone, and told him that it would be better if such a decision was not taken by the Minister of Information, but instead by other higher authorities. He agreed with me on that, but didn't tell me that he had already distributed the news to the media. The news was broadcast, and it divided the country. It was welcomed by some, many journalists and media professionals on competing channels, as well as many ordinary Egyptians who had been unhappy with Al-Jazeera's coverage. At the same time, the move infuriated the demonstrators and the political opposition.

As I mentioned earlier, the director of Al-Jazeera's office in Cairo, had disassociated himself from how the channel was handling the unrest, blaming the management in Doha, saying that matters were beyond his control. Still, in spite of my personal dissatisfaction with the channel, such a decision, looking back on it now, is worth reconsideration, especially within Egypt's new political framework.

Later that day, Ahmed Fathi Sarour, the Speaker of the Parliament asked to have a meeting of the national security committee at the People's Assembly. He wanted camera crews to record the meeting. I was notified, as usual, in a phone call from Anas.

"Dr Sarour is very interested in having his meeting on TV. It'll be just under an hour," he explained.

I was not impressed. "I can't give him an hour," I told him, "even if we broadcast fifteen minutes of this…this old way of doing things, it will be a disaster. We will lose all credibility, completely. I can give him a report of no more than five minutes."

"He will be angry," warned Anas.

"I don't care," I groaned, exasperated.

Anas accepted my point of view and told me I could do whatever I wanted. I sent a camera crew over to record the meeting and put the resultant report in the news cycle, but only as a four minute item. Sure enough, when it came out, Dr Sarour was affronted. When Anas called to tell me, I told him he could have five minutes, but that was it. I let Anas deal with him on the phone.

There was more news coming in that day of other heads of state in the region calling President Mubarak to lend their support. Again, I had to tell Anas that it was not the right time to announce on all the ERTU channels that the Presidents of Djibouti and Comoros had called to let Mubarak know they were right behind him. When I was explaining this editorial line, Anas interrupted me and asked slowly, "is it news from the Presidential Palace or not?"

"Well, yes it is," I replied, hesitantly.

"Then we have to follow the rules," he chided, as if he were a teacher disciplining an errant student, "if its presidential news then it gets broadcast."

I had no option but to run with these pointless little stories. I tried to run them quickly, and make sure my newsreaders did not dwell on them, so we could get them out of the way.

That night, at around 9.30pm, my sources called me to tell me that there had been an assassination attempt on Omar Suleiman. Not long after I got the first report, I got a call from one of our presenters. She was confused, and the words came tumbling out of her.

"Mr Menawy…I live in Masr Gadida, I don't know what's going on! Please, I don't understand…the army…the army is firing on the army!"

"What?" I asked, trying to make some sense of what she was saying.

"I'm at Masr Gadida," she repeated, a little more slowly, "there are army vehicles shooting at the guards in front of the army building and the guards are returning fire. The army…is there something wrong?"

I still didn't really understand what she was talking about, but it quickly dawned on me that this must be related to the attack on the new Vice President, Omar Suleiman. I called all my sources to confirm that it was true. Some of them admitted that it happened, some denied it. They all told me not to report anything.

As Omar Suleiman was leaving his old office at the Intelligence HQ, he was ambushed outside the Triumph Hotel in an upmarket district of Cairo, Masr Gadida (known as Heliopolis in English).

The car was moving along a broad avenue, where the two opposing lanes of traffic were separated by a grassy central reservation. The Vice President was travelling in a convoy headed by a top of the range BMW 7 series while he travelled just behind in a black armoured Mercedes. The Mercedes was part of a small fleet purchased by the government in response to the assassination attempt on Safwat El-Sherif and the rise in terror attacks in the mid nineties. Before that, the only armoured car in the country was the one that Sadat had used during his rule. When the BMW passed the entrance to the hotel, gunmen, who had been hiding in the grass in the middle of the road, opened fire. When the firing began, the army guards in front of the hotel shot back at the convoy, which they thought was shooting at them. The cars in convoy sped away. One man was killed in the BMW. The Vice President was unharmed.

I never found out who was behind the attack. My best guess would be that the attackers were from an Islamist terror group, but I really have no idea. I don't think it was anybody from within the government. In spite of the suspicion and distrust at the top of the regime, nobody would have done that. It wasn't how they worked.

Some journalists said after that when President Mubarak was handed a report containing the results of an investigation into the attack, he read it, closed it and then just asked everyone to forget about it. I don't think that was a true story.

Towards the end of the night, I started getting phone calls from my contacts. They told me that I was to be chosen as the new Minister of Information in the next cabinet, and I would be appointed tomorrow.

"Please, no," I begged.

"We think this is the only solution," one of them insisted, "You are the only one we can have now. We need you to accept this responsibility." I knew why they wanted me. Anas was part of the

Gamal group. They were trying to marginalise Gamal in the new cabinet, and would sacrifice Anas to achieve their ends.

"I don't want it. Please…this is the worst time to offer someone such a position," I pleaded. The appointment was a poisoned chalice. I knew that for sure. Even so, despite my protestations, I kept getting more phone calls telling me that I had been confirmed. Each time I said no, but that didn't stop them, they just told me to get ready. I had picked up hints and suggestions about this for years. Some senior people were trying to drive a wedge between me and Anas, trying to make us lose trust in each other, hinting that I could take on Anas's job. I never took it seriously and never encouraged it, never tried to advance down that path. Once, they offered me the job of head of the ERTU, but I turned it down. I'm a journalist, not a manager. I like to do the news, I like politics. I don't like positions. I had always made it clear to Anas that I didn't want his job. Sometimes he was convinced. I really tried to be sincere.

We finished late that night. There was no point in going home. People were sleeping under desks and in the corridors. We used the building's small clinic as a makeshift dormitory. I had been on a small tour that afternoon around the offices and studios. I checked all my staff in the various departments, in Channel One, the Egyptian Satellite Channel, Nile International, Nile News, as well as the radio people. I shook their hands and gave them some encouragement, trying to raise morale. I tried to reassure them that we were not working for a particular person or regime, but that we were all working for our homeland, for the country we lived in, and that our duty was for each person to play their part in protecting it. Though it's a 28 story building, our operation only took up floors 2 through 7, easy enough to cover.

I retired that night to the comparative luxury of the sofa. It was in a room connected to my office. The door was near the desk. It had those half swinging doors like the ones you see in old Western saloons. It was an unusual door to have in an office environment, especially in a government building. It gave my office a distinctive flavour, making it the talk of the building.

I couldn't sleep that night. I kept thinking about what I would do if the government cast this stone around my neck and made me a minister. I was praying, please, *please* no.

JANUARY 31ST – MONDAY

Another night passed in the Maspero building. We were all concerned for our loved ones at home, since we were getting a torrent of panicked calls in the building. The only thing we could do was to check on them by phone from time to time. My two sons, both young men at 19 and 21 had volunteered for the local popular committee, helping our neighbours to protect our homes.

I had a rough night, helplessly hoping that I wouldn't discover I had become the country's new Minister of Information in the morning. I had no interest in the job; I did not want to act as the government's official mouthpiece. The job would be made harder due to the fact that Anas was very close to the President and his family, he was almost considered a third son. His relationship with the family was one of the reasons that other senior members of the government tried to have him ousted from the cabinet. I didn't want to be a pawn in their manoeuvres.

The walkie-talkie standing on my desk hissed, waking me up. I opened my eyes, joints aching from a night on the sofa. A voice on the other side announced to the band that the minister was on his way to cabinet. I was so happy I wanted to jump up and down. It meant that Anas had kept his job and I wouldn't have to take it.

I received a call a little while later from the official who told me the night before to get ready to take on the role. He apologised, and I thanked him. He explained that the President and his son Gamal insisted there was only one candidate for Minister of Information, and that was Anas Al-Feky. Despite protestations, they would not relent, knowing that they needed Anas, a key ally in an important position. Their refusal to concede the loss of Anas was the biggest favour they ever did for me.

Things started to relax a little that day. We didn't see the large numbers of people out on the streets that we had seen in previous days. People had calmed down, and were waiting to see how the new cabinet turned out.

I told my contacts in the army and in the palace that this was the time for the government to show they were serious about reform. The public had given them an opportunity, they had made their move, now it was the government's turn. I even suggested to all those I knew who had access to power that it would be a good idea to bring some opposition politicians into the cabinet.

A new, vibrant cabinet could have been a way out for the government, but unfortunately, such thinking was naïve, as the powers that be reverted to their usual myopic policies.

Since Friday evening, the public had been waiting for the roster of new ministers, as was promised by the President.

The new appointments were announced at 2.30pm. A torrent of disappointment swept the country. We have a saying in Egypt that dates back to Roman times: "The mountain gave birth, and brought forth a mouse" (or *Parturient montes, nascetur ridiculus mus* in Latin). It was very fitting that afternoon.

The presidential decree had three articles. The first named Dr Ahmed Shafik as the new Prime Minister. The second named Field Marshal Mohammed Hussein Tantawi as Deputy Prime Minister and Minister of Defence. The third listed the new ministers.

It was a curious selection. There were 14 new ministers, most of whom were unknowns. 16 ministers were straight from the old cabinet. After looking through the list, I called Anas at the Presidential Palace and told him there was something missing. Two posts had been omitted. There were no ministers for either Tourism or Education. The Palace had addressed this oversight by not mentioning it at all. They may have simply forgotten, or hoped nobody would notice. I told Anas that I would put out a statement on behalf of the government saying there were still negotiations ongoing for the new positions. Anas asked Zakaria Azmi, the Presidential Chief-of-Staff at the palace. Apparently, in all the excitement, they had indeed forgotten about the two ministries.

The only major development was the dismissal of the businessmen from government. It also confirmed that Tantawi would remain as Defence Minister and not be forced out. The confirmation went against all the rumours and leaks swirling around Cairo that claimed that he would be losing his job as Defence Minister.

Rashid Mohammad Rashid, Minister of Trade, was out from a job that I thought he was actually doing quite well. I later heard that he refused to participate in the new cabinet despite being offered a position by Ahmed Shafik and the President himself. His name was often mentioned in the palace as a possible candidate to succeed Ahmed Nazif as Prime Minister. Mubarak had sought to dismiss Nazif the previous summer, going so far as to hold meetings with ministers excluding him and telling ministers not to report to him. Gamal Mubarak, together with the prominent businessman Hussein Salem, asked Rashid to convince the President to keep Nazif, which Rashid succeeding in doing, at least until the current crisis.

Ahmed El-Maghraby, the Minister of Housing, was also gone. He was one of the powerful figures in the previous government and was at one point touted as a future Prime Minister. He was unpopular, connected to the sale of state land, allocation of state properties and an increase of land prices. His real estate company built some of Egypt's most famous new housing projects, such as the Palm Hills development, one of the most exclusive in the country.

Minister of Tourism Zohair Garanah, who was rumoured to be using his position as minister to win favourable government contracts for his tourism companies was also not on the list.

The most important minister to lose his job was of course Habib Al-Adly. The Interior Ministry had handled the protests particularly badly since they began, and the police had proved unable to keep law and order. Despite his continual reassurances to his colleagues, Adly had proved himself poorly suited to the job. In addition, he was one of the most hated figures for the public, and one of the reasons that this unrest had started in the first place. Though he was a strong ally for the Presidential Palace, he had to go. He was replaced by Mahmoud Wagdy, former assistant to the Interior Minister and Director of the Prison Authority. The man had a good reputation after what he had done with the country's prisons. He improved conditions and initiated the Mazraat Torah project which produced products, such as handmade wooden crafts, which were then sold to the public.

The most important ministers who stayed were Tantawi, Minister of Defence and Foreign Minister, Ahmed Abu El Gait. Mofeed Shehab, a leading member of the ruling National Democratic Party and State Minister for Legal Affairs, also kept his job.

Ali Moselhy, the Minister of Social Solidarity stayed on. He was a controversial character directly connected to the rise in food and fuel prices, and the resultant crises. The Minister of Petroleum stayed on, though he was highly unpopular with the public due to his close association with the gas exportation deal to Israel.

The new cabinet totally lacked a sophisticated political dimension. They didn't bother to include any opposition politicians, nor did they appoint any popular figures even from within the NDP. Once again, the government was trying to hold on to power, and toss little scraps of reform to the public.

If this new cabinet had been appointed before the start of the protests, then the public would probably have just accepted it. However, since the protests had begun, the rules of the game had changed, and the government would have to be more sensitive to popular opinion. At that point, the public was expecting a totally new, reform-minded cabinet.

The reaction out on the streets was contemptuous. We had reporters out among the protesters when the announcement was made, in contact with the studio over the telephone. When the anchor asked how the public greeted the news of the new cabinet, the reporter told him, there was nothing to say. The people were speechless, despair etched on their faces.

Egyptians were sitting in front of their TV sets, waiting for some good news that could possibly end the state of mutual antagonism that was threatening to tear the country apart. There was a genuine hope that the government could meet the public's expectations, not only those of the protesters but also address the real Egyptian urge for change. None of that happened.

I found out later that the new cabinet was born out of the power struggle between the Presidential Palace and the military (backed by the intelligence service). The military tried to convince the President of the importance of reform and lobbied for the inclusion of populist figures in the government. The suggestion was rejected by the President, backed by his son Gamal.

I was a harsh critic of those that announced widespread public dismay within minutes of President Mubarak's first address. This time, however, the reaction was immediate and unequivocal. It was a disappointment to anybody who even had a vague understanding of Egyptian politics, let alone the protesters. It was not what was expected from a regime in crisis. It was a unsubtle attempt to secure power in the face of mass civil unrest.

I understood, from that point on, that Gamal Mubarak was essentially trying to dictate the government's response to the crisis by himself. President Mubarak depended on his son to manage the government in this time of crisis, with the help of Zakaria Azmi and, it seemed, Anas.

I remember a conversation I had with Anas where he pointed out how the protests forced the regime to reform. He said that there were many within the government that were dreaming of and calling for change, but they never actually believed it could be accomplished.

Anas's actions were governed by his loyalty to the President; he had always been loyal, and now his loyalty was finally tested, he stood firmly with the old man. He was bound by duty to support Gamal's actions, even if they would ultimately prove to be damaging. He mentioned many times how much he appreciated and respected Mubarak, and made it clear, to me at least, that he would stop working for the government when the old man ended his tenure as President.

Unsurprisingly, the crowds in Tahrir Square began to swell once more after the new cabinet was announced. There were new calls and slogans being chanted. It was the first time we started hearing the word, *millioniya* (a million). The new call was for a million people to come down and protest the next day, Tuesday, a week after the unrest started. They were not interested in anything the government had to say or offer. They simply wanted Mubarak gone.

It was announced that this Friday wouldn't be a "Day of Rage", but the "Friday of Departure". They declared that there would also be a million people on the streets and each person there would be calling for Mubarak to leave.

As the government had been totally unable to heed the protesters' calls for reform, it was determined that the President himself was standing in the way of change. It was therefore decided that the President had to go. Whilst there were portions of the public who were content to see him see out his term, the government's somnolent attitude to the unrest suggested that it needed to be brought down completely in order for a real progressive change to take place in the way Egypt was governed.

The protesters and their chants became more aggressive. There were countless scenes of Mubarak's picture being burned or defaced, something which simply would not have happened in public even a month before. This show of anger was a recent addition to the protests, and wasn't really so apparent at the beginning of the unrest. However, as the protests dragged on, people got angrier.

Later on, after we received the footage in the studio, I told Anas that it was sad that we had reached this point, and it was sadder still that the President had allowed the situation to deteriorate as far as it had. Now even his own people were burning his picture.

"There is pressure on the President," I said to Anas.

"What are they demanding from the President now exactly?" Anas asked in exasperation, "Are they asking him to be naked? Is he supposed to strip?"

"If he's got to strip to solve this problem, then he should strip" I told him, "he shouldn't go through this political striptease."

Anas often appreciated what I had to say, unfortunately, he mostly had his hands tied on important matters, having to wait for orders from the Presidential Palace.

Two hours later after the cabinet announcement, I got a phone call from Zakaria Azmi.

"Forget about the presidential decree we gave you," he began, "article 2 will be changed."

"Why?" I enquired. I had thought Tantawi's position was secure.

"There will be no deputy prime minister." Tantawi was indeed safe as Defence Minister, but he didn't want the deputy prime minister job. I found out later that Tantawi had called Azmi at the palace and told him, in no uncertain terms that he would not be taking on the additional position. It was unusual, one would have thought that the new job would have made him more secure, and more powerful.

The palace faxed through the new decree, identical to the first, bar the omission of reference to the deputy prime minister. I set about editing the footage of the new ministers taking their oaths.

While I was looking over my editor's shoulder, the phone rang. It was Anas, still at the palace, telling me exactly the same thing Azmi did in his phone call a few minutes before. I explained I already knew about the change, but I was still puzzled by it, so I asked him why Tantawi had refused the deputy premiership.

He thought for a moment, "Maybe it's because of rank," he suggested, "Tantawi is older than Ahmed, so he can't be his deputy." Ahmed Shafik was also a military man, and held a senior rank, though obviously not as senior as Tantawi. I wasn't convinced by such a convoluted explanation. Even though Tantawi would end up as acting head of state, I believed then, and still do now, that Tantawi only really cared about running the army. He didn't want to get drawn into the mechanics of civilian government.

After the decree was broadcast, it was clear that the country was upset. It was depressing for me too. The government had squandered yet another chance to get itself off the path that would eventually lead to oblivion. People knew the government wasn't serious about change. At best, they were just trying to buy themselves time.

As the protests had diminished somewhat, we tried again to get our cameras out to Tahrir Square, but to no avail: our crews were beaten back whenever they approached. Though we kept trying, we couldn't suffer the alarming rate of attrition, as our crews repeatedly came back with broken equipment. In addition, I had to get permission from the army every time I sent a crew out onto the streets. We were forced, again, to use CCTV feeds from adjacent buildings, as well as footage from other news agencies. Getting the CCTV footage was particularly tedious. I couldn't use it without getting permission from the relevant building's security service. Once permission was obtained, I could feed from the national network, to which all the country's security cameras are connected. However, even then, the footage was grainy, or distant, and I'd have to get hold of the operator if I wanted the camera to zoom in or change its angle.

We were constrained in the studio as well. There were still instructions that we were not to have anyone from Tahrir Square, or even anyone from the opposition in, to talk on air. I tried to mitigate the pro-government thrust of our coverage by not inviting in the more aggressive pro-regime politicians and commentators, but the imbalance was there for all to see.

We got a very interesting statement from the army that day. The army had made a decision to unambiguously declare that they were not against the demonstrators. The statement read:

"Your armed forces realise the legitimacy of the people's demands and stress that freedom of expression using peaceful means is guaranteed. The military is aware of your legitimate demands and the forces deployed on the streets are for you and for your safety. We did not and will not resort to the use of force against our great people."

It was a signal to the public, to those who were afraid to go out, or let their families out and demonstrate. The army was telling them that they would not be attacked.

I also received a statement from the Ministry of Interior, which I was asked to broadcast immediately. It referred to the deployment of the Criminal Police Investigations Units and Central Security Forces in densely populated areas, and added that normal police services were to resume. However, the armed forces were still on the streets and had repeatedly stressed in their statements that they were in control, not the police.

The statement went on to reiterate the importance of having the police back on the streets, and requested that the citizens' checkpoints, which had been set up by the youth movements, disband and allow the police to re-establish control. This would prove controversial, as the citizens' checkpoints were set up so that the protesters could protect themselves from harassment.

We responded to the request. Through television screens we tried to communicate the importance of the cooperation between army and police, the importance of the police adhering to their designated duty and the importance of the public receiving them positively, to help them do their job.

There were no signs of any of that on the ground. There was only mutual antagonism between the protesters and the police. Many of the demonstrators actively incited people not to welcome the police back onto the streets. They had frightened them off once before, they could do it again. There were even calls to assault the police if they were deployed, with a view to dismantling the whole institution of state security.

I went up to Anas's office when he got back, at around 3pm, to congratulate him for keeping his job. As I strolled into his office, I was shocked to discover that he was having a meeting with the editorial team from his current affairs show, Egypt Today, his daily mouthpiece. For the last couple of days he'd been hinting at getting the show back on air. Each time, I vetoed the idea, telling him that it wouldn't say anything relevant to the current situation. I was angry, I didn't think he would go behind my back like that.

He feigned pleasant surprise when he looked up and saw me. Making conversation, he asked, "What do you think people think of the new government?"

"The feedback is very bad," I responded, in no mood for pleasantries.

"Do you think it's a good idea to go on air now with this?" referring to his show.

"What are you going to say?" I countered, "The government put us in a very bad situation, what can we do? You are missing the chances. Even the chance to get a new government with popular legitimacy, you didn't use it!" I noticed the expressions on the faces of the team sitting on the armchairs in his office. They knew there was a problem.

I would have expected this behaviour from the other misguided barons at the palace, but not from Anas. I didn't even bother to come in, so instead I just stood in the doorway, looking vexed. How could anyone speak to the public to defend the government's behaviour? "This cabinet is shocking" I barked, "and it makes a mockery of people's ambitions and wishes. This is the worst way to manage the situation, they are pushing for confrontation! It's not the right time for late night shows!"

"OK," he said, "come and join us. We can talk about it."

"I'm very busy, and I have studios to run, I don't have the time for this discussion!" I snapped. I turned around and walked back out the doorway. I left his office infuriated. The government was pushing things to a point of no return.

The momentum of the demonstrations was growing. It seemed that there were more protesters in Tahrir Square since I last looked at the monitor. I went into the control room and told them to put Tahrir Square on the screen on a live feed. It would have to be from CCTV, or borrowed from other news agencies, but it would do. The presidency hated having to watch the demonstrations on their state TV. Whenever we had it on, I got calls from Anas telling me the palace had called and wanted Tahrir Square off the screen. We would initially agree, then simply resume the feed when we felt sufficient time had passed. Perhaps they wouldn't notice.

When I came down to the office, there was talk of Mubarak giving a speech that evening, laying out the government's position. This idea was rejected in favour of a speech by Omar Suleiman. He went on air that evening; it was a convincing speech.

The only thing I didn't like was when he began his speech by saying "I have been assigned by the President..." It would have been far more prudent not to refer to the President at this stage. The public would not take kindly to the impression that the President was still controlling the government and its response to the uprising. The problem was that Suleiman was a loyal character, and would always defer to a higher authority.

After we broadcast the new Vice President's first official statement, I received some bad news. Anas informed me that Gamal and his cronies had organised some pro-Mubarak counter demonstrations to take place in front of the Maspero building. We were to give them prominent, live coverage. Anas's instructions were strict. He seemed reinvigorated now that he knew his job was secure, and his loyalty rewarded.

I accepted his command, put the phone back down and slouched on my chair, letting out a long sigh.

I started getting tedious phone calls from NDP officials and business tycoons asking me to put out a call on TV for protests "in a bid to preserve the country's legitimacy". I had to say no. That would be a horrendously provocative act. I was finding it extremely difficult to try and keep neutral under pressure. I didn't want us to start blatantly taking sides. More importantly, I didn't want to start contributing to any violence that would potentially flare up on the streets.

I would not incite people onto the streets to blindly defend a regime that didn't know what the hell they were doing.

A few minutes later, I saw a few dozen, then a few hundred people congregating on the Corniche outside the Maspero building. They were organised, carrying printed banners and pictures of Mubarak. Their slogans were mostly proclamations of loyalty to the President and calls for stability in the country. I reluctantly told my people that we had orders to put them on air, and sent down a camera crew to catch them on the street.

After a few minutes, I asked the producer to split the screen, showing footage of the Tahrir Square protest on one side, contrasted with the pro-Mubarak demonstration on the other. Despite the fact that the occupants of Tahrir Square numbered in their thousands, the pro-Mubarak demo seemed more vibrant. We had a professional crew filming them, with high quality cameras, close ups and the freedom to use different angles. The Tahrir Square footage, though also live, was distant and grainy, borrowed from a CCTV feed.

In spite of the imbalance, Anas was screaming at me down the phone.

"Aren't you watching?!" he yelled.

"No, I'm not watching." I lied, "What's happening? I am not in my office."

"The presidency called and they're furious with what's on screen," he shouted, "this is our moment! We have demonstrations on our side!" Whenever Anas leaned on me, I knew he was being leaned on by his superiors. It was obvious that he had received a dressing down on the phone from Gamal and Zakaria, angry about the coverage.

Even then, I still felt bad. We got angry phone calls on air from a journalist and some other protesters. The journalist chided us, "I was very upset with you, as the state TV station, to have tens of demonstrators live on air while you don't show the thousands in Tahrir Square."

He was absolutely right.

It was, possibly, one of the least professional moments of my career.

However, for the first time since the unrest started, I managed to get some opponents of the government on TV. Not in the studio, but finally we had people calling in, demanding Mubarak step aside. The protests had been going on for almost a week and only now could we get any representatives on air to put forward their point of view. I dealt with the inevitable ferocious response from Anas by not bothering to answer the phone when he called.

That night, thoughts were swimming through my head. I tried to think of a possible solution to all this. I was looking for an exit. I asked a few of my colleagues if they could think of anything, I asked some of my friends who had been out in Tahrir Square. The general consensus was for Mubarak to cede authority to Omar Suleiman. It was the only honourable option left to him. I took notes during all these conversations; flicking through them, I decided to write a speech for Mubarak.

I'd never done that before. I'd never been asked. I wasn't a speechwriter, it just felt like the right thing to do.

I wrote:

A statement to the Great People of Egypt

Great people of Egypt,

We are now going through exceptional circumstances in the history of Egypt and you all know that I have served our cherished homeland as an officer, commander, Vice President and President. I carried my soul upon my palm, pronounced the testimony of Islam and ran into our country's wars. I took the oath on the honour of fighting for Sinai until I have reached the glorious October war in the year 1973 and our great battle in Taba.

Throughout my presidency, I have passed many milestones and overcome obstacles, both international and national. Allah knows that I have neither betrayed this responsibility nor have I ever compromised on the independence of our homeland or the dignity of our soldiers, our great warriors.

Great people of Egypt,

When our youth began protesting and calling for change, my decision was to give them a full chance without the use of excessive force as I would have been cruel and violent like other leaders in other regimes. My experience and my eternal love for our great people halted me from placing my authority above the national interest.

Great people of Egypt,

Our youths saw, as one of their rights, my obligation to let them enjoy the freedom to choose their own future according to their wishes and lead them to reach their ambitions in and around this evolving world. I was worried that our youths would be swayed in dangerous directions, taking the country with them, but events have arisen to ensure their courage and good thinking. I do not wish for our youths to build their future on ruin and I do not want them to go back to year zero, as it would take them longer to reach the point we are already at.

Great people of Egypt,

It was a great honour for me to be part of your history, but I will leave you the future assured and satisfied wishing that you would keep your nation and honour together…

I declare that I will not run for the year's presidential election. I step down from presiding over the National Democratic Party. A few minutes ago, I accepted the resignation of Policies Committee Secretary Mr Gamal Mubarak from the National Party to seclude political life after years of hard work for a better status.

I also declare the delegation of all authorities of the Republic's President to the Vice President of the Republic except the decision of war until I hand in power in a democratic framework to a new president.

Great people of Egypt,

I am not sad about what happened; I am one of you who will be happy to win the battle for democracy after winning the battles of war and peace.

I love the flag of my country and the soil of my county and the people of my country, and I wish our precious Egypt the great future that our people and our history deserves.

After I had it all written down, checked it and redrafted it, I lay down on my sofa. I decided to send it to every one of my contacts who was in direct contact with the President. Staring at the ceiling, I wondered how to get this address to the President, or at least get him thinking about putting into effect its key points.

FEBRUARY 1ST – TUESDAY

I woke up early in the morning, having come up with a plan to get my speech read by the powers that be over at the palace. I went down to an office on the ground floor and called one of my senior contacts in the intelligence service and asked him to put me through to a secure line. I didn't want anybody listening in to what I had to say.

I told him that I'd spoken to a lot of people, colleagues, other ministers, army officers and protesters and we'd all agreed there was only one conceivable course of action.

I explained that it was obvious that the country's political officials were in disarray. The poor quality of their decisions demonstrated that none of them understood the magnitude of the current crisis. They strongly believed that this crisis would be dealt with in time, that it would just pass as others had done, even if it was more profound than the usual. They believed that a partial response would satisfy people. I described the chief crisis manager as a crooked bank teller, who takes out a few pounds from each packet he gives out, hoping the client won't notice the discrepancy. I didn't give a name, though I meant Gamal Mubarak.

Gamal believed that it was possible to get the body politic to compromise on a deal as long as they got just a small part of what they demanded. He always operated like that, and it became particularly apparent during the crisis.

The complete absence of President Mubarak in the decision-making process had become apparent. The President received toned down reports of the unrest, and was assured that there were capable people managing the crisis and that there were simple solutions to the problems. As such, President Mubarak deferred the handling of the crisis to Gamal and those around him.

I gave him the full picture, as I saw it. I informed the official down the line that the situation would not resolve itself unless the President addressed the public in a different manner and tone than the ones he had used thus far. He had to appeal to public sentiment directly and announce that he was handing all his powers to the Vice President, only keeping the constitutional authority to declare war and dissolve parliament. Everything else must go to the republic's Vice President. I mentioned that I had a draft address to this effect, which I would be sending them at once.

Before hanging up, my contact assured me that there were meetings taking place with the President as we spoke: senior officials were trying to convince him to hand over some of his powers to the Vice President. He told me that progress might be made on this by the end of the day. He expected that the President would probably agree because of the current chaotic circumstances. I added that there were still ongoing attempts to break into the television building, and it was almost breached twice in the last few days. I told him we were having difficulty convincing employees to keep working, especially with the slow and unresponsive reaction of the state towards recent events. I brought to his attention the fact that those employees also had brothers, sisters or relatives in the demonstrations. It was hard for them to keep doing a job which they considered had questionable ethical merit in the service of an ambivalent and callous government.

The call ended.

I walked up to my office, feeling both relieved and guilty. I was pleased that my confidante in the intelligence service had agreed with me, and I'd articulated what a lot of people were thinking. Conversely, I was worried that I was pushing the President too hard, when perhaps it wasn't my place to do so. Yet, I was certain I had said what needed to be said.

When I got back to my office, I remembered there was one other point to add, so I called again on a normal line and pointed out that if there was a manager incapable of doing his job, he would assign his deputy to run the business while he took an enforced holiday to recover. I hinted that the solution may be for President Mubarak to leave for Sharm El-Sheikh or Germany to receive treatment for some unspecified malady. My contact got the message and assured me that it was among the suggestions being tabled for discussion. He bid me goodbye, saying, "may God help us".

My crew in the palace kept me abreast of developments over there, and I knew that a round of meetings had been called between Mubarak, Suleiman and the new PM, Ahmed Shafik. The President and the First Lady had seven camera crews in rotation, leaving one constantly at their disposal.

My people at the palace told me that the President would address the nation by midday; this was later confirmed to me by the intelligence service, the GIS. I didn't know if this was because I'd been pushing them for the speech, nor did I know what happened to the content I gave them. Gamal summoned Anas to the palace.

Anas had a few cars parked outside, and took his 4x4, not his usual vehicle. When he turned on to the 6th October Bridge, a short way down the Nile from the Maspero building, somebody in the crowd must have recognised him in the passenger seat. Within seconds, a mob began to attack the car, hurling stones and debris at it. The driver was forced to swerve round, and double back on himself to a chorus of shouting surrounding them. The bulky vehicle managed to get back on the Corniche and accelerate back to the TV building.

When it passed through the army cordon, the car was found to be dented from multiple impacts, but Anas and his driver were unharmed. He was, however, stuck, and unable to get to the palace.

Anas called me up telling me that he couldn't make his appointment, chuckling with nervous laughter. He was forced to follow developments from his office from then on.

I got another call from my contact in intelligence that afternoon. He told me that the President would be appearing on TV today even though the initial noon deadline had passed.

"Is he going to do what we talked about?" I enquired.

"Not exactly," he admitted, "but it will be a start."

"What does that mean?"

"He's very stubborn, we've tried to negotiate with him," my contact claimed, "but he's very stubborn. He doesn't want to listen!" Admittedly, though he was stubborn, those around him would not speak to him frankly, let alone advise him to step down. Mubarak was a strong character, people were daunted by him.

I heard that twice from two different people with access to the President that day. They both claimed that Gamal was controlling everything, making the important decisions, yet his father refused to believe that was a problem. He let himself be led. If there was ever a difference of opinion between Gamal and any one of the President's advisers, Mubarak would instruct his staff to follow Gamal. Even if an advisor was older and more experienced, like Suleiman Awad was, Gamal would win out.

When it comes to dealing with Egypt, the trick is the play on emotion. We're a sentimental country. If a politician can handle the sentimental character of Egypt, then they will win over the country. Every country has its own defining characteristic, its key. For us, it's sentimentality. That was the case when the President lost his grandson, and it seemed every Egyptian felt that they lost a member of their own family. The incident almost stopped a previous uprising against him. Likewise, when Mubarak was ill in hospital in Germany, nobody wished him any harm, the whole country just wanted him to get better. If the President had to play on the country's emotions, that was the only way he could win it back.

We had been waiting all day for the speech, as afternoon turned to evening and still, there was no news. I found myself staring at the live link to the presidential studio once more.

The President finally appeared on my monitor at 10pm. He never used to keep us waiting for hours on end, but he seemed to take forever these days. Gamal would often keep people waiting. The younger son was obsessed with detail, and would dither when it came to any decision of importance, or for that matter, anything trivial.

Every development and decision during those 18 days was late coming. The changing of the Prime Minister, the sacking of Ezz, the televised speeches, the appointment of a new cabinet; everything was late. For every delay, every hour, the government lost opportunities, missed their chances and enraged the public further.

I was informed that the speech would be pre-recorded, and was to be broadcast as soon as it was finished. Mubarak arrived with his two sons and Suleiman Awad, his press secretary. Before he started, the President had a brief chat with Awad. I could hear it picked up through the microphone.

"Have you heard?" asked the President, "Baradei told them that he was ready to be handed power."

Awad nodded his head and brought up another potential Eygptian President, "They went to Amr Moussa [head of the Arab League]" he revealed, referring to the protesters, "and chanted in front of the Arab League saying 'come down Amr'!"

"He said I am ready to serve my country in any position" sneered the President, with a mocking smile etched on his face.

"Terry Larsen [Terje Rød-Larsen, special envoy of the UN Secretary General and a friend of Amr Moussa] called me an hour ago and said to tell the President that they are backing him. He said Egypt would lose a lot if he left. He was ready to come, especially to talk to Amr Moussa" revealed Awad, "I told Larsen the President will speak soon."

The President did not comment on Larsen's offer.

"Did you announce that I would be speaking on TV?" he asked.

"Yes," Awad answered, "many times." Evidently, the President was not aware that the whole country was waiting for him.

He began to speak. It was a very sentimental speech, appealing to the nation's emotions. He was talking as an Egyptian man, to his fellow Egyptians.

The most important point he made was, "I want to live on this land, and I want to be buried on this land. This is my nation. I served this land."

The major political statement was the concession that he would not stand for re-election when the presidential elections came around in 2012.

After the speech had been fed through to our system, Anas called and said I had to get hold of a couple of videos. He wanted the music video for a song by the popular musician Amr Diab, "*Wahid mina* – One of Us." Though the song never mentioned the President by name, it is very much Mubarak's song, and the video features numerous clips of Mubarak looking alternately brave, noble, wise and gentle. He also wanted a specific documentary, a personal documentary about the President. It was mostly the President and his wife Suzanne talking about their lives. Anas told me they were to be played immediately after the speech on TV.

After the broadcast, people were sympathetic to the old man. The music video and the documentary were effective. He had told the nation he would be stepping down, and overseeing a peaceful transition of power, something of a rarity in Egypt.

I got a phone call from the army when the documentary was running, a couple of minutes after Suzanne Mubarak appeared on screen. They told me that it would not be wise to have Suzanne on TV, as she was deeply unpopular. I agreed. On their suggestion, I had the programme edited to remove her screen time.

People knew that she had access to power, with her own clique of ministers and officials to do her bidding. She often suffered negative comparisons with Nasser's popular wife Tahia. They disliked Suzanne in the same way they hated Jehan Sadat. Many deeply conservative Egyptians did not like the idea of these powerful, liberal women meddling in their national politics. In contrast, Tahia Nasser was largely absent from public life. The hatred directed towards Suzanne, though largely justified due to her ambitions for her son, was in spite of the fact that, in many areas, Suzanne Mubarak had a very positive influence. She was a keen supporter of universal literacy, culture, women's rights and a campaigner against people trafficking. If it wasn't for Suzanne Mubarak, we wouldn't have had the new Biblotheca Alexandria, the giant national library and cultural centre in Alexandria.

Ten minutes after the speech, the arrangement was to broadcast a statement from the speaker of parliament, who announced that he would take the necessary legal action to respect the legal sentences concerning the invalidity of the parliamentary elections in some constituencies, in accordance with what was said in the President's speech.

The feedback for the speech was very positive. When Mubarak finished speaking, the crew in the studio couldn't hold back their smiles. Some of the presenters on the commercial TV channels cried on air (as I said, it's a very sentimental country). Even some of the youth protesters were pleased, although by no means were they all happy. But, they had actually managed to force a major concession out of Mubarak. Many of the more established opposition figures were pleased as well. There was still a tangible current of opinion that was unhappy, pushing for his overthrow, most notably, the youth groups such as the April 6th and Kefaya movements, as well as the Muslim Brotherhood, among others.

There was a lot of sympathy for the old man. He was the "family elder", to use a phrase coined by his predecessor Anwar

Sadat. The talk among people in the street, and on the late night talk shows on satellite TV, was about the man, not the policies. Trying to get an understanding of him and to empathise with him, even though it was felt that Mubarak was no longer the best man for the job, and that he may have committed mistakes. But, hard as it may be to believe now, many people were reluctant to see him treated badly. They felt he didn't deserve it. That was how a lot of common people thought, those who listened to his speech that night.

I felt after the end of the speech that this was another great opportunity for President Mubarak, and that he should make use of it to break the impasse. It was surely possible to find a compromise for all sides concerned on the political front. It was feasible that the government could respond to the demands of the demonstrators, whilst keeping the 80 million or so people that make up Egypt on board. Also, Egyptians had never had a peaceful transition of power before – the prospect was quite exciting.

At the same time, it would preserve the image of Mubarak, as a person truly linked to this country and concerned for its safety. He would be ending his political career, not only as the first President to decide the direct multicandidate elections, but also as the first President to hand over power, and the first President to hold the title of former President without it being the result of a coup, death or assassination.

I felt a little guilty. When it had finished, I looked at the friend who I had been watching with, an officer in the intelligence services, and asked, "Do you think I went too far with him? Was I wrong to push him to give authority to the Vice President?" He didn't cede any authority in the speech, maybe I wanted too much of him. My friend murmured some reassuring words from the sofa. I got up from the sofa and went back to my desk, to carry on working.

I went up to Anas's office. He was happy with the speech, as was I. However, despite the breathing space the speech had bought the government, it was then that the mistakes started happening again.

I heard him talking on the phone to Zakaria Azmi and Gamal, telling them that everything was fine and they had nothing to worry about. Anas turned to me and told me there would be some more pro-Mubarak demonstrations happening soon.

Half an hour later, people started arriving at the television building. Somebody set up a sound system and began to play patriotic songs. Very loudly.

Anas called me and asked how many demonstrators there were. I looked out the window.

"Not many," I laughed, before joking, "17. I was even thinking of sending down three of my staff to make them 20!"

It was ridiculous, there was no need for this. If they left people alone, people would surely come out in support of Mubarak. People wouldn't come out demanding that he stay, but now he had said he was leaving, there would surely be demonstrations of gratitude for the old man. In spite of the many thousands in Tahrir Square, among the many millions of Egypt, there was still a great deal of respect for him. In Arabic, there is something called a "Salaam Selah," it's a salute given to departing military officers, in thanks for their many years of service. That's what people wanted to give Mubarak. I thought it a fitting epithet and chose it for the title of an article I wrote on the subject.

When I went back up to Anas's office, he got one of his secretaries to open his office window as wide as possible. He telephoned the President, saying "Mr President, everything is good, can you hear the people in the streets?" He told the President how his own family members were crying, overcome with emotion when he gave his speech. Anas hung up the phone, content. I shared his feelings, as did many Egyptians.

I thought it was all a bit too much, too soon, though.

The protests were organised through the ruling National Democratic Party. The different local representatives and party members would get in touch with each other over the phone. They would then co-ordinate their efforts, getting their supporters to gather in the designated place. From each of the local areas, they would march towards the centre of the city. However, going about and organising a demonstration like that, late at night, would not guarantee more than a few hundred supporters, at most.

Phone calls began to come in from the NDP, and some semi-official bodies, telling us where the pro-Mubarak demonstrations would be starting from the next day, which streets, which squares, etc. When I was asked, I told Anas that we would be ready to cover them.

Every caller wanted a camera for their own little demo, each one of them telling me that theirs would be the biggest. They were all most insistent about television coverage. I started to get suspicious. Why did everything have to be so exaggerated? I had a feeling that this aggrandisement would be counterproductive.

By concentrating the footage, we would make all these demonstrations seem artificial and forced, even if there were some genuine, ordinary people among them. My vision and sense dictated that it would be best to let Egyptians simply express their feelings. A lot of people felt sympathy and wanted stability. That was it. Gratitude to the President for the things he said he would do in the speech; after all he did say he would be stepping down in a few months. Despite all this, preparations were still underway to send cameras all over town to capture the choreographed demonstrations.

The music blasting out of the sound system on the street below was deafening, and it went on for hours. It was already late when they started. It certainly wasn't a spontaneous display of affection for Mubarak. It was organised and they had even set up a small stage. The songs they were playing were songs we used to hear on great national occasions, during military parades or graduations at military colleges.

How peculiar, I thought. The whole city was silent, save these two parties, completely opposed to one another, going on just a few hundred metres apart. I joked with my colleagues about how I preferred the demonstration in Tahrir Square on purely aesthetic grounds. At least there was some peace and quiet occasionally in Tahrir Square at night. Outside our building, they went on until four or five o'clock in the morning.

It was a rough night.

FEBRUARY 2ND – WEDNESDAY

In the morning, I sent out a few cameras to cover the imminent pro-Mubarak demonstrations. The demonstrations, though, were real. There were far more people there than one could reasonably expect the NDP to assemble overnight. Many ordinary people came out onto the streets, as I thought they would, to celebrate the end of Mubarak's tenure. There were hardline pro-Mubarak fanatics there of course, but the overwhelming mood of the people seemed to be "thank you and goodbye."

Citizens began arriving from different parts of Cairo, some came out from Sharrabiya, Abbasseya, and Khalifa, while others came from the governorates of Aswan and Assiut, declaring their support for the President. They also chanted slogans condemning the opposition figures, Dr Mohammed El-Baradei and Ayman Nour, whom they described as "outsiders" to the nation, who sought to destroy Egypt. The protesters carried banners reading: "We will solve our problems with our elders without outside interference."

Since the previous night, I had been calling all my contacts in the NDP begging them, "Please, you have a million square kilometres in Egypt to have your demonstration, you have the whole country, just leave this one square kilometre in Tahrir Square."

If the pro-Mubarak demonstrations pushed their way into Tahrir Square, there would be open conflict with the anti-government protesters and we could have a bloodbath on our hands. I was worried that the sudden feeling of empowerment the government would get after the renewal in support for the President might lead them to try such a tactic.

I decided to test the government. I picked up the phone and dialled Anas. In Mubarak's speech, he mentioned that the government would respect the court orders regarding disputes brought over the parliamentary election. Egypt maintains a separation of powers, to a degree, so when cases were brought to court challenging the election of certain MPs to parliament, the courts often ruled against the government.

I asked Anas if the government would be affirming some of the main points made in the speech. I specifically asked if the government would be respecting these court orders.

"Do you think that what Mubarak said means that the government will put these court orders into effect? Will they run by-elections in the seats where the courts have declared the results null and void?" I asked.

He didn't have an answer for me, "Hang on a minute" he muttered as he picked up the other phone and dialled Gamal, relaying my enquiry.

Gamal's answer was not encouraging. "Look, leave it as it is now and we'll see what we can do about it later." Clearly, he did not place any importance on the reform the speech promised. He was dangling the carrot in front of the electorate. I also realised that, due to the wording of the speech, by doing nothing the government would not necessarily be going back on the promises the President made. The President said that they would *respect* the court orders. He did not say they would *obey* the court orders.

I also pleaded with Anas to use his influence to ensure that the pro-Mubarak demonstrations would not go near Tahrir Square.

When it came to the coverage of these new demonstrations, I opted to give them the subtitle of "demonstrations for stability." Anas called and challenged me when he saw the coverage on his television screen, "Why don't you call them 'demonstrations for Mubarak'? And why are you still giving coverage to Tahrir Square?"

"It will sound better like that," I replied, "it'll be more credible."

"No, it's *our* day today!" he ranted, "if you don't do it today, when will you do it? It should be support for Mubarak!"

"But, it's better to…"

"No," he cut me off, "it's our day!"

I partially followed what he said. If the government would employ half-truths and empty promises, then so would I. I told my staff to use both "demonstrations for Mubarak" and "demonstrations for stability". I ordered my staff to go back to just using "stability" in the later news cycles.

The whole day, Anas was on the walkie-talkie with Nabil El-Tablawi, the building's chief of security, checking the movements of the crowds outside as he looked down on them from his panoramic office window.

At around 2pm, I glanced out of my window, and was forced to do a double take. I saw a band of horses and camels making their way over the Nile on the 15th May Bridge. I noticed that their riders were the same handlers who give tourists mounted tours of the pyramids in Giza, in an area called Nazlet El-Semman. I asked my staff about them. One of my reporters told me that, angry at lost income due to the revolution, a troop of tour guides got together in the morning and made their way from Giza, in the far west of the city and rode in to downtown Cairo. They were certainly a sight to behold as their animals strolled across the roads amidst the gathering crowds. I counted about 20 as they passed by.

After a while, I was told by my staff that there were clashes between opposing sets of demonstrators in Tahrir Square. We checked the CCTV feeds. The fighting had been going on for a short time, having started at around 1.30pm, with the odd stone hurled between the two sides.

The night before, after Mubarak's speech, many of the casual protesters who had been occupying Tahrir Square had gone home. The thousands who stayed overnight in the square were the more committed activists. We also received information from inside Tahrir Square that some demonstrators were unwilling to leave as rumours spread that they would be arrested by the army upon leaving the square. There were other reports that some of the more zealous protesters were making it difficult for others to leave. This was not helped by the fact that the army controlled some of the exits to and from the square.

When I heard about this, I called the army and asked them to release a statement confirming that nobody would be harmed or followed by soldiers on their way home. It was imperative that protesters did not feel under attack from the army.

I also called the operations room of the army and asked them for instructions on how people could leave the square. I was told that people would have to negotiate their way through the crowds to the south side of the square, and ask the officers stationed next to the American University in Cairo building. I put this information, complicated as it was, on TV.

All the while, I could see out of the window streams of Mubarak supporters moving down the Corniche towards Tahrir. Moreover, these demonstrators seemed to be coming from every direction. Seeing the masses of people, all heading towards Tahrir Square, I panicked.

I decided that the line for our coverage should be enough demonstrating, for *everybody*. Neither in support nor in opposition to the government. It was probably the only angle that would make us unpopular with both sides, but I thought that it may go some way to avoiding any further bloodshed. Having only anti-government protesters out in force was one thing, and the initial protests on Tuesday had been predominantly peaceful, but adding pro-government demonstrators to the mix could only lead to open conflict in the streets, which many Egyptians just didn't want to see in their country. Instead, we should resort to dialogue, which was something that a great many people had been calling for since the unrest began. We repeatedly called upon everyone to stop these demonstrations and protests. If everybody continued like this, then the result would not be good for Egypt.

I gave my instructions to the broadcasters going live on TV to stress through their comments and discussions that we rejected all of today's demonstrations, and, as Egyptians, we should settle our differences around a table, not on the street.

Our calls went unheeded, there were already so many thousands out in Cairo, and all of them were angry – angry for different reasons, but angry all the same.

After the speech the night before, the palace and top NDP officials started mobilising supporters, in the same way they did for the elections. Today, they were able to swell their numbers with volunteers. Many Egyptians, unaware of the official demonstrations, took to the streets anyway in support of the President.

There's a line at the end of an Al Pacino film, *The Devil's Advocate*, where Al Pacino, playing the Devil, exclaims "Vanity, definitely my favourite sin!" I can see why vanity would appeal to Satan. It leads intelligent men to do foolish things. The government and NDP, who thought that they had lost power, suddenly found themselves gaining strength once more. It was their vanity and hubris that led to what happened next.

Gamal started making phone calls abroad. It was inappropriate to call foreign officials at this time, but he called the British Foreign Secretary, William Hague, and gloated. He told the British politician that he was mistaken when he said that the people weren't behind the government, claiming that the pro-government protesters were evidence to the contrary. William Hague is an experienced politician and mentioned on BBC radio that he had spoken with Gamal and warned against the dangers of state-sponsored violence, diplomatically avoiding mention of Gamal's tone. However, it was extremely immature and arrogant of Gamal to make such a call.

The anti-Mubarak slogan, continuously shouted, was *Irhal*! (Leave!). The pro-Mubarak slogan was *Misha Yamshi*! (he's not leaving). They also referred to Mubarak as *Al-Rais Al-Ab*, (The President Father). The government supporters were adamant that the old man should not be humiliated, especially as he had already announced he would be stepping down, albeit not immediately.

Various marches were rolling along major streets around Cairo, from both sides of the Nile. People came out of the side streets to join them. The smaller roads led onto the larger thoroughfares, which would usually be choked in traffic. The marchers had their arms raised, passing along the streets with empty shops and restaurants either side. The demonstrators were chanting slogans in support of the President. In contrast to the slogan heard a few days earlier: "The people want to overthrow the regime," the supporters chanted "The people want Mubarak as President!" In addition, they chanted sentimental messages and expressed their apologies to Mubarak: "Wake up…come round, the President is like your father," "Oh Gamal, tell your father…the Egyptian People love him" and "Oh Mubarak! Oh pilot…we offer you our apologies." When it came to their enemies, men like El-Baradei, they chanted "Oh Baradei…Oh spy agent…take a bag to Israel."

On the Corniche, just outside the Maspero building, thousands had gathered, weeping and chanting the same slogans, emphasising their support for Mubarak and their opposition to the Tahrir demonstrations.

The vanity of those in the circle of power when they saw their supporters out in full made them think they could just "cleanse" Tahrir Square by flooding it with opposing demonstrators. Even if the army and intelligence didn't accept that this would be possible, they did not stand up to the palace. The government and its supporters should have left the square alone. Their plan to end the protests quickly could only have ended in disaster.

The government thought that since they had protesters dotted around central Cairo, they would be able to encircle Tahrir Square. From there, the anti-government protesters could have been pushed out, and perhaps even some would join the pro-Mubarak demonstrations, to show their gratitude.

I didn't read it like that. All day, I had been begging anybody I knew in power not to touch Tahrir. The Tahrir Square protesters had survived attacks from the police on Friday and were prepared for a stand-off, far more organised than the rabble on the Pro-Mubarak side. Many of them had also been trained for such a confrontation.

In the early afternoon, something incredible happened. I could barely believe the monitor. The camels and horses that I'd seen wandering about earlier were storming Tahrir Square.

Their owners had trekked out all the way to central Cairo with their animals and had headed to the TV building so they would be picked up by the cameras and be seen to be showing their support for Mubarak. Some of them had turned away from the crowds, heading back over the 6th October Bridge after they had paraded along the Corniche. However, the remainder peeled off towards Abdel Moneim Riad Square, close to Tahrir. A spirited charge emerged from under the jumble of overpasses that spilled out from the 6th October Bridge, to the north of the square. They charged down the open road next to the Egyptian Museum. The shocked protesters leapt out of the way, allowing the leaders of the charge to power through. However, some of the slower riders were mobbed, the crowd pulling them off their animals. Some were dragged to the green railings to the side of the road and were viciously kicked and punched by the furious protesters in the shadow of the great pink walls of the museum. One was pressed against the railings while a man pulled at him from the other side, repeatedly thumping him over the head.

The story went that riders were used by the pro-Mubarak agitators to raid Tahrir. The footage was splashed across the world's media, reminding people of camel charges from films like Lawrence of Arabia. Not something one would expect to see in the 21st century.

I've looked over the footage many times. There could not have been more than 15-20 animals who actually charged into the square. Some of them were loaded with two riders. Some broadcasters claimed there were scores of mounted riders, but this is not the case. It was also claimed that the riders were beating protesters with clubs and knives, though I didn't see them wielding any weapons. All I saw were the thin canes that they use to control the animals, similar to a jockey's whip. The whole thing was over in about a minute. It was a stupid thing to do, they should never have been brought to the square. The animals should never have been subjected to it either. Aside from the issue of animal cruelty, the horses and camels were these men's livelihoods, and they could have been killed.

I thought it would be wise to contact somebody who knew what was going on with regard to the animals. My staff managed to get hold of the Governor of Giza, Sayyed Abdul Aziz, who is responsible for Nazlet El-Semman, where these men were from. He explained on the phone, live on TV, that these people were not members of the police force as reported; instead, they were indeed the tourist workers of Nazlet El-Semman. He reiterated that these camels and horses were how these men made a living, and that they have come riding these camels and horses as ordinary citizens who want their voices to be heard, to make people aware of the fact that they had lost business during the uprising. It was not a cynical, calculated attempt by the government at harassing the Tahrir Square demonstrators. It was a group of men, far from home, who got carried away, many of whom paid the price when they were subsequently beaten up by the protesters.

I got a phone call from Anas in the early afternoon, ordering me to announce on air that people were moving towards Tahrir Square, and the roads towards the Square were safe to travel.

"I can't say that," I declared.

"Why?" he demanded.

"Simply because I can see that the road to Tahrir is not safe, there's fighting going on," I answered.

"Is there?"

"Yes," I responded, "I cannot say that there isn't."

I put the phone down on him. After a while he called back again.

"Say that Tahrir Square is safe. There are no clashes," he commanded.

"I cannot say that because there *are* clashes in Tahrir," I announced, "and I'm not going to say there aren't."

When he realised that I wasn't going to relent on this one he gave up. He just put the phone back down.

I was not in a good mood after seeing what was happening in Tahrir Square. A party official called me up to check on me. He asked me how I was, and I grunted some courtesy back at him.

"Abdel Latif, why are you so panicked? Take it easy, stay calm. This afternoon, you and I will take two deck chairs and a parasol and sit in Tahrir Square."

I paused for a moment, not quite sure how to respond to such optimism that clearly wasn't grounded in reality. "I don't think so," was all I could think of to say. I bit my tongue, despite the fact I was angry, under pressure, overworked and tired.

Even though the government had tried to marshal their supporters to finish the thing quickly, the situation was totally out of anybody's control. The discovery that the protesters who remained in the square were strong, organised and ready to respond to aggression was a complete surprise to the authorities.

Some people, I honestly do not know who, discovered that the protesters in the square were fighting back and decided to hire their own fighters to even up the odds. These *baltagiya* (thugs) were not too difficult to get hold of. During elections, for instance, thugs are often brought out onto the streets. It was rumoured that the NDP used them, rich businessmen used them, even the Muslim Brotherhood has used them. Contact is made with certain unsavoury characters, who then organise their own crew to come in and act as fists for hire.

At around 6pm, some of these thugs made their way to the top of the buildings surrounding Tahrir square, and the fighting suddenly got far more vicious. As we watched the CCTV feeds, we started to see flashes on our screens, as petrol bombs (Molotov cocktails) were lobbed across the streets. The army later stated that the Muslim Brotherhood and other Islamists, who had formed a substantial portion of those fighting in the square, had also managed to occupy the rooftops of surrounding buildings, using them as a launchpad to hurl petrol bombs and other improvised missiles down on the square. One of our colleagues in the television station who lived in Tahrir Square called for help that night, asking us to call the army. She lived in Tahrir Square and said that Islamists had taken over her building, kicking out all the residents. The army was able to reclaim the building, allowing the residents back in the next day.

The two sides formed opposing lines on the street, with the anti-government protesters lashing out from Tahrir Square, as the pro-Mubarak supporters tried to break through their lines. After a while the running battles spilled out from the area directly around Tahrir, to the streets beyond. Everybody out on the streets was polarised amid the chaos, there was no longer an impression of "thank you and goodbye," you were either for Mubarak or against him. Many Mubarak supporters were calling for revenge against the protesters and the political forces who staged protests calling for the overthrow of the regime. Several public figures called upon the military to step in, one statement asked "the military institution to ensure the security and safety of Egypt's youth who were gathered to demonstrate peacefully in Tahrir Square and other streets, neighbourhoods and Egyptian cities".

The statement, signed chiefly by businessman Naguib Sawiris, Egypt's former ambassador to the United Nations Nabil El Araby and writer Salama Ahmed Salama, noted that "the violence witnessed in some of Egypt's streets now will only lead to more political tension and blockage of any prospect of easing the current crisis." The statement added, "we have high hopes in the military institution to save the nation and the citizens from this crisis and rescue the lives of Egypt's youths."

Pro-Mubarak groups rushed into Tahrir Square, coming from the main surrounding streets, while the demonstrators in Tahrir Square tried to block the roads. They chucked rocks at each other until the Mubarak supporters managed to penetrate the square, though most of the fighting was at Abdel Moneim Riad Square, and the side streets. They shouted for the President, raising slogans in his support. The side streets witnessed clashes between the two sides that ended when pro-Mubarak supporters succeeded in driving out the opposition.

Both sides were attacking each other, both were involved in the violence that ensued.

When I saw some of the petrol bombs fly into the garden of the Egyptian Museum, I called the military again, and demanded that they do something to prevent the museum going up in smoke with Egypt's national treasures inside.

As this was happening in Tahrir Square, the Prime Minister was busy giving interviews on TV. He did three interviews with three different channels, each one within ten minutes of the one before. Each interview was informal and Shafik didn't do any official posturing. He was wearing a simple blue jumper and talking in a simple manner to the people. Shafik did not deliberately intend that his first TV appearances on the commercial channels be so relaxed as the country descended into chaos. However, he promised to open an investigation into the "Camel Battle" and to hold those responsible accountable.

My dismay at what was going on pushed me to bring in religious figures, both Christian and Muslim, to ask those out on the streets to calm themselves. We asked sheikhs to come on TV. We asked the country's intellectuals to come on. Everybody we had on, both holy and secular, had one message for the country: just calm down. The Sheikh of Al-Azhar addressed Egyptians on television, calling to bring an end to sedition, and to cease mutual hostilities, while reminding the country of the famous Islamic hadith which states: "If two Muslims fight each other with their swords, the killer and the killed will go to hell."

The armed forces did not get involved, but were content to stand as they did over the previous few days with orders not to engage. They issued a statement, requesting "Egyptians to look into the future and that the army and the people are capable of changing the existing situation." They directed their words to the youths saying, "We have received your message and learned your demands and we are up all night to secure the nation for you, generous people of Egypt." The statement raised some questions: can we walk safely in the street? Can people go out to their schools and universities? "The Armed Forces are calling on you, not through the authority of power but with the desire for Egypt to restore normal life to the country."

It was an emotional statement, as was the case with most of the statements issued at the time. It tried to address the emotions of the Egyptians, but what was clear is that there was no warning against demonstrating. Basically, there was no explicit and rigorous request not to demonstrate.

The fighting between the two sides caused many casualties. Many people lost eyes during the night after being hit on the head by stones. I believe that those in Tahrir Square fought with more passion. They were fighting for a reason. Their belief made them stronger. Those attacking them were just fighting for money or the sport of it.

We heard the ambulance sirens screaming down the street as they raced towards the square. Despite what seemed to be a constant stream of emergency vehicles, there weren't enough to carry away all the injured.

The Muslim Brotherhood also issued a statement, commenting on the day's events, which said that it holds the regime responsible for the thousands of citizens killed and injured, and refuses any negotiation with it, saying that it sought to prevent the people from achieving their objectives so that they could end what the movement termed their "blessed Intifada." They called on the people to come to the protests in their millions so that the people could regain their sovereignty and dignity. The Brotherhood went on to say, "we greatly appreciate the heroic role of the Egyptian people, whose protests and marches have continued since Tuesday, the 25th of January. Yesterday's march was one of the greatest rallies in global history, where several million participated nationwide, reflecting the true will of the people, which proves that all elections conducted by the regime were rigged, giving it false legitimacy."

In the early evening, around 6 or 7pm, I got two calls from the army. The first said we were to issue a statement, that said an "unnamed security source" called on all demonstrators to leave Tahrir Square immediately and that elements of the Muslim Brotherhood were firebombing the crowds from above. I put the text on the screen in two points. One point said that all demonstrators were to leave the square, the second was that some Ihkwan "elements" were throwing petrol bombs from rooftops surrounding Tahrir Square to encourage civil conflict.

A few minutes later I got the second call, where they asked us to broadcast an official warning across our TV channels:

"Because of agitators on their way with firebombs (literally translated as *fireballs* in Arabic) to Tahrir Square, we plead with all citizens to evacuate the square immediately."

They asked me to repeat it over and over again.

When the text came in, I called all my contacts in the army, intelligence, cabinet and the palace asking what was going on, as I couldn't quite believe the warning I'd been given. When questioned, they all agreed that the warning was correct and should be broadcast.

It reminded me of an old black and white film, very famous in Egypt, which features a scene of a man going into a pharmacy to buy medicine. The transaction seems to go smoothly save for the pharmacist's blunder, silently revealed to the audience in a visual aside. The pharmacist hands the man deadly poison packaged within the benevolent confines of a medicine bottle. When the error is discovered, the characters in the film commandeer the local radio station, announcing: "Don't drink the medicine! This medicine is poison." The cry was repeated over and over. Now I was calling on the country not to drink the medicine.

We put the warning on a loop, repeated across all our radio and TV channels. While the warnings were going on, I called all my friends in Tahrir Square, and begged them to leave, in case they got hurt. When they asked me what was going on, I had to confess that I didn't actually know, I just wanted them out of there and safe.

We had a reporter from Nile TV, the English language station down at the square. Before he went, he came to me to ask permission to get down to the square.

"Yes," I told the young reporter, "go!"

He looked me in the eye before he headed off, "But" he said, "I will broadcast what I see."

I looked him back in the eye, telling him, "Don't broadcast *anything* but what you see."

We couldn't give him a camera as we needed approval from the army, so he had to file his reports to the studio over the phone. We called him and told him to hurry back when the reports of firebombs started coming in.

I sent out a call to all of our staff, some of whom were heading to Tahrir, that they should all get away from the square. I pulled back a camera crew that I had sent there earlier.

The battle continued. Rocks and debris were launched at the opposing sides. The facades of the giant stone buildings around the square were damaged, windows were smashed, cars were destroyed. Molotov cocktails were still splashing on the pavements.

The army called again. They asked me to stop broadcasting the live feed from Tahrir Square. They didn't want it on the screen. I was told, using the English word, that the picture would be "ugly". I called around my contacts again. They were all in agreement.

I had no idea what to do. Perhaps I should just show people praying, or have my anchors repeat warnings not to let the country burn. Maybe some patriotic songs. There was only one live shot I had that wasn't trained on the square, and that was from the camera set up on the tenth floor trained on Qasr El-Nil Bridge. An empty bridge.

I was given no choice. I was overworked, doing lots of different jobs. I was simultaneously running the three TV stations, several radio stations and fielding calls from the ground, acting as a contact for the army and the public. I'd been doing this for days on barely a few hours sleep. At the same time, I had to manage all these different parties, both inside and outside the government, as they jostled for position. The pressure was unbearable.

It was coming up to 9pm, so I decided to at least run with the 9 o'clock news. Since the uprising began, we'd abandoned our regular news bulletins. When I talked it over with my staff, we decided we should at least do things properly, so we put together the evening news.

I was in the control room and the news was running when I suddenly fell into a pit of depression. It was, I felt, the lowest point of my professional career as a journalist. I felt that the people around me, who believed what I had told them, who were facing personal attacks from their friends and relatives for working with state TV, were seriously doubting themselves. Perhaps they wouldn't bother coming in to work tomorrow.

I stared at the machines in the office, then looked up at my monitor, not showing the chaos developing less than a few hundred metres down the road. I looked at my staff. Their eyes were sunken. When they turned to me, their eyes seemed to say "What's happened? This isn't what we believed in…this isn't what you told us to do."

I thought about all the mistakes that had happened, that we had made. I couldn't do anything about the mistakes I had made: they were out of my hands.

Something snapped inside my head. Perhaps there was something I could do. I stood up and announced to my staff, "Right, that's it, we're changing the broadcast. Everyone, get hold of everything you can on Tahrir Square."

I raced around the control room, there was suddenly a flurry of activity in front of the banks of monitors as people raced to get hold of material and control the broadcast. Commands were hastily bashed into keyboards and machines. I got hold of Ahmed Wagih, one of my field reporters, told him to grab a cameraman and get himself down to Tahrir Square straight away.

"Everyone!" I shouted, "don't take any instructions from anybody but me. Get the link to Tahrir Square back onto the screen. NOW!"

I picked up the telephone, and furiously dialled the army, the palace, the intelligence service, everyone who had just dictated to me what I was supposed to be showing on my channels. "LISTEN!" I shouted, "from this moment, I'm not going to do ANYTHING but what I want to! I will not be taking any instructions! If I don't believe that what you're telling me is true, then I WILL NOT broadcast it! I'm warning you, get that guy on the ninth floor off my back! No one will be giving me ANY ORDERS if you want me to stay! Either that, or I'm leaving, and if I leave, ALL my people will be LEAVING WITH ME!"

I called round everyone with the same message. If they wanted me to stay, I would stay, but I would stay as a professional.

They got the message. From that moment onwards, we didn't broadcast anything unless we thought it was right to do so. I started doing this job because I wanted to run a professional media organisation. That was how I intended to finish it.

They tried to interfere, of course, but the editorial choice was ours. I know that they put in a call to Anas and told him to let me do my job.

Uprising and revolutions are not peaceful. It's the nature of what they are. People are always going to get hurt, on all sides. It was a grim night, that night. A lot of people were killed or injured. And everybody was responsible. The President, Gamal and his clique, the NDP, the Brotherhood, the protest groups, everybody.

Most importantly, for far too long I allowed our coverage to be dictated by higher powers. Because of that, I was also responsible.

FEBRUARY 3RD – THURSDAY

By the early hours, my staff had all heard about the phone calls that I made the night before, demanding that we be able to exercise editorial control over our output. Some of them had been in the office while I made them. It was useful to have witnesses.

I was often keen to hold my phone calls with officials – be they from the armed forces, the presidency, the intelligence service, or Anas – with a member of staff in the office. I did this for two reasons.

Firstly, I wanted to prove to them that the stance which I urged them to take, was a principled one. I wanted them to be reassured that their positions went beyond the limits of professionalism. I wanted them to sense that they were undertaking a national duty, shared by us all, in a bid to save this country from the danger it was facing.

Secondly, I had a feeling that the events of those few days would prove to be controversial in the future. History was being made. It was important that we had people to bear witness to our actions.

In the early hours of the morning, which followed a sleepless night, I called a staff meeting. I wanted everybody present: presenters, editors, producers, the lot. Before I started talking, I studied their faces. Unshaven, baggy eyes, messy hair, or veil, it was quite a sight, but they seemed content to be working through the fatigue. They were comfortable with their jobs, because we were now committed to doing our jobs properly, without having to defer to higher powers, we were not just a tool to be manipulated. It reinforced the idea that, when we were forced to make important decisions, or see through a confrontation, all our allegiances were to our nation and our profession.

Despite being reassured in what we were doing, we were all anxious and concerned about what had happened the night before. Egypt, for the first time in its modern history, almost came close to civil war. The tension running through the office affected our broadcasts. It was drawn on the faces of the presenters of our morning show, *Sabah El-Kheir Ya Masr*, (*Good Morning Egypt*). The credits opened with two presenters who normally looked so cheerful, just looking scared. Before one of them spoke, he announced, "Pray to Allah that He saves Egypt from the sorrow that overshadows it!"

After a while, at around 6am, Ahmed Wagih, the reporter I had sent into the battlefield the night before came back with his crew from the Tahrir and Abdel al Moneim Riyadh Squares. He told us about seeing rocks flying through the air and petrol bombs landing on the streets. He was joking about arriving back in one piece. "You wanted to get rid of me as usual, but I always come back to you," he laughed, "I never knew you liked me that much!" He asked me what he should do with the material he had filmed. I told him to simply report what he saw, I also let him know that he didn't have to stick to the standard three-minute report, he could have as long as he needed.

"Take your tapes and head to the editing units to give us the story of what happened, as it evolved," I ordered, "and as you have seen it, without taking sides."

It was gripping stuff. He said that the opposition protesters in the square were far more organised than the broad swathes of youth usually present for the large demonstrations. He noted that their skill and tactical ability came as a surprise to the pro-Mubarak supporters. He further elaborated that those supporters did not resemble those that took part in the morning protests, many of whom came out to demonstrate spontaneously. Instead, they seemed to have been hired or instructed, as if they were on a mission.

We aired his report later that day, and which I honestly consider to be some of the best coverage anywhere of what happened that night. Many of the demonstrators refused to watch us by that point, and our integrity was being questioned in the international media. Well, all I can say is that I'm damn proud of the journalism that we produced that morning. Wagih was even used as a studio guest to give an eye witness testimony of details of events.

Reports started coming in of protesters shot dead, in and around Tahrir Square. The reports were all the more worrying as the protesters were apparently killed by sniper fire, by carefully and deliberately placed shots. This was in contrast to previous gunshot deaths during the uprising, which were the result of reckless or poorly trained recruits opening fire on crowds, or in some cases, bystanders caught in crossfire.

It was never revealed where the gunfire came from, we just heard shots fired. It was only later that people suggested that the culprits may be snipers.

As far as I know, the Interior Minister had a group of 20-25 highly trained, elite officers, similar to the SWAT teams of American law enforcement agencies. This elite team was trained in special weapons and tactics, and that included sniping. There are many elite forces like this across the world, training their whole careers for a moment that may never come. I had heard through the government that one part of the team were protecting the Interior Ministry itself, near Tahrir Square, and another group was stationed at the State Security building in Nasser city. I had heard that they were used to repel armed attackers from the Interior Ministry on the 29th of January.

I have no evidence as to who fired those shots, or who gave the order to shoot. The protesters blamed the Interior Ministry and the NDP, some even blamed the army. The regime blamed the Muslim Brotherhood and Hamas. Official reports blamed gunmen who had crossed into Egypt from Gaza and Sudan. All I know is that the Interior Ministry did have teams of trained snipers stationed in Cairo that night.

This state of confusion prompted me to contact those in charge, to ask for an urgent and immediate investigation into what happened over the past few days, especially into what took place on the previous day and night. It was important to announce the outcome of those investigations, with haste, so that public confidence could be restored. I underlined the need to make public information on whether any foreigners had been involved in these events, as some reports had stated, particularly as some had been arrested by the armed forces and at the citizens' checkpoints.

It was important to investigate all of these things. I gave my instructions to the broadcasters to say on air that we, in Egyptian television, demand an immediate investigation into recent events.

I got a call that morning from a member of Omar Suleiman's staff. A dialogue between the new Vice President and the opposition had begun that day; however, they were having trouble finding some representatives of the youth movements. The meetings had already begun, and the youth movements, who initiated the current unrest, were conspicuous in their absence. The youths subsequently criticised their exclusion from the discussions. They felt that it was unfair that they, who caused the dialogue to be called in the first place, were passed over in favour of opposition parties which they saw as weak and ineffective. I was asked if I knew anybody. I had a few names and phone numbers of people I knew who were involved in the protests, and gave them to him. The problem was that this youth movement didn't have a titular leader. In a group of 20,000 protesters, there would be at least 200 ringleaders. There really wasn't a mainstream youth movement at all. Instead, it was a broad spectrum of young people (and old, for that matter) without any unifying ideology.

The meeting had not been announced to the public beforehand. It included a number of traditional opposition politicians, though, as yet, no members of the Muslim Brotherhood. There were 21 political parties present, including some of the old established ones such as Al-Wafd, Al-Tagamaue' and Al-Nassery. Also present were quite a few smaller parties set up in the past few years, though they didn't carry any real weight. Many of them were only formed to create the false impression that, at the time, there was a genuine multi-party system.

The Interior Ministry issued a vague statement saying that they had arrested foreigners in Cairo. It triggered public suspicions that any foreigner could be a spy. Subsequently, foreign journalists were being subjected to attacks in and around the square. The atmosphere had become very dangerous, especially when the two opposing sides were out in the streets. Egyptians can be very suspicious of foreigners, especially at a time of national crisis. The current anti-foreigner sentiment was fuelled by rumours of the presence of foreigners among opposition demonstrators, and their activities in some parts of Cairo and Alexandria distributing publications and flyers inciting the people to revolt against the government. It was also a result of what had been reported, and proven in some cases, that outsiders had provided support for the demonstrators, in the form of food, beverages, and it was rumoured, finance. However, in the cold logic of the streets, all foreigners, the most visible of whom were the journalists, were agitators, encouraging the overthrow of Mubarak. Even Egyptian reporters, including our own, were subjected to attacks. One of our correspondents was stabbed, though we managed to get a call from him on air while he was in hospital, telling us and his family that he would be all right.

The previous day, many foreign media organisations, including the offices of Al-Arabiya and Al-Jazeera were assaulted by Mubarak supporters, due to their belief that these channels were taking a biased stance against the President and were plotting against the country. I got calls from many colleagues who worked for the foreign press, demanding that we do something to stop them from being targeted. A journalist I knew, Hala Jaber, a British-Lebanese woman who worked for *The Sunday Times* told me she'd been getting calls and emails from friends in trouble. I told her to give me their names and contact details. She emailed me the details. I called the army, and asked them to protect them.

At Nile International, they received a call for help from an Egyptian fixer working with a group of foreign journalists. The fixer said that thugs surrounded the journalists in Tahrir, chasing them out of the square. Some of the journalists took cover in the the Ramses Hilton hotel, near Abdel Moneim Riad Square, close to Tahrir, where many of the foreign journalists were staying. I called the armed forces, who sent a unit to secure the Ramses Hilton hotel. The thugs tried to enter the hotel, smashed a door I believe, but the army surrounded the place before they were able to enter.

After I called them, the armed forces sent a unit to secure the Ramses Hilton hotel, near Abdel Moneim Riad Square, close to Tahrir, where many of the foreign journalists were staying.

I put together a statement, in our name, from the Egypt News Centre and broadcast it across our channels. It stated that we had received many calls of distress from foreign journalists who were subjected to hostility and attack. It called on the citizens of Egypt to protect journalists and help them do their jobs. After the statement was broadcast, I called Anas and told him what was happening. In turn, he got the State Information Service (SIS), an affiliate of the Ministry of Information, to issue a similar statement. Some of the journalists who had initially called me, telephoned me again to let me know that they had seen troops deployed, protecting foreign media offices. However, the prospect of the army surrounding already embattled journalists made it seem as if the state was repressing them further.

Anas called me, at around 11am. He sounded more formal than usual, telling me "Get two of the presenters ready to go to the Council of Ministers building." I asked two of my presenters to get ready, and make their way over there. A few minutes later, he called me again, "Get ready, the Vice President wants to do an interview."

"OK" I replied, "do you want me to send someone now?"

"No," he answered, "he wants to do it with you."

"Have you any idea what this is about?" I enquired.

"No. All you have to do is go there and do the interview."

I checked with my technical people and asked if we could do a live feed, and a proper location interview. We thought about it for a short while, looking at the CCTV feeds of the streets, still filled with protesters. The director told me that because of the danger on the streets, they couldn't get a SNG (Satellite News Gathering) vehicle out there. It was highly likely that the van would be attacked, an unacceptable risk for the crew to take. The best they could do was bundle a crew of about three people with portable equipment into a car and send them over. When they came back, we could edit the footage together and broadcast it.

I would go separately. After changing out of my jeans and into a suit and tie, I started preparing for the interview, and asked for my car to be readied. After gathering up my things, I went down to the car. It was the first time I'd been out of the building since the previous Friday. I had no time to dwell on the novelty. The challenge that we had to overcome was actually finding the way to reach the Council of Ministers building. The first obstacle was to escape the siege surrounding the television building. Contact was made with the Republican Guard, who were in control of the perimeter of the Maspero. They secured an exit for us, and we set off down the roads. I sat in the back rather than in my preferred front position, just to be safe. It would normally have been a five-minute journey, taking a route that should pass straight through Tahrir Square.

We were forced to take a massive detour. We headed over the 15th May Bridge, passing over the island of Zamalek, reaching the other side of the Nile. The Council of Ministers was of course on the same side of the Nile as the Maspero building, but we thought it wise to cross right to the other side and double back. We reached the other bank of the Nile at Agouza, Giza, before driving down and crossing back over on the University Bridge before finally reaching the Council of Ministers. The five minute journey lasted about 45 minutes.

We were also delayed by having to cross improvised checkpoints erected by the concerned citizens of the popular committees in order to protect their neighbourhoods. In the absence of the police, these checkpoints had sprung up all over town, some of them guarded by armed men. My two sons later told me that they had helped out, manning the one near our home. We had to stop at each one we passed, though when they saw who I was, they apologised, explaining they were stopping every car that came by.

"There was a foreign lady who came in a car through here," one of them explained, "when we tried to check her car she became confused, and when we tried to stop her she sped off in the car, hitting one of us. We couldn't catch up with her."

"We stopped one of the buses from a foreign private school in Maadi," another one piped in, "we found a large number of meals to be sent to the people in Tahrir Square."

"We are not thugs as they are trying to portray us," announced another, "there are many channels and newspapers trying to give the impression that we are, but we are trying to protect this country and save it from falling into an abyss."

Before I left them, they asked me to convey their sentiments on the television, and to let the public know that they were only trying to defend their homes. I told them I would do so.

It was the first time I'd seen Cairo so tired. It was the first time I'd seen the streets of Cairo through my own eyes, rather than through live monitors or recorded tapes. It was truly shocking. I wrote an article about it the day after, I called it, "The Cairo that I Don't Know." I wrote about how I've always loved Cairo, I think it's the best city in the world. I fell in love with it long ago. That day, I didn't see the Cairo I knew. People looked exhausted, sad and upset. People were sad for what Cairo had become, and they were angry at those responsible, whether they be the government or the opposition, the youths or the Brotherhood, be it one or many, or all of these elements put together. After spending days patrolling the streets, the concerned citizens who took the security of their neighbourhoods upon themselves, looked so tired, as if they could barely go on any longer. Shops were smashed and looted of all their merchandise. Pavements were broken. There were hardly any cars on the street, a stark contrast to the chronically busy roads familiar to residents of the capital. The few cars that remained on the roads drove recklessly, and with impunity. We often complain about how drivers in Cairo lacked respect for the rules of the road. Now, there were no rules. Cars zipped along roads, heedless of the fact that they might be driving in the wrong direction down a one-way street, or that they may be driving through residential streets at speeds normally reserved for the motorway. As the giant billboards atop the buildings showed smiling models advertising their wares, the faint smell of burning still hung in the air, and the traces of arson were still visible. Scorch marks seared up the sides of the towering apartment blocks, or left dark patches on the roadside.

I was encouraged by the fact that young men had come out on the streets, and, irrespective of political allegiance, tried to restore order and safety to the roads. Their tenacity and resourcefulness was admirable. Unfortunately, the fact that they were out on the streets at all illustrated how the police and security services had abandoned their duties, though I did spy one traffic officer on my way back, heroically struggling to keep order at an intersection.

I remember thinking about how everyone was responsible for what Cairo had become and we should all have tried to find a way to fix it. All the political groups were to blame, even those youths who sparked the initial protests back on January 25th, they too are responsible for the way Cairo turned out to be. As to those who have practised intimidation and bullying, they are criminals. I finished that article I wrote by saying, "I exclude the criminals and invite the others, whom I hold responsible for what happened in Cairo, to return to build it once again, and I put in the forefront those young people who have changed the equation of understanding and awareness, thus I invite them to think, for maybe they can find an innovative approach to repair what we have devastated."

When I got to the cabinet building, I thought about the last time I was there, a few weeks before when I interviewed Ahmed Nazif. I even saw the same faces milling about the corridors. When I walked up to the room where I was to do the interview with Omar Suleiman, I saw Dr Ahmed Shafik, the new Prime Minister, giving a press conference. One of his usual boring long-winded ones. Sometimes they would go on for two hours or more. I sat down in a nearby room, waiting for the Vice President and my crew.

Dr Shafik spoke about what happened, expressing his sorrow, and promising that it would not happen again. He confirmed that an investigation was underway, as it fell under the remit presented to him by President Mubarak, to investigate the security vacuum. He talked of Mubarak being the "father of the nation," as all of the top officials did, and that he should not be treated this way. Despite his promises of immediate action, the committee to undertake the investigation was not actually set up until six days later, in spite of the urgent need for it. I made a mental note at the time to badger Anas to remind the Prime Minister how important it was to get started in this as soon as possible.

I don't know what happened, but when I was told that the Vice President was ready to see me, my crew still hadn't arrived.

ABDEL LATIF EL-MENAWY

I was taken into another office where I found Omar Suleiman waiting. We shook hands. I had met the man before, though this was the first time I had spoken to him since the uprisings began. He is not the kind of man to waste time with small talk, asking "How is the situation with you at the TV station?"

I answered truthfully: "The situation is very bad. We are having problems." He listened to me intently, calmly taking in everything I had to say. "Things are getting worse," I added.

Despite the weight of the crisis, he seemed confident that he could find a solution to it. He told me that what was needed was for all the parties to be convinced of the importance of dialogue as it was the only way to resolve the situation.

Before we started, I told him the names of a few of my contacts in the army and the intelligence services, telling him that I had been in touch with them the whole time.

He nodded sagely, "Yes," he acknowledged, "I know. Keep in contact with them." What I suspected at the time, and what was later confirmed to be the case, was that my contacts would always tell Omar Suleiman whenever I called, sometimes deferring to him before they called me back with their answers to my queries. "What are we going to talk about?" he asked.

"The key issue is to create a state of trust among Egyptians," I replied, "to find a way forward to overcome this crisis from which we are all suffering."

When I do interviews, I tend not to have a set list of questions, preferring instead to simply talk, making sure I cover a series of points which I lay out beforehand. I don't like to broadcast pre-recorded or edited interviews, I'd much rather do them live to air or live to tape. I think that good interviews grow, as the discussion takes hold and the interviewer and subject become comfortable with one another.

We began the interview. Because my camera crew were nowhere to be found, I was forced to improvise. I remembered the press conference I saw in progress on my way in to the building. We had two electronic news gathering (known in the trade as ENG) portable cameras recording the event. One for Channel One and one for Nile News. They weren't the proper cameras to use for an interview like this, but they would do. I grabbed the crews and told them to set up. We couldn't get the lighting right, we only had the ambient lighting of the room, which gave the interview a slightly amateurish feel. It wasn't ideal for Omar Suleiman's first interview.

He sounded knowledgeable and confident. I was shocked to notice on the recordings afterwards how weary I sounded. It was the result of all the stress I was enduring over the past few days. It was almost as if I was striving to have my voice heard.

Fatigue was also apparent in the Vice President, except he still managed to sound more assured. He had been busy, taking on his new role and still running the intelligence services. When I met him, he had just concluded the first session of the national dialogue.

He identified four separate agendas which affected the state's response to the unrest since it erupted on the 25th of January, aside from the youth movements that actually started it all and the disaffected public who joined them. The agendas which he referred to were those of the international community (including foreigners in Egypt), the Muslim Brotherhood, existing political parties and powerful businessmen. He stressed that the response of the government to the youth movements would have to take into account the potential actions of these four actors, who were also formulating their own responses to it, and in some cases, would use the sudden crisis and the absence of the state to further their own ambitions in Egypt.

In spite of the technical problems we had, all the news stations took the footage. Back at the Maspero building, in the control room, we have a bank of about 20 screens, displaying all the other major satellite channels, CNN, Sky, Al-Jazeera, BBC, RT, Euronews, Al-Arabiya, etc. When we broadcast the interview, suddenly all the screens changed, almost simultaneously, and cut to our interview. A friend of mine, Abdul Rahman Rashid, the manager at Al-Arabiya, called me up later on, "What's happened?" he asked in jest, "suddenly I saw your face on every screen in my building!"

The interview went on for about 40 minutes. As I mentioned before, Omar Suleiman was well respected in Egypt. Some people saw him as the solution to the current political crisis, not just the one that had been going on in the last few days, but in the last few years. Out of all of those at the top of government, he was seen as the safest pair of hands. He had a certain sort of charisma, not in an extrovert way, but he holds himself well. He is known as a hard worker, and apparently works out in the gym every day. It is also well known that he has a heart problem that affects his stamina.

His reputation has suffered in Egypt because he was intimately involved with managing some of Egypt's most sensitive, and unpopular, international relationships, namely those with Israel and the United States. During his career, he has also been frequently attacked by Islamists, as he had made no secret of his suspicion of Islamic political movements, inside and outside Egypt. He was also seen by the youth demonstrators as far too close to President Mubarak and the old regime to be serious about reform.

He did another interview around the same time with Christiane Amanpour for the American network, ABC. The interview was in English. Omar Suleiman is known for choosing his words carefully; however, he is not the strongest English speaker. In this interview, he did not come out so well. He bluntly blamed a great deal of the unrest (not just in Egypt, but also in the rest of the Arab world) on foreign interference and Islamist currents in Egypt. It is worth mentioning that he is not a politician, rather, he is originally a military man. His statements were not helped by the fact that he referred to the Muslim Brotherhood as the "Brother Muslimhood".

He told Ms Amanpour that in order to have democracy, Egypt needed a "culture of democracy", however, it appeared to suggest, that he, an Egyptian statesman was saying that Egypt was not ready for democracy, when he was actually inferring that democracy was something learned and developed, rather than something that could be instantly and successfully enacted. During the interview he did with me in Arabic, he was far more nuanced and selective in what he had to say. He made more or less the same points, but more effectively.

I got back to my office at around 2.30 in the afternoon, after negotiating the same extended route back through the city. When I returned to my office, I reviewed what had happened throughout the past two hours. We had heard that the Muslim Brothers in the square were telling their fellow demonstrators that they should not leave the square or else they would be victimised and chased down by the army. In response, we re-broadcast a notice on television that anybody was free to leave Tahrir Square and would be protected by the military if they did.

At the same time, calls began to come in from different youth groups to head back to the square and stand by their brothers who held out against the assault by the Pro-Mubarak rioters.

A case in point was the on-air interview that one of our anchors, Rasha Magdy had with one of the young protesters in Tahrir Square. The young man said that he had been involved in the demonstrations of January 25th and 28th, staying in the square until the President's speech on the 1st of February. When he listened to that address, he decided to return home, convinced that they had succeeded in forcing a change. However, when he got home and saw the carnage unfolding on television, he considered it a betrayal by the government. Yet, he still believed the President's promise to step down and begin reform was a positive outcome after the demonstrations, and something to be welcomed. When the anchor asked him whether he was convinced by that, he underlined his conviction. "So," she asked him, "will you go to Tahrir Square tomorrow?"

"Despite all that, I will go to the square and call on all of my friends to go down too," he declared.

The other theme that we picked up on in our telephone interviews with protesters was the resentment that they were excluded from Omar Suleiman's national dialogue. One of them, a young man named Sharif, spoke about it on television. I remember him saying, "I went home after the President's speech, but we have to go back once again to the square, we shouldn't leave it, they are now sitting and talking to the opposition, which should not be the case – the opposition has never achieved a thing and if they could, they would have done it on their own. We are the one who launched the revolution but the authorities are debating with them and leaving us out!"

At the station, we were still receiving reports that journalists were being attacked, though less reports of that were coming in. I don't know who was targeting them, it could have been the police, paid thugs, angry pro-Mubarak demonstrators, even angry anti-Mubarak demonstrators, anybody. Any accusation, however, would be guesswork. I do believe, however, that to co-ordinate such attacks would require a degree of control which nobody really had at the time. The harassment of journalists was certainly not planned or thought out, it would have been the result of passions stirred up in the heat of the moment.

After we broadcast the interview with Omar Suleiman, there were positive reactions to his proposals among the commentators and politicians we had calling into our studio, as well as on some other domestic news channels. However, the situation in Tahrir Square was different. Those leading the protests in the square, who had decided to continue their demonstrations until the end, were not satisfied at all with the proposals made by Omar Suleiman, even though he reiterated the promise that neither the

President nor his son would run in the upcoming presidential elections.

The announcement that the assets of four major party officials, including Ahmed Ezz, would be frozen received a positive reception from the crowds, but it wasn't enough. These announcements, which would clearly prove popular with the public were always released the day before large demonstrations. This tactic of announcing concessions to the public like this, the day before a protest was widely adopted throughout the following months in Egypt, in order to mitigate the size and aggression of the coming demonstrations.

That night, Egypt was torn in several different directions. The demonstrators in the square, and the Islamists, were both pushing for the protests to continue until Mubarak was gone. The Presidential Palace was desperately trying, and failing, to cling to power without conceding to any of the demands made on them. The armed forces acted as guardians to the demonstrators. They would not attack them, yet they would take decisive action to end clashes between opposing sides. On the other side, there stood the Egyptians who just wished the whole crisis to end.

With all these different forces brought into play, the streets were gripped with tension and suspicion.

That day, the renowned Egyptian musician Ammar El-Sherei, in an interview on a commercial TV channel, savagely criticised the Egyptian state media. I requested a summary of the interview from my staff. Since the beginning of the unrest, I had not been following developments on other TV channels. I had to concentrate on what I was doing. After I read through the summary, I called him up, for I knew him quite well, and told him, "Ammar, if you have a criticism, why not air it on Egyptian TV itself, rather than on another television station?" He wasn't expecting that. I told him that if he had something to say, he could do so with us. After I finished talking to him, I asked my staff to call him live so that he could give his views on air.

The anchor on air at the time was Ahmed Bosseila. Ahmed began by asking him what he thought of the Vice President's address.

"I'm not here to talk about the interview with the Vice President," Ammar responded, "I am here because Mr Abdel Latif El-Menawy told me that if I have a criticism concerning the Egyptian media, I can direct it through the TV station of my country, the Egyptian television."

Sure enough, Ammar began to explain the problems with our coverage of events. Many of his observations were totally valid due to our constrained circumstances, especially towards the beginning of the protests. However, his other criticisms were somewhat bitter and cynical, which frustrated the staff in the office. He said some things that weren't true, for instance, that Channels One or Two were broadcasting comedy films during the demonstrations, which was not the case. He also made some barbed comments about our presenters, accusing them personally of gross distortion.

I could see some of my staff in the office getting upset as they watched what was going on on the banks of monitors. I initially had no intention of going on air when he called in, but I decided that somebody had to stick up for their reputations as nobody had done so thus far. I hadn't appeared live on air since the crisis began, as I wanted to focus on management rather than comment. So it came as a surprise, as much to me as to the producer, when I announced that I was putting a call through to air.

When I was put through, I began by countering something that Ammar had said about him being allowed to speak freely on television as evidence of a change of approach. "I would consider it a confirmation of the approach which we tried to implement from the beginning, that Egyptian TV is the television station of all the Egyptians, and we have chosen to stand by the side of the security of the homeland and of the citizen," I explained.

"We decided that this institution would play multiple roles, roles it had not been assigned, but taken on nonetheless. We decided to do this when we discovered that the entire state had collapsed and the only parts that remained were the armed forces in the streets, and the TV station here."

"Our coverage was not intended to intimidate people, instead it was a means of communication between people to contribute to resolving the crisis suffered by Egyptians. The demonstrations which came out in support of the President were not asking him to continue in his post, but were more like, as described in one of my articles, a salute, given for a commander who has just finished his duties after thirty years of service to his country, even if there were errors committed during that time."

"We, as a television station, have made mistakes, the responsibility for which does not only lie with us, but with all sides. We were forced to make those mistakes, but when we discovered those mistakes, we were the first to correct them. We miscalculated events on the 2nd of February, as happened with many who were running the country that day."

"Ammar's claims are an injustice against this place and those working here to secure this country, to get it to the other side of the river and not let it be drowned halfway…we refuse to be among the riders of wooden horses stepping on the corpse of this country, and when the facts become clear, what we have been doing for the well-being of this nation will become evident."

"I thank all my colleagues working here, who decided to take up this stance, not for the sake of individuals or regimes but for the sake of a nation to save it from the brink to which it has been pushed."

When I thanked my colleagues, I heard applause. It was the applause of those working in the studio's control room and inside the studio itself. When I had finished, almost all my staff came to thank me. I could even trace the ghost of a smile on a few of their faces.

One of my staff pointed out that we had a lot of footage of attacks by the protesters going back to the first day of the unrest, which at the time I was unwilling to broadcast, as I didn't want us to appear to be intimidating the protesters. He suggested that we broadcast the pictures, so that people would know that we had them, and why we hadn't put them on air.

We showed attacks by demonstrators on the 28th of January which took place at the Maassara metro station. These were harsh and violent assaults, including the destruction of all the surrounding public property. We commented on this footage, saying that we were broadcasting the incident now that it was over. If we had wanted to intimidate people, as we had been accused, we would have broadcast the material at the time.

That evening, I had a very interesting conversation on the phone with an army commander. He was a high-ranking officer, very close to the senior decision-makers.

"Look, Abdel Latif," he said, "the decision you are concerned about isn't an issue any more. Whatever they do, the end has been decided."

It took me a second to work out his cryptic message, which he shrouded in a Koranic verse. It suddenly became apparent: Mubarak was going to go. Maybe not tomorrow, or even the day after, but soon, very soon, he would step down. Events that could not be stopped had been set in motion.

There were calls on the street for another *millioniya* (million person protest) for the next day, Friday, and the slogan would be *Irhal!* (Go!)

In the last few days, everybody, within the regime and without, had by now put their differences aside. They were now calling out one word.

Go.

FEBRUARY 4TH – FRIDAY

One of the unexpected outcomes of those events at the beginning of 2011 was the sudden, worldwide fame achieved by Tahrir Square. Aside from its position as a central geographical location in Cairo, it also became a symbol that would later be adopted by protest movements around the world, becoming a new word in the global lexicon of resistance.

Tahrir Square, when it was first established, was called the Ismaili Square, in reference to Khedive Ismail, who built the square, as well as the Nile Palace Bridge in the 19th century. Following the 1919 revolution the square's name was changed from Ismaili to *Tahrir* (Liberation). At the time, several stories circulated as to why its name was changed. There were those who said it was named Tahrir in reference to the liberation of the people of Egypt, while another, more credible, story claimed that the square was so named after Hoda Shaarawi, the famous Egyptian feminist, and the women accompanying her, who cast off their veils in the square, liberating themselves, as they joined in the revolution.

Later though, yet another explanation was put forth, that the square earned its current name in the July revolution of 1952, in reference to the liberation of the country from corruption and the monarchy after the Free Officers toppled the monarchy in Egypt.

The square simulates the design of Charles de Gaulle square, the home of L'Arc de Triomphe in the French capital Paris. The square is considered one of the few squares in Cairo that has a well-determined layout. From above, it becomes clear that it is bisected by several major roads and thoroughfares running through the square. It also lies in the vicinity of nine government ministries, including the Interior Ministry, the Ministerial Cabinet, the Ministries of Justice and Education. Also nearby was the burnt-out shell of the National Democratic Party headquarters, which towered over the protesters camped out in the square.

Tahrir Square had become a real focal point for the country, as the protesters continued their occupation. They had survived all the tricks, bribes, concessions, violence and coercion that the Presidential Palace and the NDP could throw at it, yet still they remained.

The Presidential Palace's only notable achievement in the past week and a half was to unify all the strands of opposition in the country in a concerted campaign to oust the President. At the same time, the apolitical portion of the population, which is a considerable number of people, moved from a position of ambivalence to hostility. This was in part due to the very ugly scenes of pro-Mubarak demonstrators and thugs confronting the Tahrir Square protesters the previous Wednesday.

Throughout the previous night, I had given instructions to my presenters to repeatedly affirm that we, the Egypt News Centre, were asking the government to investigate what happened on the 2nd of February. The investigation should be transparent, public and be set up quickly.

The other reason why public opinion turned against the government during this tumultuous period was their constant tardiness in making concessions to the public. Constant delays were part of the genetic makeup of Egyptian government officials. The previous day, the Prime Minister, during his press conference said that a committee would be set up, post haste, to investigate what had happened. It was almost a week before the government announced the actual formation of the committee, the next Wednesday. In the period in between I repeatedly nagged Anas and my army contacts to do it as quickly as possible.

Another Friday was upon us, which meant that the whole country would be gathered for Friday prayers. Events played out as the week before, with crowds gathering outside the mosques and churches after prayers. This time, there were no police trying to block the way, and no violent clashes on the way to the square.

That Friday, Ayatollah Khamenei, the Supreme Leader of the Islamic Republic of Iran got involved. He chose to give his weekly speech after Friday prayers in Tehran in Arabic, and directed it towards the people of Egypt, calling on them to revolt against the regime and called on the army to overthrow it. He said that the regime of Egypt was against Islam and for Israel and Zionism. Such a statement did not go down well in Egypt.

The hostility to foreigners on the streets was palpable. We had people calling in to our offices and the studios complaining about them. Somebody called in the day before, telling us that he was in Mohandiseen, west Cairo. He was on Gamaat al-Dul al-Arabiya, a wide street, home to plenty of fast food outlets and clothes shops. He said he was at Al-Tahabe Al-Dumiyati, a Egyptian fast food restaurant, and could see two foreigners stop at the restaurant and order 800 sandwiches, and claimed that the workers at the restaurant asked him to call the army or the TV to tell them of this suspiciously large order of sandwiches. The implication was that the purchase of so many sandwiches was a foreign plot to feed the protesters of Tahrir Square.

This paranoia of foreign involvement in the uprising also manifested itself in the infamous case of the free Kentucky Fried Chicken meals. Back at the beginning of the uprising, we were getting lots of phone calls from all sorts of people. At one point, we got a phone call from a famous actor called Hassan Youssef. He was a handsome and prolific actor in his youth, well known for his comedic portrayals of dashing playboys. He was very popular with the public, who felt that he was one of their own. He ended up marrying the famous actress Shams al-Baroudy, one of the most beautiful women in Egypt, well known for her stunning outfits and glamorous roles on the screen. By the 1980s, both of them had found religion. Youssef grew a beard, quit acting and Shams took to wearing the veil in public.

When Youssef's call made it on air, he scolded the protesters, "Go home!" he cried, "why are you doing this?! That man is a good man, give him a chance! If there are any mistakes he can fix them! Don't listen to other people, there are some people there…they are giving them money, they are giving them food from Kentucky Fried Chicken!"

The anti-government activist who chose to highlight that one sentence, out of everything that all our callers said on air since the crisis began, understood propaganda. The flow of information from Tahrir was rapid during those 18 days; the KFC story spread across the nation until it was on the whole country's lips. The implication was that rather than it being a random accusation from an elderly actor over the phone, that Egyptian state television had declared that the entire protest movement had been covertly sponsored by Kentucky Fried Chicken, or a foreign agent who was using American fast food to manipulate the protesters. It became a rallying cry.

Food was distributed in Tahrir Square. Many protesters, especially the older ones, brought food that they'd prepared at home, or bought from the supermarket. People were even setting up makeshift kitchens in the tent village that occupied the island in the middle of the roundabout. A few foreigners also came to Tahrir Square to show their solidarity with the protesters, supporting the calls for Mubarak to leave. To say that all the tents, blankets and food were brought by each protester to provide for themselves and that no foreigners came to help at all would be a dubious claim to make. However, the organisational aspect and the question of foreign interference became a stick with which the government could beat the movement. Because of the reactionary position adopted by the government, the Tahrir protesters became particularly sensitive to any claims regarding external support, be it foreign or domestic.

A famous interview broadcast at the beginning of February on the Mehwar TV channel with a female activist claiming to be part of the April 6th movement contributed to the suspicion. The young activist told the interviewer that she, with some other members of April 6th, had received training abroad in Serbia with the *Otpor!* movement. The interview caused an outcry among the public. The April 6th movement denied that she was associated with them. However an April 6th leader, Mohammed Adel later came on another TV channel, and stated that the female activist, Nagat Abdel Rahman, was with them but not part of the movement. She was also accused of being a spy for the police by some members of April 6th. The two presenters who conducted the original interview were later fired.

As the morning rolled on, I noticed the protesters out of my window, wandering up to Tahrir Square along the Corniche. There were definitely newcomers today, from different places, entire families, fathers, mothers, children. They were carrying their food and beverages on their way towards the square, which was walled by citizen checkpoints manned by the demonstrators, checking the people's identity cards as they entered the square and making sure they weren't carrying any weapons. They wouldn't allow anybody on if they were carrying any sort of weapon, or looked suspicious, or were employed by the security services. People parked their cars on the 6th October Bridge, four lanes deep, getting out to watch what was going on in the square.

In an unexpected move, Field Marshal Tantawi visited the square to see for himself what was going on. He was promptly surrounded by demonstrators. He told them, "The man told you that he will not run for another term!" When he noticed bearded protesters around him, Muslim Brothers, he called on them to "tell the Brotherhood Chief to sit with them!" By this he meant that they should convince the head of the Muslim Brotherhood to participate in the national dialogue, as they had formally refused to take part so far. The Field Marshal's visit was cordial, and another indication of the army's tolerance of the ongoing demonstrations. It further encouraged those who were reluctant to go down to the square to come along.

A great many public figures made appearances in the square that day, particularly now that the balance was firmly tipped in favour of the demonstrators. It was also a good opportunity to have their picture taken, to prove that they had visited the square and supported the uprising. Some of the personalities who came down were thought of as apolitical, such as musicians, actors, footballers and sports commentators. Some of the famous faces to turn up in the square had not been seen in public for many years, such as the film star, Sherihan, who came out and wished the youth success in their aspirations. Sherihan's appearance was particularly notable, as her personal life was subject to constant rumour and speculation concerning her relationship with members of the ruling family.

Among the more established political figures to come to the square that Friday was Amr Moussa, Secretary General of the League of Arab States. The occupants of the square began to gather round as he told them that he was considering running for president. Although, when we contacted his press office, they said Amr Moussa wanted to calm the situation, and not present himself as a possible candidate in the presidential elections.

Prince Ahmed Fuad, the son of King Farouk, the last king of Egypt, a man who considers himself the rightful heir to the Egyptian throne, issued a statement on the situation, offering consolation to its victims, hoping Egyptians would recover, and praying to God to protect beloved Egypt and its people.

Jehan Sadat, the widow of late President Anwar Sadat, came out to publicly deny that she had left Egypt after a newspaper published news of her departure. She insisted that she was staying, expressing alarm and regret at what was happening. She was especially concerned at the embattled state of the National Democratic Party founded by her husband.

We could never shake the accusation that we were against the protests and acted as a tool of the government. We tried to put screens up in the Omar Makram Mosque, just off the square, but we couldn't. We tried to put up screens inside the square itself but the protesters prevented us from doing so. We tried to go through loudspeakers, I called anybody that I thought could help, businessmen, technicians, government officials, activists, but we got nothing.

The 4th of February was to be a *millioniya*, a day with a million protesters out on the streets. That day some protesters claimed a million had gathered in Tahrir Square. Some disagreed, and put the figure at two million. Others stated, unequivocally, that there were at least four million in the square. Crowds are notoriously difficult to gauge, and protests, universally, are subject to optimistic estimates on the part of their participants. Numbers from international media outlets varied wildly, though some journalists were quoting the two million figure. How these estimates were arrived at was never explained.

The army tried to work out how many people were there by working out a grid to calculate the area of Tahrir Square. The army found the central area of Tahrir Square itself cannot take more than 150,000 people. Taking in the wider area and some of the surrounding streets, this figure increases to about 450,000 people at a density of six persons per square metre.

When we broadcast that there were hundreds of thousands of people in the streets, rather than several million, we were once again accused of spreading false information. Even though we explained how we arrived at the figure, people did not care. Looking back, it would have been futile to approach the issue in such a way. To be a protester in Tahrir Square, looking around and seeing thousands packed together in every direction, the only conclusion to be arrived at would be that there were millions there that day. There's a saying in Egypt: "You don't pay taxes for words". It means that you can say whatever you want, and evidently, people did.

We still did not have a camera in the square, and were forced to use feeds from other news channels or the CCTV feed.

Meanwhile, on the other side of the Nile, in Mustafa Mahmoud Square in Giza, several thousand pro-President Mubarak supporters had gathered. It was a real challenge to broadcast developments from both squares. Whenever we broadcast an update on what was happening in Mustafa Mahmoud Square, we were accused by those in Tahrir Square of being biased towards the pro-Mubarak supporters. When we broadcast developments in Tahrir Square, we were attacked by the pro-Mubarak supporters in Tahrir Square. When we broadcast pictures on screen of both demonstrations on the screen simultaneously, both camps accused us of giving one side more coverage than the other. At the times when we were covering neither, both groups accused us of distorting our coverage by ignoring them. When trying to put out balanced coverage, we discovered that there is just no pleasing some people.

Demonstrations also spread throughout Egypt's cities and provinces. Our correspondents reported on the size of these demonstrations in the different governorates. It seemed clear that, nationally, the public had swung behind calls for Mubarak to step down, either completely, or by transferring all his authority to his Vice President.

Closer to home, the demonstrations in Tahrir had once more spilled out onto the surrounding streets, and specifically around the Maspero building. We were yet again under siege and subject to the constant threat of invasion as the protesters tried to breach the army's security cordon around us. Instructions by some of the self-proclaimed leaders of the protesters commanded them to tighten the noose around us, and search for any weakness in the army lines so they could break through. Every attempt was seized upon and halted by the army protecting us.

However, their trials were not all without some success, as some people managed to overcome the barriers and infiltrate the building. However, they were promptly arrested by the soldiers, including two people who managed to break into one of our offices. Fortunately, they were picked up before they managed to do any real damage.

Meanwhile, the army decided to put the start of the curfew back to 7pm. This had no effect whatsoever.

That afternoon, I received a call from the office of the Attorney General informing me that Rashid Mohammed Rashid, the former Minister of Trade and Industry, had been hit with an asset freeze and a travel ban, despite the fact that he had already left the country. As soon as I heard, I called Anas to tell him. Anas was completely taken aback and immediately called the palace to speak to Zakaria Azmi and Gamal. They were both as surprised as he was, when he told them. Anas called me back, asking me to sit on the news until he had it confirmed by the President.

I had to refuse his request, telling him that it was a statement from the Attorney General, and as such, it should be aired immediately. I put the statement on the news cycles.

The news made me terribly upset. I knew Rashid well. I was convinced he cared deeply for Egypt, and had been trying his best to improve the economy, under very difficult circumstances, and considerable resistance from the status quo.

After the news had been put out across all our channels, Rashid called me from the UAE, in a state of considerable distress, "I don't understand what happened," he quavered "I had refused to enter the ministry, even after the Prime Minister had called me several times, and even after the President called me in person, but still I apologised because I felt that the situation was different, and that there was a need for new faces. I travelled on Tuesday after informing them all, the President, the Intelligence Chief, the Prime Minister, and the Attorney General." He was truly shocked and saddened at what had transpired, repeating, "They all knew that I had left the country. I even nominated my main assistant to be the next minister." Indeed, Dr Samiha Fawzy, his assistant, was chosen to succeed Rashid. All the while we talked on the phone, he kept murmuring "I don't understand what's happening."

Afterwards, Rashid appeared on several TV channels, including Egyptian television, to comment on the statement. He repeated his assertion that he had travelled under normal conditions and that he had left the country with knowledge and consent of all the relevant ministries, adding that he was ready to face any charges against him. He stressed that he did not intend to escape from Egypt under any circumstances. He added that he had served the government for six and a half years and was not running away from justice. He also pointed out that he had left and returned to the country once before during the current unrest, having travelled to and from Davos.

The charges against Rashid surprised even the protesters themselves, he was a generally popular minister. Rashid wasn't the only one hit with a travel ban. Several other major businessmen had been prevented from leaving the country. There were other announcements of charges against other former officials accused of corruption and embezzlement of public funds. The charges had come about because of a sudden flurry of reports filed against officials at the office of the Attorney General. There were 25 separate complaints against Habib Al-Adly alone.

I was under severe pressure the whole time. I would lock myself in the bathroom, in an attempt to calm down and control myself.

Two or three times during those difficult days I broke down and burst into tears. The first time I wept was about five days before, when I thought that everything around me had fallen apart. My phone was alive with people screaming on the streets and pleading for help, all I could hear was gunfire outside my window and smoke billowing through the air. The only thing I saw that resembled something like the state were the few officers stationed inside my building and the smattering of soldiers outside, nestled in between reams of barbed wire. When I heard what had happened to my friend Rashid, and when I couldn't see a positive way out, I had to just let it all out once more. It was fortunate I managed to make it to the privacy of the bathroom before any of my staff could see me. I always strove to give off the outward impression of strength.

I decided that once this was over, I would resign my job. Either Mubarak would somehow hang on, or the people on the streets would force him out. Either way, I would be gone. My dream of forming a genuine public broadcaster and being part of Egypt's reform had turned into a nightmare. I would stay for a while, to try and help with the transition. I didn't want to just run away. My determination to see out my job and tie up all the loose ends was affirmed after I was attacked by some employees of the ERTU after Mubarak stepped down. I wasn't going to be forced out, I wanted to leave of my own volition.

I didn't tell anybody except my friend Mohammed. Mohammed, an intelligence officer, was a trusted confidante who stayed with me in the Maspero building during this whole period.

I met Mohammed in 2006, the year after I first started working at the ERTU. He was fairly young back then, in his mid-thirties. At the time, I was trying to rebuild a news studio, and it was proving to be a real challenge. I asked the engineering department for the material and products I needed, intending to get the studio ready for use by January (it was November). They told me that it would take a least six months to get hold of what I asked for. I was impatient, and wanted to get the job done quickly.

Someone introduced to me this young officer in the intelligence services, who had been posted at the state TV station, working in the technical section. I told him that if he wanted to show me what he could do, then he could help me get what I needed for this studio by the end of the year. He took on the challenge, even going so far as receiving some pieces of equipment at the airport and bringing them straight to me. He succeeded in helping me put my new studio together on time. The studio looked great, it had state of the art screens, glass panels and a depth to the visual field. I was proud. There is a culture of lethargy and complacency in Egyptian state institutions, something which I was not used to, having been working abroad before I started there. I was pleased to be working with someone so proactive. He liked the way I worked and he wanted to be part of the changes I was trying to make.

I realised that he was somebody I could use. Together we built another studio, and a brand new HD news channel (sadly, the channel didn't manage to get on air – it was supposed to be launched on the 22nd of February, but was postponed due to the unrest).

We had been friendly over the years. When the uprising started, and we were forced to remain inside the building, he chose to stay with me and help, even though he didn't have to.

As the day dragged on, the momentum of the movement to get rid of Mubarak continued to grow. It was a national feeling. The closest thing to it was when I was in London in 1997 and witnessed the British national mood plummet into depression after the death of Princess Diana. Though in Egypt, the mood was defiant rather than melancholic.

Cairo was awash with rumours about Mubarak, each one more damning than the last. One of the more prominent stories was that Mubarak had $70 billion stashed away in foreign bank accounts. I don't think that was true. That figure was never substantiated, though for me, it was the sheer amount that seemed unbelievable. After all, who's got $70 billion in the bank?

That Friday was a tipping point. I realised that we were closer to the end than we were to the beginning.

FEBRUARY 5TH – SATURDAY

The crisis had been going on for ten days, and a pressing concern for a great many Egyptians was the problem of how to return to normal life. Food prices had finally come down slightly, after they had shot up in the first few days of the unrest. Egyptians were waiting for banks to open so they could cash their salaries and pensions, or even just withdraw some money. Fortunately, it was announced that the banks would be opening the next day. In Egypt, as is the case in most of the Arab world, the weekend lasts from Friday to Saturday, so Sunday is actually the first day of the working week.

Public transport was up and running again; we put footage of the moving trains and buses on TV, to show that Cairo was moving again and was returning to something approaching normality. Many Egyptians had not been able to get to work and were beginning to get worried about their jobs, and how they would provide for their families. Even though the country generally supported the calls for Mubarak to go, they also wanted their lives back.

In previous days between two and five thousand people were camping out in the square overnight. By Saturday, they started staying out in the square in greater numbers.

The inhabitants of Tahrir Square all had different reasons to stay. Some wanted to stay because of their ideological affinity to certain groups who had declared they would be staying in the square till the end. As I said earlier, the Muslim Brotherhood had been forced to support the protests after the government blamed them for starting them. In addition, there were a great many youths from the new protest movement, driven by the fortitude and determination of the young, they would stay there until their demands were met. They believed that any change on the ground was enforced by their presence at the square, so they were duty bound to stay.

The day started with another press conference held by Prime Minister Ahmed Shafik after a meeting with the President as well as the ministers concerned with economics and finance.

The meeting was staged to create the impression that the President was still running the country, putting the needs of the citizens ahead of his personal priorities. The public were briefed that the meeting was called so the government could call for basic goods to be made available and for economic changes. This was meant to be the "social justice" that the protesters had been calling for.

It was possibly the longest press conference I have ever attended. At one point, the prime minster mentioned that "a few foreigners" had been captured in Tahrir Square, though they never mentioned their nationalities or gave any further details. However, the premier and his ministers spent most of the press conference droning on for what seemed like hours about ensuring the stability of living conditions and the promise of price controls.

They were unaware of the public desire for far more fundamental change, or at least unwilling to implement it. Rather, they went back to their usual manner of long-winded answers and promises shrouded in statistics.

The Governor of the Central Bank also attended the meeting with the Prime Minister, though he didn't attend the press conference. His name is Dr Farouk Al-Okdah. He is a very clever man and handled Egypt's banking system competently over the last few years. Because of his management, Egypt's banks were able to weather the international banking crisis relatively well. He doesn't talk to the media often. I met him in 2008, when we ended up having an argument about the importance of the media in economic affairs. I trusted him, and thought him wise. It was a shame that he wouldn't speak to the media, for, to me, he seemed far more capable than many of those ministers who did.

Anas called me after the press conference to tell me Dr Okdah would be giving an interview on TV, and that he had asked for me personally. He needed to talk to the country about how the unrest had affected Egypt's economy and its banks.

When he arrived, he came up to my office to have a brief chat before we recorded the interview. He mentioned the discussion (or argument) we had had three years before. We laughed about it. The conversation turned to more serious concerns. He told me that we were passing through a gravely dangerous situation, but the Central Bank was coping. He reassured me that the banking situation in Egypt would hold up because of the banking measures Egypt had taken in the previous years, which pulled it through the international financial crisis. These measures would pull us through this one too. Despite the apparent optimism, he warned me that we couldn't go on for much longer like this. The economy had already lost 3 billion pounds since the unrest started. He went on TV to let people know that the banks were still working, and Egyptians wouldn't be losing their savings. Before we started, he said he would only talk for 10 minutes; we ended up talking for 45.

Meanwhile, the national dialogue headed by Vice President Omar Suleiman was still ongoing, behind closed doors. Almost every political party was present, no matter how small or marginal. For the first time, the leadership of the Muslim Brotherhood joined in the meetings, as well as public intellectuals (the wise men) and some representatives of the youth.

The dialogue was mainly focused on issues people had been demanding for years, like the annulment of the emergency laws, free presidential elections, the release of political detainees and an easing of restrictions on establishing new parties.

The dialogue went on, even as many voices in Tahrir Square were demanding that there could be no discussions until the President was gone. There was also a demand, and from my point of view a particularly valid one, for resolving the disputes which arose out of the previous November's bitterly contested election results, one of the main reasons why all of this started in the first place. The government rejected that request outright, citing problems to do with constitutional amendments connected with the nomination of a new President.

The palace, especially those around Gamal, were particularly adamant it would not call a new parliamentary election, claiming, bizarrely, that discussing the constitutional amendments would hinder the whole political process of reform.

It could be argued that if the government had called a new parliamentary election, the President could have hung on to see out his term for a few months, as the country's political focus may have shifted to the upcoming election rather than be calling for his removal. Another lost chance.

I believed at the time, and suggested as much to my presenters, that to dissolve parliament and have new elections would mean that changes to the constitution would take more time. Otherwise, this would mean that the upcoming presidential election scheduled for September would be under the old constitution, which people didn't want. It was very complicated.

Some of the opposition activists came to the meeting with some radical requests. One even suggested that the government should hang Habib Al-Adly in Tahrir Square.

The government made mistakes because they couldn't think outside of the box. They could have accepted the court orders which overturned electoral results, they could have dissolved the parliament just after they changed the constitution, but they didn't. It became apparent that in the Presidential Palace, there was no wish to solve the problem.

The protesters in the square knew this. That's why they were staying there.

That morning, Major General Hassan Al-Roueini, the military commander for the Cairo area, went to Tahrir Square in an effort to convince the demonstrators to allow traffic through the square.

"The people are losing money," he declared, "we need to move around, we need to open the way for traffic!" As he addressed the crowd, he went on to chastise the protesters, declaring, "the *Ikhwan* were standing on the rooftops of these buildings and throwing firebombs down." The statement was shouted down by the crowds, who countered that those throwing the firebombs were thugs. Roueini turned to them, "No! They were *Ihkwan*! I told Al-Beltagy [a Muslim Brotherhood leader] either you tell them to come down or I will take them down myself." The crowd continued to deny his claims. "What are you doing here?" shouted the general, "I'm a 58 year old man, and you are trying to bluff me. I know what I'm saying. Don't play games with me. They were *Ikhwan*!"

His attempts at opening up the square for cars were unsuccessful.

Meanwhile, Mubarak, as the leader of the NDP, decided to change the leadership of the party. He announced that Safwat El-Sherif, Gamal Mubarak, Zakaria Azmi, Mohfeed Shehab and Ali El-Din Hilel (the big six, minus Ahmed Ezz, who had already been removed) had resigned. Dr Hossam Badrawi was named as the new general secretary for the party (taking both Gamal and Sherif's position).

It was a signal to the public that Gamal would not be a candidate in the forthcoming presidential election, as being a party leader was a precondition for running.

Badrawi, a trained doctor and successful businessman, was a well-known exponent of education in Egypt. It was generally expected that he would be made Education Minister some time ago, however, Ahmed Nazif personally disliked him. In addition, Hossam Badrawi had some liberal ideas which were not received well by either Gamal or the President. He was seen as something of a troublemaker.

They thought that this appointment would appease the people. However, they misunderstood that party arrangements did not matter much to anybody outside the party. It was a welcome development, but an inconsequential one. To prove the point, that day the party building in a little village called Samasta in Beni Suef, Upper Egypt, was burnt down. At the same time, one could still smell the smoke from the burnt crust of the party building in downtown Cairo. People did not care about the party.

As I mentioned earlier, every night a few thousand people stayed overnight in Tahrir Square. However, during the day, the number increased by many tens of thousands reaching peaks of hundreds of thousands (though, of course, accurate numbers are difficult to ascertain). One of the tricks to having a successful demonstration is to make it a fun place to be, even on the days (like today) when there wasn't actually that much going on. It was a real carnival atmosphere. When visitors entered the square, they were received by singing protesters, welcoming and saluting them.

Tahrir Square became an attraction in Cairo. Many people simply went there for the experience of seeing it. Children nagged their parents to take pictures of them with the tanks. I even saw a child riding the gunbarrel of a tank like a horse. The army was very patient and let people play around them.

I disagreed with some of the army officers on this issue. The army should have respect, it shouldn't be an attraction at a fun fair. There was nothing wrong with the army declaring that they would protect the rights of the people, but that did not mean they should allow children to play with their weaponry (because a tank is a weapon) or permit people to scrawl graffiti on their vehicles. Some officers at the top agreed with me on this, though they did not make a fuss about it as they didn't want to get into a confrontation with the people.

After lunch, one of my colleagues came back from Tahrir Square with a smile on his face. "I've just had a fantastic meal," he announced, "I've had Kushari [a pasta, rice and lentil dish popular in Egypt], tea, and sweets. At a very competitive price!" Other stalls were selling popular street dishes, soft drinks and tea.

There were even a couple of marriages in Tahrir Square, as amongst the crowds, imams married young couples out in the February sun. It was something to behold. It contributed to the romance of the occasion, and certainty that they would prevail. People thought, "If people are getting married there, then how could we possibly fail?"

New slogans were chanted, funny ones like "Please go! I want to have a shower!", "Please go! I want to go home and see my wife!", "Please go! I've been here two weeks!" and "Go…it means *Go*!"

The square was divided into different sections. One section, where the Islamists were, had prayer areas and stages for religious lessons and sermons. Another part was occupied by the leftists and socialists, Nasserists, in fact, every stream of opposition was there, lending their support to the campaign to oust Mubarak. The blind Sheikh's politically charged songs were drifting through the air. A friend of mine who was out in the square said that he spent most of his time in the section run by the Muslim Brotherhood, simply because it had the best toilet facilities.

For the youth it had become the place to be. Even if they had never expressed a political opinion before, they still went there.

It also became a place to gain publicity. Those with ambitions to be president, men like Amr Moussa, Mohammed Al-Baradei and Hamdeen Sabahi all addressed the crowds in the square.

That day, Essam Sharif, the man who would be Prime Minister after the fall of Mubarak, made his first appearance on Saturday in

Tahrir Square. The former academic and Minster for Transport had resigned in 2006, apparently after being forced out by the government, though he remained part of Gamal Mubarak's Policy Committee since. His appearance in the square went down very well with the public and led directly to his appointment as Prime Minister.

Film stars, sports stars and singers were also still lining up to be photographed in the square. One singer, Sherin Abdul Wahab, famous for singing to Mubarak on many occasions, came out on stage in the square and claimed that she was forced to sing for the President. I've seen her get ready to sing for the President. Nobody forced her.

To illustrate the slightly fickle nature of some of Egypt's famous faces, another singer came out with a pro-Mubarak song in early February called "We're sorry Mubarak". The same song was released a few days later, this time with anti-Mubarak lyrics, "We're sorry our country". It had exactly the same tune!

That day, we received the first reports of an explosion at the gas pipeline in Sinai pumping gas to Israel. The issue of gas to Israel was a taboo subject amongst the Egyptian governing class, they never wanted to talk about it. For years, I discussed it with Cabinet Ministers, the Oil Minister, the Prime Minister, the Intelligence Chiefs, asking why they never talked about it.

The issue was sensitive because it was seen as a betrayal of the Palestinians. The accusation was that by selling Israel gas, Egypt was powering Israel's war machine to be used against Palestine. More importantly, the gas was sold to Israel for a much lower price than anything available domestically for the Egyptian consumer.

It was actually a lot simpler than people realised. The gas deal was an aspect of Egypt-Israel relations designed to maintain the peace between the two countries. The gas was sold to Israel at a favourable price for the time, in a 20-year contract. However, as energy prices rocketed over the next couple of years, the price remained fixed in the original contact.

It was a mistake to not to allow the price to fluctuate according to the market value. It was a bigger mistake to keep quiet about the deal, and never explain to the public the reasons behind it. Perhaps there was a secret aspect to the deal hidden in the contracts, but they certainly made it worse by refusing to speak about it. Whenever I brought it up, the answer was always the same: they couldn't talk about it because of "national security".

The sabotage of the pipeline was most likely carried out by Bedouin groups, possibly with some involvement from (or at least communication with) Hamas, taking advantage of the lack of government in the area. It was more opportunism, this time from people who have had a long history of friction with the central government. It was the first explosion of many, and they would go on for months.

That afternoon, I don't remember why, but I went up to see Anas. For the last couple of days we hadn't been in contact with each other so much. I noticed that he phoned me less, and he had been giving me fewer orders.

We were discussing the general situation when, during a lull in the conversation, he pulled back his chair, reached into his drawer and pulled out a handgun.

"Look," he explained, "they could invade the TV building at any time, and I don't trust anyone but myself. That's why I asked the head of security to get me a gun. You should do so as well."

I was stunned.

"No," I insisted, "I'm not going to carry a gun!" I know how to use guns, I went to a military school and had done my national service in the army, but I wasn't going to carry a gun.

I left Anas's office slightly shaken. I was beginning to worry about him.

The previous week, I hadn't been home at all. Late that night, I decided to go and see my family. My main concern was to explain to them what I was doing. I have three children. Marwan is 21,

Omar is 19 and my daughter Haya is 14. They had friends in Tahrir Square. My daughter is very close to me, she knows about politics and current affairs from the long talks we used to have. I had three very politically aware and astute children. Now, the state TV, where their father worked, was under attack from the protesters during the biggest political upheaval in their lives. I wanted my family to know what I was doing, that I wasn't serving any single person, but I was serving the country.

Sometimes my wife Rula would call me on the phone and beg me to leave. "Please leave that place," she would cry, "don't give your life for this regime! They don't deserve it."

But I wasn't serving the regime. Somebody had to take responsibility for the state media. I had taken on the burden.

I didn't tell them that I would be coming home. I got back at around 2am. Everyone in Egypt was awake. Nobody was sleeping. I passed through all the checkpoints, though they let me through when they recognised me.

After I got home, surprising my family, I sat talking with them for three hours, explaining what I was doing and why I was doing it. I didn't give a damn about the regime, that certainly became clear when I was sitting with my loved ones. But, I could see the country was collapsing. I wasn't against what the people in Tahrir Square were asking for; I was against people using the crisis to bring the country down and ferment strife between Egyptians.

I told them that there were opportunists, either from inside or outside who would use the change we were going through to try to push forward the change that they wanted, that maybe wouldn't be in the best interests of the people.

All I wanted was to help see the country through to the other side of this crisis. It was my job, and I never wanted to see a television screen go black, because then I would have failed.

They asked me a lot of questions, who was doing what, why

certain people did certain things and whether there was any truth to the rumours they were hearing.

I felt relieved afterwards. When I had finished talking with them, I was finally able to have a proper shower. I had a shower in my office, but it only gave me 2 litres of hot water. I worked out that lasted exactly 90 seconds, forcing me to keep my showers down to a under a minute and a half. It was so much better to enjoy the unrestricted flow of water in my own shower, for as long as I wanted. It was wonderful just to be at home for a bit, even for a few hours.

When I was dry, I headed straight back to the office.

FEBRUARY 6TH – SUNDAY

When Sunday came around, there was a feeling among the more organised elements of the opposition that if they did not finish it quickly, people would start to leave the square, and the momentum that they had built up till now would dissipate.

I also heard that my name was being bandied about in the square. I, personally, had become a target. I had good friends in all the opposition groups, the Brotherhood, Gamaat Al-Islamiya, the leftists, the liberals, I even had good friends in the government. When my mother died, and people came to offer their condolences, someone from Gamaat Al-Islamiya had come to speak to me. I noticed that the man behind him was an intelligence officer, his job at the time being to catch members of Gamaat Al-Islamiya. There was someone from Al-Azhar and someone from the Cathedral. We have different opinions, but we have mutual respect. Some of the leaders of Gamaat Al-Islamiya know that I am opposed to them ideologically, but they considered me their friend.

I have always tried to stand in the middle. Egyptian politics has always been tumultuous, with all sorts of dangerous games being played. I sought to remain aloof from all that. After all these years of trying to stay neutral and keep friends on all sides of the political spectrum, finally, after all my efforts to build up a state media based on public service, my reputation was being shredded in Tahrir Square.

I also learned that morning that my wife and son had received threatening phone calls, on our home number. The brooding voices on the other side telling my terrified wife that they knew where we lived, and that they would be coming to get us. I told

Anas about it; he immediately picked up the phone and called the new Interior Minister, telling him that my family were receiving threats, suggesting they send security officers. The Minister agreed and they sent over some guards.

I didn't actually want armed guards at my home. They would surely make my home more of a target. I went back down to my office and called the Minister asking him not to send the security officers to protect my family.

"No, it's fine," he reassured, "we don't want you worrying, we want you to concentrate on what you are doing. We want you to be satisfied that your family is secure."

There was no convincing the man, and two armed guards were sent to my flat. It had to be said, he took the safety of my family very seriously.

That day, the issue of the martyrs started to appear in the newswires. It was a major point. It was, in fact, a turning point in the uprising.

Suddenly, all the channels had stories of the families of those killed in the protests. The story of the young man who was going to marry in a couple of weeks, brutally murdered, or the story of the mother talking to her son on the phone, only for him to be killed a few minutes later. The young girl who was expecting a child, each one a tragedy.

It was very organised, as all these stories hit the domestic and international media seemingly at once. I later found out that the protest groups were advised to start bringing up major issues that would grab the attention of the media by some of the more experienced liberals, many of whom had knowledge of western political processes.

Though common in the western world, the human interest story is largely absent from the media in the Middle East. It has been known for a long time in Europe and America that photographs of human faces and their personal stories are far more effective than reeling off statistics. However, it was never really employed by political forces in the Arab world.

As well as the protest groups who already had exposure to the western media by virtue of their youth and familiarity with new media, some political advisers also suggested to the Brotherhood that they start exerting pressure and gaining support by highlighting those who had already lost their lives in the struggle.

I know quite well an Egyptian liberal, secular academic, who had been on good terms with the government, though had turned against them as events moved on. When he was in the square, he gave political and media counselling to the Muslim Brotherhood. When he found them, they were panicking, as they thought that the initial impetus of the protests was waning. When they explained to him their concerns, he asked "Do you have a media institution or are you working without a media plan?"

They replied that they only really depend on friendly media outlets such as Al-Jazeera. The strategist advised them to identify youths from within the group who didn't look particularly religious and use them as their face for the media. He also said it may be worth bringing in some of the families of the victims of violence from the beginning of the uprising. Before they were brought on air, it would also be advisable to brief the families on what they should and shouldn't say in front of the camera. He suggested that they had powerful media tools on their hands, and that they should emphasise the human cost of Mubarak's oppression.

The Brotherhood did not even have a media group dealing with the uprising to coordinate their public relations. With the new media advice, they were able to put together a far more effective media campaign, and come up with much more successful soundbites and statements. One particularly powerful soundbite, heard on the news channels, was a quote form the father of a boy who was killed in Suez, "The prophet Mohammed ruled for less than twenty years, who is Mubarak to rule for more than thirty?" It was a powerful question.

By putting stress on the human stories, they moved into a different gear. They would have a different subject every day. One day they would talk about the martyrs, the next Habib Al-Adly, the next the media and Anas Al-Feky, etc. I didn't understand it at the time, it was only later, after talking to certain people connected with the protesters, that they had been advised to mount a coordinated media campaign.

I later found out from the academic that he asked an Indian journalist working in Egypt to act as a media coordinator and PR officer to coordinate the media campaigns for those in the square. He then gave him a list of journalists, both Egyptian and foreign, to help out in the campaign.

The issue of those who died was, and still is, particularly sensitive. It is undoubtedly true that many were killed during the protests, however, not every life lost during that period, and subsequently labelled as martyrdom, was directly related to violence during the protests.

The most famous case, particularly in the West, is that of Sally Zahran. The sepia tinged image of the smiling girl, with wild, frizzy hair and youthful eyes was flashed across the world. It was reported that the 23 year-old was clubbed to death by pro-Mubarak thugs on their way to break up the protest in Tahrir Square. A beautiful young girl cut down in her prime by the Mubarak government.

However, with few police out on the street and the government in hiding, it was always difficult to ascertain what actually happened before the story made its way around the world on the blogosphere and in the satellite news reports.

Sally Zahran's mother gave an interview, some days after Mubarak had stepped down, and claimed that Sally's death was not the result of being beaten at all, but a tragic domestic accident. She tearfully explained how her daughter had been at a protest that day, returned home, and was subsequently forbidden to go out again. Locked in her room, an argument ensued. It was unclear as to whether she was straining to view the protests out the window, or whether she had somehow tried to climb out of her bedroom, or whether it was some kind of defiant act of suicide.

She did not die in Cairo, as the reports asserted, but in Sohag, where she lived, on the west bank of the Nile, roughly half-way down the country, about 200 miles south of the capital.

Some protesters have accused her mother of lying, though I do not believe that her tearful explanation was made under duress, nor do I believe it was a calculated lie, particularly as she spoke out after Mubarak had stepped down from power.

However, it would be difficult to deny the galvanising effect the death of a beautiful young woman had for the domestic and international image of Mubarak's already under-fire government.

The picture later became a source of great controversy in conservative Egyptian society, as the picture of Sally Zahran showed her unveiled, when she had supposedly taken to wearing the veil in later years.

Without a doubt, lives were lost in the violence that enveloped Egypt's cities, but, at the risk of saying something incredibly controversial, I do not believe that every life lost during that tragic period, was a down to Mubarak's thugs or government violence, though they may have been regarded as such.

The appearance of the families of the martyrs on television created a new focus for the media. I believe that the whole media, us included, were swept away by the stories, and, in some cases, did not properly discuss the circumstances surrounding them. The issue was conclusive in pushing public opinion even more vehemently against the regime, if that was at all possible by now.

FEBRUARY 7TH – MONDAY

Dr Mohammed El-Baradei was in Cairo many months before the unrest started. When he arrived, he was very vocal in his statements that Egypt should change. Even before he returned to Egypt, he made an announcement in Vienna that he would come back to Cairo and would get involved in politics. This was very surprising to Egyptians, as he was not really known as a politician.

He had served three terms as the head of the International Atomic Energy Authority having been appointed in 1997, with support from some African countries and the United States. He was not, in fact, the Egyptian candidate for the position. Mubarak was actually pushing for Dr Mohammed Shaker, the former ambassador to the UK to lead the IAEA.

Back then, I was working in London and had a good relationship with Dr Moustafa El-Feky, our ambassador in Vienna at the time. We had a chat one day in Vienna, back in 1997, when he told me that Dr Shaker would not be getting the job, as he lacked the requisite international support. He observed that it would be better for Egypt if they got behind Baradei. He passed on this advice to Cairo, though it was not acted on. Dr Shaker travelled the world lobbying support, but to no avail, as El-Baradei took the seat.

Even after all that, the government was still proud that such a high-profile international job had gone to an Egyptian. When he won the Nobel prize in 2005, Mubarak honoured him with the Kiladat El-Nil, the highest state honour bestowed by Egypt. Whenever he visited Egypt, he would be received by Mubarak personally for high level discussions. He always looked happy to meet Mubarak.

Still, Egyptians never thought that he had any political ambitions within Egypt.

I met him once in 1999, for a newspaper interview. He was a gentleman, a very professional man, an executive. It was clear he was in control of the organisation, and he had a good relationship with his staff. I never got the impression, however, that he was a charismatic leader. He was calm and tactful. He answered difficult questions methodically using diplomatic language, and never gave confusing or contradictory answers.

One day in late 2009, one of our correspondents in Vienna, Mustapha Abdullah, called me to say they were having a lunch to celebrate his leaving at the IAEA. He said El-Baradei was preparing a statement on the situation in Egypt. The statement was to be delivered to the international media. He sent me a copy.

The statement said that he would be willing to put himself forward as a candidate for the presidency under certain conditions. He gave the impression that he would be the candidate, if the public wanted him, but he wanted guarantees that the election would be free, fair and transparent.

Many people asserted that he might not be the best candidate for Egypt; he was regarded as something of a foreigner, who had not lived in Egypt for 30 years. There was also resentment that this man, who was very much an outsider, having lived and worked abroad for so long, was laying down conditions on Egypt for his candidacy. Due to his lack of charisma and his distinctive features, the political elite at the top of the regime used to call him "Mickey Mouse".

From 2009, Baradei's name was mentioned by opposition groups in Egypt as a possible presidential candidate, who would act as a unifying force for various different strands of opposition. However, he fell out of favour with some opposition groups, particularly among the newer movements.

In spite of this, he was still a potential leader of the protest movement.

When he came back to Egypt on the 19th of February 2010, there was a discussion among the public, wondering what the government was going to do. He was a major international figure; would they meet him at the airport?

My opinion at the time, which I told Anas and other contacts, that it would be best if someone greeted him at the airport, perhaps the Minister for Higher Education, the Minister for Energy or the Minister of State for Foreign Affairs.

I thought we could take him from the airport to our studio and go straight to air, and let him say whatever he wanted to say. Unfortunately, my ideas were not accepted. I was only able to run with "former head of the IAEA returns to Egypt after finishing his position abroad."

At the time, I said, publicly, that Baradei wants to have an Eastern Europe style democratisation movement in Egypt, with people on the streets to bring the regime down; however, it would not be acceptable for Egyptians to have someone from outside come and lead such a revolution. I wrote that anybody could gather 100,000 people and take over the triangle of Maspero, Tahrir and Abdul Haleq Thalat Street (where demonstrations used to take place) and bring down the government. This would be like a stroke, cutting of the country's blood supply. Even if the body was healthy, a stroke could still kill it.

My point was that to assemble several hundred thousand people, out of a country of 80 million wouldn't be beyond the realms of possibility for many different political groups, but it wouldn't necessarily be the best way to force political change. It was, therefore, incumbent upon the government to take measures to prevent it having that stroke, to enact political reform and open up the government, to adopt a healthy lifestyle, as it were. However, just as an old patient is resistant to the doctor's advice, the government was unwilling to make the necessary changes needed to survive.

When I wrote those words, I didn't realise that something like that would actually happen.

That morning, when I was working in my office, I got a call through my walkie-talkie: "There's a young man outside wanting to come in the building. He says his name is Omar, he says he's your son. Shall we allow him in?"

I was touched. He wanted to surprise me. I told the solider on the other side of the band to let him pass, though not to tell him that I knew he was coming.

I called home and found out that he had driven by himself to Zamalek. He parked the car there and walked over the 15th of May Bridge to the other bank of the Nile and up to the Maspero building, surrounded by soldiers, concrete blocks and barbed wire.

He wanted to surprise me, so when he came in to my office, I pretended to be so. He came to give me support. It was a wonderful gesture for a son to give his father. He stayed a while, and we talked, looking out of the window onto the Corniche below.

"Did you see all the tanks around us?" I asked him, "it's like in a war. And we're the most secure part of the country." I wanted to give him the impression of safety. I tried to make it seem that any kind of invasion was unthinkable. Unfortunately, just as I had been slightly dishonest with him about my ignorance of his visit, I was also being untruthful about the safety of the building. I think he knew that I was holding back my fears. He offered to come back for a little while every day, just to check in with me. I said no. He should stay with his mother and siblings.

I did not like lying to my son, but, in actual fact, the possibility of protesters invading the building was very real and of constant concern. It seemed more likely that they would get in every day. I made him promise me that he wouldn't come back to visit. It was far too dangerous.

The building was a massive target in the middle of town. All of the opposition forces would have loved to have got hold of the state TV. It's always one of the first things that rebels go for in a military coup. However, having said that, they could have just torched the whole place, as they did the NDP building. If there were tens of thousands in the square, then a few of them, every day, would mount an expedition down the Corniche and attempt to break through the security barriers.

At least three times, I thought the game was up. Once, I gave the order for everyone to get ready for evacuation. I told the security men to forget about me and just try to get all the staff out safely. I told them not to try and fight off the invaders, for, if the army could not stop them, then nobody could.

In the early afternoon, I got a phone call from an old friend, an opposition activist who was at Tahrir Square, Dia Rashwan. He's a nice guy from Upper Egypt, and a very clued-up political expert. I've known him for years; we were at university together.

He told me that he was calling on behalf of a few different groups, Islamists, leftists, liberals, etc, and that we needed to find a solution to this situation. Everybody was standing stubbornly in their position. The people on the streets would not leave before Mubarak; meanwhile, Muabark didn't want to go anywhere.

"What can we do then?" I asked.

"I believe that, and this isn't just my opinion, we can solve the problem by sticking to article no. 93 in the constitution. The magic solution is article no. 93. The article gives the President the right to give his authority to the Vice President, and to only keep the authority to declare war and dissolve parliament."

He asked me to arrange contact between them and the army leaders, including Omar Suleiman. I told him I would make some calls. Dia told me that if they could arrange this, and get the President to accept, then most of the protesters in the square would accept it. But, if there is only dialogue, and they don't offer the public anything, then the situation will continue. I had been convinced for some time now that this was the right way to go: it was the rationale behind the speech I wrote back on the 31st of January.

I called Omar Suleiman's assistants, and my contacts in the intelligence service. I told them the idea and gave them Dia's name and number.

I found out later that they did manage to meet.

At the same time, I knew that the attitude of the Presidential Palace was stubborn and nothing would happen. They still thought they would manage to get through this without making the President step down.

It was similar to the a way of thinking, all too prevalent in Egypt, that if one is in debt, then only part of the debt has to be repaid, and the debtor will accept it. It was the way Gamal thought, and the group around him. They thought they didn't have to do what they had to do, or pay what they had to pay, and when they did pay, they were late in doing so. Each time, they dragged their feet before they offered any concessions to the public. There were plenty of opportunities when they could have bought themselves much more time, and could have saved themselves from public anger, but every time, they were late.

Since the 2nd of February, we had started getting people from Tahrir Square on TV. We had open discussions with them, and many of them enjoyed it. Each person would come, claiming to lead a group called, the "25th January Revolutionaries," the "Tahrir Group" or something like that. It showed that there weren't any major leaders. We had phone calls complaining that these people didn't represent the square, then others would come to TV claiming they represented the groups out in the square, unlike the previous lot we had on. We tried to get everybody on, but it was difficult.

One youth leader came, and while he was waiting to go on air, he was told that he would have to wait a little while, due to a problem with a schedule. "No," he fretted, "I told all my friends and my mother that I would be on now, they're waiting for me!"

Many of the youths we had on TV did not have a political background, some of them just went out on the street because they wanted change.

That day, I had a long chat with the building's head of security, Nabil Tablawi, an ex-general in the intelligence service. He used to come from time to time to my office to chat, but mainly to have an espresso. My office was well-known as a good source of coffee. I had one of those coffee machines that comes with little capsules which I had a friend bring me back from Paris. I love coffee, I loved that little machine.

Nabil complained that the Minister was calling him on his walkie-talkie every couple of minutes, asking him how many people were in the square. If Anas couldn't get through to him on the walkie-talkie, he would call him on the internal line. Nabil was laughing about it.

"He's calling me every two minutes!" he moaned, "every time I hear his voice come through, I just think, *what do you want now?! Enough is enough!*" That made me laugh, it was comforting to know that there was someone else who shared the experience of being pestered by Anas.

"Did you hear the story about the head of the engineering department?" he continued, sitting down with his espresso. I told him I had not. "I was at a meeting with the head of the Republican Guard and the head of engineering. The general asked the engineer what would happen if protesters invaded the TV station, got someone like El-Baradei to come on TV and demand the government dissolve. They wanted to know how they could shut down the signal. The engineer sat for a while explaining to the general the measures that could be put in place to secure transmission, even if it was deliberately cut. He said he would be able to connect it through a different point. If the electricity was shut off, he would be able to secure enough electricity to keep the studios working. Then he took the man on a tour of one of the studios to show him where Dr El-Baradei would sit. He pointed out where they could adjust his lighting and how it too could be secured. The general was furious, shouting, *"what are you saying? I'm asking how to stop the broadcast not to secure it!"*

The silly little story goes some way to explaining the genuine worries that we had that the station might be hijacked.

We had made contingency plans for keeping our broadcasts going if we lost control of the Maspero building. I asked the head of engineering if we could use the emergency studio in the presidential compound. We had never used it before – I wondered if it would be usable. The head of engineering submitted a report to Anas saying that it was indeed ready to go to air.

I knew that wasn't true. My sources in the compound admitted that the studio wasn't up to the job at all. I told Anas that we would have to find an alternative. Anas gave orders to prepare an emergency studio at Mount Mokatam. They were historically considered the main backup ERTU studios. They had recently been renovated at considerable expense, so we may as well have made use of them.

Every inquiry I made, I would be greeted by the same response, *"tamamm ya efendi"* (everything's fine). It didn't appear that way to me.

I always considered these emergency measures like the safety procedures taken onboard planes, when they tell passengers what to do in case the plane plummets down from the sky and is forced to do an emergency landing. Most airline passengers never believe it would happen. In our case, we had the emergency, we just didn't have the landing.

When I was sitting in my office in the afternoon, I got the news that the new Culture Minister had resigned for health reasons.

The new Culture Minister was a man called Dr Gaber Asfour, a very famous writer and thinker, the head of the higher council of culture. He had been a candidate for the job for a long time.

After he got his position, a mere two days later, he was talking about his longterm plans and goals. He was talking from the heart, very passionately.

"Is it true that Gaber Asfour resigned?" I asked Anas.

"Yes, he did." I don't think Anas knew, but he was not surprised.

"Did anything happen in the cabinet meeting" I enquired.

"Yes, we were sitting and talking." Anas began, before narrating the incident that occurred during the last cabinet meeting: "Gaber started saying that he was taking part in this government as it was a government of national unity. He was asking why there hadn't been an investigation into what happened on the 2nd of February. He was also asking why there were still two ministries empty, and perhaps we should get some people from the opposition to fill the vacant posts. Mohfeed Shehab tried to stop him, but Dr Asfour brushed him aside, demanding that he be allowed to finish. He went on to say that he was very upset after what had happened on the 2nd of February, that it was very difficult to see injured and dead people in the streets. I knocked on the table and shouted, asking *who said it was a national salvation government?!* Dr Shafik, the Prime Minister made no comment."

Dr Asfour just went home and turned his phone off.

I heard Anas tell the same story over the phone to the President himself. I don't think the President was bothered by the news at all.

A famous name we started hearing over this period was Wael Ghonim. Wael Ghonim was an activist. Nobody had heard of him before. Born in Cairo in 1980, he was raised in Saudi Arabia, in Abha, until he was 13, before moving back to Cairo. He studied at Cairo University, and the AUC. He worked in IT and computers. He was a regional marketing manager for Google in Dubai. He founded the *Kulona Khalid Saeed* (We Are All Khalid Saeed) Facebook group, one of the most active pages during the uprising, which was used to organise many of the protests. He took some days off from Google, returning to Egypt just before the 25th of January. He supposedly didn't tell his colleagues at Google, nor his American wife, that he was coming to Cairo.

The Egyptian security services had been trying for several months to work out his identity, but with little success. On the night of the 27th of January, he was kidnapped and arrested in the middle of the night by people wearing civilian clothes and was taken to the SSIS headquarters. His family kept looking for him, but could not discover his whereabouts. The Egyptian authorities did not confirm his arrest, despite the best efforts by his family and Google. They held him for about 12 days, ostensibly to find out who else was behind the Kuluna Khalid Saeed Facebook page. They didn't torture him, they kept him in the state security building, questioning him. They weren't just trying to work out who was behind the page, they were trying to work out who was behind him.

His friends demanded that he be freed. The Prime Minister had him released that Monday in an effort to assuage the protesters, and create the impression of a new era of openness and respect for the rights of demonstrators in Egypt.

Wael Ghonim appeared on television, on a late-night talk show called Al-Asharaa Massa, after his release and broke down in tears when he talked about the violence that had erupted in Cairo while he was detained. The pictures became famous the world over. As I said, Egypt is a sentimental country, and the sight of young man in tears would surely move the country. It was another turning point in the crisis. If there were any Egyptians that wanted Mubarak to stay on as President before the nation bore witness to the young man's tears, there certainly weren't any more.

I asked my people to call him. We asked him twice to appear on our TV station. The first time he just refused, saying he wouldn't appear on Egyptian state TV. The second time we asked, he turned us down again, saying that state TV had "blood on its hands."

FEBRUARY 8TH – TUESDAY

At 6.40am I looked at my phone and saw I had received a message from someone whom I consider to be a friend, Hamdi Qandil – an old presenter, famous in Egypt, who had been on Egyptian TV since the 1960s. His programme was a mixture of news and comment, driven by his inimitable, opinionated style. In the last few years, he had become a particularly vocal critic of the government. Back in 2004, during the conflict in Iraq, he appeared on his programme and 10 minutes in, walked out, quitting right there and then. We had respect for each other, even though in recent years he was becoming more of a politician than a journalist.

The message he sent me that morning read: "Please don't connect your name with this media prostitution in the Maspero. From what we know about you, you should resign quickly and publicly."

I'd had many calls like that in the last two weeks, asking me to leave. My answer to these messages was always the same, that I was serving the country, and I am in position of responsibility which I cannot abandon.

The opposition demonstrations had spread to every aspect of Egyptian society. The demands for better wages and living conditions were universal, so workers in every factory, union, faculty, business, industry started protesting outside their places of work, demanding better opportunities. Protests took place outside factories, newspapers, power stations, anywhere.

Looking back, those final days are something of a blur. The unpredictability of the uprising had settled into a routine. Tahrir Square remained occupied, protesters were still trying to storm the building where we worked. Newcomers kept coming to the square. University professors arrived en masse on Tuesday, campaigning for political change and better conditions for themselves. The arrival of these academics brought even more intellectual weight to the protests. The protesters were planning another *millioniya* for that Friday.

Some demonstrators called it the "stubborn week". The government had settled into a malaise, as the protests in the square grew, the government remained silent and inactive. However, there was at least one development that Tuesday. The formation of the committee to investigate the violence on the 2nd of February was announced, six days after the event.

There was considerable resistance within the military and the government to force Mubarak's hand. The reasons for this were as much cultural as they were political. Asking Mubarak to leave was against Egyptian customs. Egyptians respect their elders. Mubarak was also one of the heroes of the October War of 1973. The military remembered the heroes of the October War.

On the international stage, Angela Merkel offered to receive Mubarak in Berlin for treatment. This was significant, as Mubarak had previously sought medical treatment in Germany. Omar Suleiman simply responded that Mubarak did not need treatment and would be staying. Mubarak would stay to run the "roadmap for reform" and oversee the peaceful transition of power.

Omar Suleiman announced that the new president would take his oath on the 14th of October. If the unrest was to end quickly, then the country could work towards that point. He said that the Muslim Brotherhood should be part of the dialogue now. They had been seeking legalisation for over 60 years; now they had it.

Importantly, he didn't accuse the youth of fermenting trouble. He said that the government now respected what they wanted. At the same time, he mentioned foreign interference in Egypt's internal affairs, asserting that there were signs of foreign activity in the form of financial assistance and weaponry smuggled in through Sudan and Gaza.

On Tuesday, the focus of protester's ire was against the media in general and Anas Al-Feky in particular. This was another part of the media campaign run from Tahrir Square; it was a shrewd tactic to keep changing the topic, so that the national and foreign media would not tire of the same stories. It was well organised. In the morning, 24 NGOs went to the Attorney General's office to demand that the Egyptian judiciary investigate Anas on the charge of spreading false information.

Tahrir Square was still a carnival in the centre of town, replete with shows and galleries. They even had something they called "The Museum of the Revolution", featuring exhibits such as a police officer's helmet, a martyr's jacket, a police baton, etc.

Solutions were being offered to remedy Egypt's economic problems caused by the uprising. For the demonstrators, it was imperative that the protests not be the cause of any lasting economic trouble, lest they lose the public sympathy and credibility that they had so far achieved. There was a romantic idea among the youth where they asked Egyptians to buy shares at 100 Egyptian pounds each (about £10 sterling). They didn't understand that even if every Egyptian did buy a share at that value, it would not come close to covering the losses incurred by the stock market collapse.

For some reason, I decided late that night that it might be a good idea to visit Tahrir Square. At about half past one in the morning, when the protesters outside the Maspero building had gone, I took Mohammed with me, headed outside and set off to cover the few hundred metres that separated us from the square. We were stopped a few times at army checkpoints, but when they saw who we were, they let us pass.

In order to get past the building, we had to pass through reams of barbed wire and concrete blast blocks. If felt like walking into no-man's land. There was so much barbed wire, and Anas kept asking for more. It became something of an obsession. After a few days of looking at it from his window, he would decide that the multitude of jagged lines was insufficient to keep protesters out and call on the army to lay more around the perimeter.

It reminded me of some African cities I'd visited, which, after the working day, are just empty. A dead city. Cairo, usually so vibrant, felt dead. It was a strange feeling, as if the dark was darker and the cold colder. The only sound was the sound of our footsteps. It was like walking through a void.

The tall, old buildings of central Cairo cast long shadows on the streets below, enveloping us in darkness.

We talked as we walked. I told him about the message I got from Hamdi, and how I felt we were walking around in circles. The country was at an impasse, all sides refusing to give anything.

"These days, we really are walking in a circle," he agreed, "we start off angry, upset, hopeful, crazy, then angry again. It's become a daily routine and we can't find a way out."

Smashed glass crunched underfoot. The burnt out cars had been cleared away, yet still the street looked a wreck. Shops, devoid of merchandise, lay broken and looted on the street.

We began to hear the rumble of Tahrir Square. It gradually got louder as we got closer. We made it to Abdel Moneim Riad Square, one of the smaller squares, from which the road led to Tahrir.

"Enough," said Mohammed, "I don't think it's a good idea to go any further. You will be a target in the square."

Reluctantly, I turned around and headed back through the cold, dark streets to the Maspero.

FEBRUARY 9TH – WEDNESDAY

Like the day before, demonstrations were taking place across the country. As the demonstrations got more aggressive, the government considered evacuating the cabinet building, due to its proximity to Tahrir.

Some of the demonstrators started to ask for mass civil disobedience throughout Egypt. Nearly all the signs of life in the capital were fading. Egypt, which at one point seemed to be heading back to normal was once more in a state of paralysis. The workers at the train station were sitting on the rails, stopping the trains, the police stations were still being attacked.

Over in Port Said, on the Mediterranean coast, the northern terminus of the Suez Canal, there was trouble. My brother-in-law is the assistant to the general manager for security at Port Said. He called me, telling me of the strife in the city that was tearing it apart. The governor's car was burnt, the police station and the governor's office was attacked. He told me they did not want to engage them, but they didn't know how to ward them off. He said that some of the more aggressive protesters were from a poor area of Port Said, encouraged to attack government protesters by other demonstrators after coming out to protest over housing conditions.

After the government decided that the risks were too great, they closed down the cabinet building after securing the road outside. Prime Minister Ahmed Shafik set up his new operational headquarters at his old office in the Cairo airport.

Hossam Badrawi, the new party general secretary went to meet Mubarak. He advised him, subtly, as it was an unspoken rule that nobody ever told the President what to do. That was one of the main problems. Hossam informed him that it might be a good idea to give authority to the Vice President, and return to Sharm El-Sheikh. He answered Hossam by telling him, "I won't run away from a battle. I was the only fighter pilot flying his plane in Egypt's sky when the air force was destroyed in 1967. That day, I wasn't a coward. If there is something I have to face, I will face it to the end. If there is something I have to do, I will do it. I'm not a coward who will run away."

When Hossam left the office, he was chastised by Gamal and Zakaria Azmi. Azmi even shouted at him. Hossam was shocked by such treatment; after all, Hossam had taken their jobs a few days before.

Hossam later stated that he told the President he didn't want to see what happened to Ceausescu happen to Mubarak, although I heard that Hossam had only recommended he defer his authority to the Vice President before leaving for Sharm El-Sheikh. He also didn't realise that the ruling clique in the Presidential Palace were very close to sacking him for his indiscretion.

After being treated so badly in the palace, Hossam came out publicly and announced to the media that Mubarak was close to departure.

The leaders of the army were afraid of pushing the palace too much, lest the palace suddenly decide to take action against the demonstrators. Field Marshal Tantawi and General Anan, in an effort to ensure they were one step ahead of the palace, asked to meet the President. They told the President, unambiguously, and unprompted, that they would not be able to use violence against the demonstrators if they were asked to do so, blaming the fact that there were just too many of them now, aside from the fact they could not attack Egyptian civilians. They were afraid that Gamal might encourage his father to issue such an order.

"How could you expect me to ask for something like that?!" he blustered, "I would NEVER ask for something like that!"

A rumour emerged after the meeting. The story was that after the two of them excused themselves, finished the meeting and left his office, they left the building and got inside their car, sitting in the compound. Unusually, the gates did not open straight away, and remained closed for some 10 minutes. The important men were not used to being kept waiting. Meanwhile, as they sat outside, Gamal was trying to convince his father to have the two army leaders (General Anan was the Chief of Staff, deputy to Tantawi) replaced with two more "loyal" officers. Mubarak refused, out of hand. He would never have got rid of his two most senior officers like that.

The President's older son, Alaa, was in the Presidential Palace the whole time during the uprising. Before, he only went to his father's office very rarely, though when the problems started happening, he was there every day. He was concerned for his father's wellbeing and asked the staff to let him know if his father got into any bad moods, though he didn't get involved politically. Alaa is a businessman, and has always kept a low public profile. He was generally more popular with the people than Gamal, and the only time he was really seen in public was in the crowd at international football matches, with his children.

It was his son who died, causing Egypt to fall into mourning back in 2009.

Alaa is a lot closer to his father. Whereas Gamal takes after Suzanne, Alaa is far more like Hosni. When Mubarak survived his assassination attempt in 1995, he called Alaa first, not Gamal. Alaa is regarded as better tempered than his brother, with humble manners, and no political ambition.

That evening in the Presidential Palace, the President was sitting in his office. His two sons were talking outside when they broke into a vicious argument.

"What did you do for our father?!" shouted Alaa.

"You don't understand anything!" Gamal accused him, "why did you come here?!"

Mubarak came out "Don't fight, I'm still alive!" he looked at Gamal, "you've spoiled everything that I achieved over the past thirty years – you and that short bastard!"

One issue that was always at the back of the government's mind was the stance of the United States of America. It was a great relief to Anas when we heard that the White House spokesman Robert Gibbs declared early on that the US would not be taking sides in the turmoil. Using very diplomatic language, Gibbs assured the country that President Obama was following the situation and encouraged the government to work on political reform. He said that what is happening is considered an opportunity for Mubarak's government to go ahead with political reform.

Gamal Mubarak took that to mean that the international community supported Egypt, as the government was debating political reform. If the government ever thought that the US had taken a stance against Egypt, they were distraught.

There were two strands within the American administration. On the one side was the Obama camp, and on the other was the Clinton camp. Those around Obama were generally younger and more idealistic. They would be much more willing to cast off their support for Mubarak. However, on the other side, Hillary Clinton and the State Department were on the whole more experienced in international affairs and more cautious. This is why the reaction of the US administration was far more muted than in Europe.

There was also a very real fear, inspired by memories of the Iranian revolution, that the United States would abandon Mubarak, just as they had abandoned the Shah of Iran in 1979.

For many years, in order to enhance their image in the US and the UK, the Egyptian government contracted with various foreign public relations companies to present a new Egypt to the world.

Egyptian officials abroad were ordered to cooperate with them. During the uprising, Gamal and Anas were both in regular contact with a British company, which they depended on for advice on how to manage the crisis.

I sat in on a conference call at one point, as Anas debated with the firm how to handle the unrest. One of the suggestions I heard was that the Egyptian government needs to enhance its image and provide new "content". They suggested that to defuse the crisis, the government needs to show real political reform to the public and the world. The fact that they needed foreign PR companies to tell them that illustrates just how detached the government was.

Anas Al-Feky, Hosni Mubarak and Gamal Mubarak prepare for the President's final public address on the 10th of February 2011.

Gamal Mubarak checks the autocue before his father's speech.

Gamal Mubarak inturupts his father's speech to adjust the President's tie.

Hosni and Gamal Mubarak in the studio in the Presidential Palace.

Alaa Mubarak helps his father prepare for the address.

Gamal Mubarak in discussion with Suleiman Awad.

The author leaves the studio's control room with General Ismail Etman, the army spokesman, after the broadcast of Omar Suleiman's announcement.

Omar Suleiman announces Mubarak's resignation on the 11th of February.

FEBRUARY 10TH – THURSDAY

In the early hours of the 10th of February, I was in Anas's office. He was on the hotline to the President. They were just talking on the phone; it seemed that Anas was searching his mind, trying to say anything to keep the President's spirits up. The situation was dire.

"Abdel Latif is here with me," he said down the phone. The President asked for me. As Anas got up to hand me the phone, he looked me in the eye, and holding the receiver to his chest, he whispered, "Try to cheer him up."

"Hello, Menawy, how are you?" asked the President. "You see what's going on?" His voice was bitter, he was upset. I never heard him sound like this before.

"Yes Mr President," I replied. I didn't know what to say. I wasn't interested in trying to cheer him up, I had other things on my mind. "I hope everything will turn out fine. Egypt will make it across this river; the country is not going to drown."

"Yes, yes," he murmured, "When this is all over, I want to have an interview, a long one. I want to tell people about everything I've done for this country over the last 30 years."

I liked the man. He was humble in his own way; he's old, he has a lot of problems, but he was a human being, just like everyone else. I just repeated what I said, "Insha'alla, everything will be fine. Insha'alla." I handed the phone back to Anas and left the office as they sank back into conversation.

After the phone call, I felt that the country was in a state of collapse, and nobody knew where the country was going. I realised that the President was in another world. He didn't understand the depth of the crisis affecting the country. He was not thinking about what he had to do in the coming days, or hours, he was thinking of how to convince the people later on of his achievements over the decades.

Later on, I had a call from one of my friends in the army. We were exchanging calls constantly, and, as the crisis dragged on, we were in contact on an almost hourly basis. He was a high-ranking officer within the intelligence services. Someone right at the top. We decided to organise a meeting over at the intelligence headquarters. I thought it best to keep it quiet. I didn't tell anyone about it, not even Anas.

As I was caught in the middle, I was forced to make a few decisions and arrange a few meetings without telling anybody. It was strange – some things I would normally defer to higher powers, but not any more. My duty had changed. As I lay on the sofa next to my office trying to catch a couple of hours of precious sleep, a line from a poem by William Henley kept running through my head, *I am the master of my fate; I am the captain of my soul.* That's how I felt, as I stared at the wall of my office. I had a job to do, and from now on the responsibility was my own.

By the 10th of February it seemed everyone was attacking the state TV. We couldn't please anybody, not the Presidential Palace, nor the army, nor the intelligence services, nor the protesters out on the streets. They all wanted to control the country's TV. I couldn't take sides, it wasn't possible. The only thing to do was to strive to be on the nation's side. Nothing else mattered. Ever since the 2nd of February, when I consciously made a decision to go forward in this way, I was getting a stream of complaints from the President, and from Anas, but nobody interfered. Even so, every day, the noise of the protesters outside our windows grew louder, I was really starting to worry for my safety, and of course, that of my staff.

When morning came, I headed off for my meeting at the intelligence HQ. Nobody knew about it but the three of us who would be in the room: me, the officer and his deputy. Part of the reason I wanted to have the meeting in the first place was slightly selfish: I needed to reassure myself and I needed support. I needed someone to show me that the country hadn't fallen apart and tell me there was a semblance of order still operating at some level. Surely there was someone in Egypt who knew where we were going.

The streets were abuzz with plans for tomorrow. There was talk of massing outside the Presidential Palace. No one knew what was going to happen. I had heard from my sources in the army that if they stormed the palace, the army wouldn't stand in their way. For the Presidential Guard, it would have been a different matter, but the army no longer felt the need to protect the President. A decision was made somewhere up the chain of command for soldiers around the palace to unload their weapons. The army's ambivalence was not kept secret. It was not so much a measure to protect against civilian casualties as another tactic to heap pressure on Mubarak.

The meeting was early in the morning, around 9am. I went down to the ground floor of the building, summoned a driver and got into the car. Even if I'm being driven, I usually ride in the front seat. Not today. It was dangerous, and some protesters were out for my blood: I had to sit in the back for my own safety and security. I was scared. It was the first time I'd been truly scared during this whole tumultuous period, perhaps the first time in my life. The opposition out on the streets had painted a picture of the Egyptian media as being against the Egyptian people. If they saw me in the car, God knows what could have happened.

As the car cruised through the streets, it was like driving through a war zone. I'd seen pictures on TV of places like Sarejevo or Beirut in the midst of conflict, now it was Cairo's turn to be the urban battlefield. There were crowds of people everywhere, we'd have to stop when we reached some streets, and make way for marching protesters, all of them shouting, chanting, carrying banners. The car had to zigzag through the streets, avoiding the trouble spots. From the back seat of the car, I could see buildings totally gutted by fire. The Arkadia Mall, the biggest shopping centre in Cairo, in one of the most exclusive parts of the city, which not so long ago would have been filled with busy shoppers, was burned to cinders. Other shops nearby had been smashed up, the debris already scoured by looters. The pavements had been battered, as the stone had been prized away for use as makeshift missiles by some of the more violent revolutionaries.

After a tortuous journey through the city, I arrived at the headquarters of the intelligence services. It's a huge compound to the north-east of the city, stacked with buildings. Everybody calls it "El-Koba". Like other government buildings it was surrounded by barbed wire and armed soldiers. Curiously, it wasn't surrounded by a mob of protesters. In fact, there was hardly anybody around at all.

I headed for the main building. I was shown up to the office with the two officers. The first thing I said was, "It's strange, you don't have any protesters here." The two of them responded with brief, strained laughter. I told them about my situation in the Maspero building. I told them about the tanks, the barbed wire and the hundreds, if not thousands of protesters congregating outside every day, some making attempts to raid the building. I told them about the people working for me, who, for 17 days now, had to hear me drilling the same thing into them, that we were working for this country, not for any one person. However, the time had come for this one person do something.

It didn't take long for me to realise that the support I sought was not forthcoming, because they needed support too. They didn't have a plan either.

The three of us talked over the situation and agreed that something had to be done, that the President had to do something. But he was stubborn. He wouldn't listen to anybody, and worst of all, Gamal was controlling everything.

I asked one of the officers, "Didn't you try and explain it to him, didn't you try and tell the President how bad everything had got?"

"Yes," he responded, "I decided last night that I had to speak to him. I decided to tell him the truth. I told him 'the situation is very bad Mr President,' I told him that something had to be done."

"Did you ask him what action he should take?" I asked.

"No."

"What did he do?" I continued.

"He was just listening. He didn't comment on anything I said. After I finished he said 'Okay, God will find a way.'"

While I was sitting with them, talking things through, the phone rang. The superior of the two officers picked it up. It was Omar Suleiman on the other side. The officer told the Vice President that I was with them in their office. He told him everything I'd said, the situation with the TV station, how the country was in a state of collapse and how tomorrow could be catastrophic. He admitted that they agreed with me, and told him that they too were worried about tomorrow.

He carried on talking over the phone. From where I was sitting, I could hear the Vice President talking down the line:

"Why don't you tell the President about this?" the intelligence man asked.

"No," came the tinny voice through the telephone, "tell him yourself."

"No. I told him yesterday, he just sat there listening. I could tell he was angry with me for saying such things. I'm not going to tell him again. You tell him."

He said goodbye and placed the phone back onto its cradle. I challenged him, "Did you ask the President frankly, to cede authority to the Vice President?"

"No, nobody told him," he replied, "but everybody around him was implying it, everybody was trying to push him in that direction."

This was the problem. Whenever anybody talked to Mubarak, they would dance around the fire, nobody would tell him what really needed to happen. There is an expression in English, they call it the elephant in the room. That's what the issue of Mubarak's stepping aside became, a great big damn elephant in the room.

We were wondering what to do, mulling over various possibilities. After a while, I made a suggestion. The President should go on television, that day, and talk to the nation. He had to appeal to people's emotions, as that was all he had left to engage with. He would have to give authority away to Omar Suleiman. It was the only thing to do.

But, again, there was the same problem. How could we tell Mubarak to do this? Who should be the one to deliver the message? I told the two of them that I had a way I could reach him.

"How?" they both asked.

"There is just one person who can do it. Anas Al-Feky. Mubarak thinks of him as his third son."

Anas was the only person who could be made aware of the danger and the potential problems that would erupt if Mubarak clung to power. He was the only one who could make the Mubarak family understand what was going on. Anas would have to feel scared, and would have to understand that the state was collapsing, as the rest of us felt it was. He would have to transmit this feeling to Gamal and his father.

We ended up talking for about an hour and a half in the office. They talked me through the situation as they saw it, going through some of the intelligence they had on the demonstrations. One of them tried to encourage me, telling me that in the Koran, Egypt is mentioned five times, whereas Mecca is mentioned just twice. He said that if God mentioned Egypt five times in the Koran, then he would protect it. This didn't encourage me at all. In fact, it was ridiculous. This man, right at the highest level of the Egyptian intelligence establishment was telling me that they were waiting for a miracle. It certainly wasn't the time for miracles any more.

After we wrapped up the meeting, I bid the two officers farewell and headed back out to the car. Before I left, I told them that I would try my best to convince Anas that he needed to speak to the President. We drove straight back to the Maspero building, running the gauntlet once more through the ferocious urban maze, doggedly avoiding the areas where the crowds and protests were at their most intense.

When I got back to the Maspero building, I went straight to Anas's office. He was sitting behind his desk; he wasn't bothering with a suit any more, simply opting for some casual clothes he'd thrown on without too much forethought. He was talking to one of our colleagues, Amr, in his office. Amr was an editor for one of our current affairs programmes, and one of his old friends.

When I walked in Anas was smiling and seemingly in high spirits. He greeted me, "Hi, how are you, how's it going?"

"It's very bad," came my terse reply. "We have a disaster. This is something that could explode in our faces at any moment. Tomorrow is going to be a very bad day."

I explained the situation to him and told him that the people would no longer accept Mubarak carrying on as he is. "They should know," I repeated, "they should do something." Anas still didn't quite intuit what I was trying to tell him, so I tried to make it as clear as I could. I told him that the protesters were demanding that Mubarak leave, and if he did not, they would head to the Presidential Palace and force him to go, one way or the other. If this happened, the army would not stand in their way and something terrible would happen.

Anas started taking notes. As his pen scurried across the page, the colour drained away from his face, his smile long since faded away. Amr was trying to join in the conversation, reiterating the same points.

"Look," I interjected, "stop talking Amr, please let me finish."

"But I'm just saying what you're saying" he responded, somewhat defensively.

"Yes, I know," I said sympathetically, "but please, I have a message to deliver to Anas."

Anas looked up from his notebook, the page scrawled with his handwriting. "So," he enquired, "what do I have to do?"

"Just one thing." I responded, looking him in the eye, "Mubarak should go on air. Today. He needs to talk to the people. He should talk in very short sentences. Direct. No bluffing. He must play on people's emotions. He can't talk politics. He has nothing to appeal to but the heart of the nation."

"What should he say?" asked Anas.

I suddenly remembered what Anas told me last night, about Mubarak's conversation with Hossam Badrawi, where he went on and on about how he was the last fighter pilot in the air during the war of 1967. I said that's how he should talk to the people.

I began making up a speech on the spot, I still remember everything I said, it having somehow seared itself into my mind. It began: "My people, I had the courage to be the only pilot in his plane flying Egypt's skies while the army and the airbases were destroyed back in 1967. I had the courage to participate in the war with Israel in 1970. I had the courage to be part of the greatest victory we ever had back in 1973. I had the courage to accept the post of President after my predecessor was killed not 20 metres from where I sat. I had the courage to work hard with you to build this country. And today I have the courage to tell you that I'm convinced that our people, Egyptians, have the right to choose their own destiny. To choose how they will be ruled. This is why I have the courage to tell you today that I am giving all my authority to my Vice President, Omar Suleiman, to run the country. I will only be watching, and oversee the first peaceful transfer of power in the Arab world. Egypt will once again be a leader in the region, as it was before." Anas was still taking notes, writing down what I was saying. He wrote down every word I said.

"This is the way to talk to people," I finished, "don't say anything else."

We took the idea of the brave man, a man who had achieved something in his lifetime, not only by himself, but hand in hand with the people. We took the idea that the brave man can step aside, and just watch and observe how the Egyptian people could be the first in the Middle East to see a genuine transition to a real democracy. If the man could just say that to people, to appeal to their emotions, but tell them that he would just stay away, I believed then, and still do believe, that things could have passed differently.

Anas picked up the phone and called Gamal. Gamal asked him "What's the news?" Anas began reading from his notebook, reading him everything that I had just said, not missing anything out. Anas told him that President Mubarak should speak to the people today. He spoke to Gamal as I expected him to. He imparted the sense of urgency, and made them see how dangerous the path they were walking really was.

Gamal told him to come to the Presidential Palace. He got up from his chair and walked across the office, opening the door to a little room he had on the side. He went in and came out a few minutes later wearing a suit, looking somewhat more dignified.

As he was leaving, I stopped him.

"Anas," I said, "I have two things to ask you."

"What?"

"Firstly, the speech should be written exactly as we have just discussed it here in this office, and I'm asking you, please, make sure that you are the one who writes the speech. Secondly, I'm asking you in the name of all the good gods, in the name of all the saints, sheikhs, angels, devils, I'm asking you in the name of all this…"

"Yeah…?"

"Please, finish it quickly. As soon as you can. Don't let it go on any longer than 4pm today."

He looked at me, "I'll see what I can do." With that, he left the office. It was about half past one in the afternoon. I was counting on Anas to get there and get the job done in two and a half hours.

That was the last time I saw Anas.

I went to my office. I had a phone call from the army telling me that they had a statement ready for me. They called it "Statement no. 1" "We have very important news," explained the voice down the line. I asked what happened.

"The Supreme Council of the Armed Forces had a meeting today." This was highly irregular. The Supreme Council is usually chaired by the President as, aside from being the head of state, the President is also the commander-in-chief of the Egyptian armed forces. As far as I knew, the President was holed up in the Presidential Palace. I asked him if Mubarak was at the meeting.

"No, he doesn't know about it," came the answer, "and he shouldn't."

He said that they were going to send news with "Statement no.1" The army would normally come to me first with their statements, watch it with me and oversee its dissemination. On this occasion, the army said that they wanted to have their statement broadcast, but they didn't want to tell anybody about it first.

"Just send it to me," I said.

Before long, I received the tape. I watched it. It was a pre-recorded video from General Mohsen Al-Fangari. It was just saying that the Supreme Council of the Armed Forces had a meeting to discuss the current situation and take the necessary steps to protect the nation and the Egyptian people. The sessions were continuing. That was it. The thing that was curious was that they called it "Statement no. 1." A name like that suggests that you should expect a "Statement no. 2".

It would be a clear message to the public. The council was meeting without the President. If he wasn't there and he didn't know about it, then it meant that the army was no longer on the President's side. It was their way of pressuring Mubarak to make a decision.

They asked me not to tell anybody about the tape. Just to broadcast it. It didn't take me long to decide what to do. I ended up broadcasting the tape. I could have called Anas, or Gamal, or the President, even intelligence, as I would normally have done. I didn't think about it. It was an instinctive decision, like the reaction one has when hitting a ball in a game of table tennis. I felt, and I knew that this was the right decision to make. The President had to do something, he had to feel the urgency of the situation, lest the country be destroyed.

I broadcast the tape on all the ERTU television and radio stations simultaneously. Within a couple of minutes I got a phone call from Anas and Zakaria Azmi, over at the Presidential Palace.

"What was that statement?!" demanded Anas, frantically.

"It was an army statement" I replied.

"Where did that come from?"

"It came from the army."

"What didn't you tell us?"

"I don't have to. This is my job."

"We used to get all the army statements before, this was important."

"Yes, I know. But this was very important."

Before he hung up the phone he told me, "Listen, if you get any news from the army, any statements, don't broadcast it, call us first."

Again, I had to make a split-second decision. I had to give them an answer that would satisfy them, something I could tell them to get them off my back.

"Look," I quipped, "the army has nothing to do with me. The news comes in a tape, carried by an officer. The officer goes to the studio, puts in the tape and presses play. I watch the broadcast like everyone else. I have no choice in the matter." This is of course untrue.

I never felt that it was going behind their back, it was just doing what had to be done, letting those involved know what they needed to know, but no more.

I wasn't part of the regime. I was a professional employed by the state and I had a role to play. I had a lot of friends in Tahrir Square protesting for what they believed in. But it wasn't my place to stand up to the President or to rock the boat. At the same time, it wasn't for me to protect his position at all costs. I was caught in a game, which I had no choice but to play. I owed it to the country to do my job as best I could. The stakes were high, my career, even my life was at risk.

When I think about it, if I hadn't acted as I had and broadcast that tape, anything could have happened. Potentially, there could have been more bloodshed, with clashes between the army and the presidential forces. What happened in Syria or Libya could easily have happened in Egypt. I was questioning myself, I was even questioning the reality of the situation. It was surreal.

There was no space for opportunism at such a time. During that whole period of revolution, I don't think anybody had the opportunity to take advantage of the unfolding crisis for their own gain. It wasn't like that. The decisions people make in such situations of great stress are instinctive.

A few minutes after I'd finished on the phone with Anas and Zakaria Azmi, I got another call from an army general, thanking me for broadcasting the statement. At the time, I didn't understand why he was thanking me, I just did what I thought was the right thing to do. Then, he asked me not to broadcast the statement again. His reasoning was that they believed that the statement had already achieved what they were hoping, to put pressure on Mubarak. He said that he was preparing a speech, and we would have to wait to hear what he had to say.

We were just coming up to the news bulletin at the top of the hour, so I asked my people not to include any footage from, or mention the statement which we had just broadcast across all our channels. When the bulletin went out, we were inundated with phone calls from the public asking what had happened. It was ridiculous.

I called the army again, and I asserted "I have to rebroadcast the statement, if I don't put it in the news bulletins, it will look suspicious if we had it on once and never mentioned it again. It will give the public, and anyone else, the impression that you have retracted the statement." The general I spoke to reluctantly agreed with me. Once I got back into the control room, I told my staff that the statement was back. At around 2:25pm, we broadcast it again.

When I wasn't in the control room, I was back in my office calling Anas. I was nagging him, pushing him to finish that speech and make sure that it would be read out by the President by 4pm.

Tahrir Square was overloaded with people. Hundreds of thousands. Nobody really knows how many. It was just rammed with bodies. The tension was at boiling point. I'd just heard that one of the senior generals, Rawani, had addressed the crowd and told them "All that you ask for will happen in the coming few hours."

We waited and waited and waited. 4pm came and went. There was a direct link in the control room to the studio in the Presidential Palace. I was waiting in front of this screen, watching it. There was nothing, only the solitary podium in front on the sombre blue background, for hours and hours. I kept calling Anas, begging him to move things along, reminding him how bad the situation was getting. The people were restless and the crowd was growing by the minute. Eventually, he stopped answering the phone.

There were thousands surrounding the TV building, chanting, protesting and getting louder by the hour. The whole building was locked down by the army. No one could enter, no one could leave. We were stuck in there. There were people in amongst the protesters trying to get the crowd to charge the TV building. This had been going on for days, and every day the army captured a handful of the more emboldened demonstrators who made a break for it and tried to get in. On that day, I really started to wonder if the army would be able to hold them back any longer.

My staff inside had gone beyond being scared some time ago. They were just tired. Exhausted. Some of them had been working 48 hours non-stop in front of their machines. To add to the strain, I was running the whole operation with a skeleton crew. Somebody from one of the stations, Nile TV, the English language channel came to me and told me they would have to go off air, as they no longer had the people to keep it running. They would just have to relay the Channel One broadcast. I asked them why, and they said "We've only got two people, a director and the presenter. We can't go on."

I snapped, and screamed at them "NO! No screen will go black! No station will close down! You must carry on!"

The two of them were brilliant. Heroically, they carried on, doing the jobs of two dozen people between them. The presenter presented, edited, prepared the scripts, did the translations on the spot. The director was a director, cameraman, switcher, audio mixer. They did everything, and went on for six or seven hours like that. They were amazing.

The only other choice was to close the station down. That was not an option. It was something we decided from day one. No station would go off air. I kept telling them, every day, this was our mission. We were on no one's side but the country's. I went back to my river analogy, I used to say it all the time, we would get to the other side of the river, we couldn't let ourselves drown.

The meetings continued in the Presidential Palace. At around 10pm, finally, there was some activity on the screen. Watching through the uplink, I saw Gamal emerge in the studio. Anas appeared not long after. They looked so tired. They were followed by a small group of advisers from the President's inner circle.

To my complete consternation, Gamal seemed to be just dithering around in front if the camera, talking with the people around him for minutes, though, at the time, it seemed like hours, about where the paper would be placed on the podium to prevent it from slipping: "Should it be here, like that, or should we place it like this?…Will it drop down?… Are you sure this is how we had it before?… Last week, when we had the speech, was this block here?"

It was incredible, I couldn't believe my eyes. The streets were alive, throbbing with bodies, Tahrir Square had become a pressure cooker and here was this ten minute discussion about a piece of paper. Then, they just disappeared. Again, all that remained was the same old blue background and empty podium.

After around 20 minutes, the President finally strolled into the picture. He was flanked by Anas, Suleiman Awad (his spokesman) and his two sons, Gamal and Alaa. They started giving the President instructions, telling him to read the first four pages from the script and the rest from the plasma screen, just out of shot, behind the camera. Then they told him after he'd finished with the plasma screen to go back to the script on the paper. The plasma screen was basically an autocue, though, at 81 years old, the President's eyes weren't so sharp, so they had to use a much larger screen. It was all so needlessly complicated.

He started reading. He stopped and started again when he made a mistake. At one point, they stopped him, right in the middle of the speech to fix his tie. When they were fiddling with his tie, Mubarak looked agitated, annoyed that he had been stopped. Anas, reading his body language, reassured the President, "Don't worry" he said, "there's time."

The President laughed, "There's time?"

After that, he carried on with his tie in a slightly different position. Once he finished, he stepped down, and shook the hands of everyone around him, as was his habit. Then he left, and that was it.

When it was over, I had a grim feeling in the pit of my stomach. This was the end. The speech was just awful. The worst speech he'd ever made in his life. It was arrogant. It was senseless. It was a disaster.

Referring to Egyptians as "sons and daughters", the President emphasised that he would "not listen to any foreign interventions, or dictations, regardless of their sources." He delegated power to Omar Suleiman, but reiterated that he would be staying to observe. It was a defiant speech, he did not give the impression that he was stepping down at all.

In any case, we had to have the speech out as soon as possible. The atmosphere on the streets was electric. Everybody was waiting, expecting the speech. As such, I had another big decision to make. The question was whether to edit it properly and cover up all the jumps we would have to make, which would take up to forty-five minutes, or whether to do a 2 minute rough cut. When I looked at the streets and saw the people getting more and more agitated, I decided that we needed something out on the air as soon as possible. I didn't have the luxury of time, it was nearly midnight and people had been waiting since 4pm. Something had to give.

Immediately upon broadcast, protesters across the country began to vent their anger, screaming into the night sky. The rage was almost tangible, as if the city had been wrapped in it. Some on the streets were even suggesting that it was a ploy to further provoke the demonstrators to justify another brutal crackdown.

Because everyone could see the jump cuts, rumours spread that this was something cooked up a few days ago, perhaps recorded in Sharm El-Sheikh. It didn't matter; the speech itself was rotten in every way. I thought that such a poor speech had no need of such polish.

I called all my contacts: army, intelligence, everyone, and asked them what had happened. They all said that they couldn't do anything. The old man was stubborn, and Gamal was trying to take charge.

Anas called me and asked me what I thought of the speech. I only had one answer "My 19 year-old boy called me after that speech, and he asked, 'Dad, why is he talking to us like this?'" that was all I needed to say. "Who did that to the speech?" I demanded to know.

"Ah, I tried, but, you know, Suleiman [Awad] and Gamal interfered. You can see that the first four pages were different from the rest, but this is all I could do," he conceded. "I won't be able to come down to the Maspero building now, everything is surrounded." He laughed, unexpectedly, "I'm not escaping, I'm not leaving you alone, eh? I'll come tomorrow morning."

That was the last time I spoke to Anas.

The people in Tahrir Square were livid, that was obvious enough. Everybody took off a shoe and raised it in the air. Sometimes, people in the West don't realise the implications of such a statement, but in the Arab world, it shows the height of disdain and disrespect.

I went to my office and collapsed on the sofa. I had the awful feeling that something big was happening tomorrow, I just didn't know what.

FEBRUARY 11TH – FRIDAY

The fallout from President Mubarak's atrocious speech the night before had been devastating. The move, aimed at satisfying the crowds, had achieved the opposite. The streets were restless with pent up anger and frustration as vexed protesters directed their rage towards the President. I knew that it would finish today, but I didn't know how.

I wasn't really sleeping. The days tended to blur into one. Each night, I could only manage a couple of hours on the sofa in the little room next to my office. The first thing I did when I opened my eyes, whatever time it was, would be to look at the screens which adorned the office wall. There were live links to our cameras in Tahrir Square and in front of the building itself, as well as live feeds from our broadcasts. Throughout the whole 18 days of revolution, I consciously tried not to follow any of the commentators, columnists or opinion formers. I was just following the news; I didn't want my grasp of everything going on interrupted by political discussion and conjecture.

At 3am, while I was sitting on my sofa, drifting in and out of sleep, I heard a noise just outside the building. I checked the cameras and discovered that the demonstrators were playing football. They were using two tanks as goals, on either side of the hastily convened pitch. When the ball hit a tank, it was a goal. They were enjoying themselves. It looked like fun. In spite of the jovial atmosphere, they spent the whole night shouting insults at the television station. I spent a short while watching the game before sinking back onto the couch.

As the sun rose over the city in the morning, people began flooding into Tahrir Square to join the already sizeable vigil of demonstrators who remained overnight. People weren't turning up to work, they hadn't been for days. The rat race had been suspended in favour of popular dissent. I made my usual round of calls to my contacts in the army and intelligence. Yet again, they seemed to be as clueless as anyone else, idly waiting for something to happen.

Rumours abounded of ideas to take the protests to a new level. I heard of one aquatic demonstration being planned, where demonstrators were going to launch themselves into the Suez Canal, obstructing shipping. Thousands of life jackets had been prepared.

The convivial atmosphere which I'd witnessed outside the Maspero building the night before had faded away. Once again, the crowd began swelling and the masses began attempting to penetrate the ring of security around the TV station. The army was desperately trying to marshal people out of the way. Apparently, some had broken through the cordon overnight and had staged an occupation on the bottom floor of the building, bringing in blankets and supplies to last them for the long haul. This was an unsettling development. The rest of the building was sealed, with no one getting in or out.

Rumours began to circulate the city, suggesting that Mubarak wasn't in Cairo but in Sharm El-Sheikh. He was also rumoured to be in Saudi Arabia. It hadn't been helped by the hatchet job we'd done editing his speech the night before, which blatantly looked pre-recorded. Rumours spread quickly in Egypt. We have a name for those who grind the rumour mills, the "Coffee Generals", often journalists themselves, they sit in coffee shops all day churning out their own analysis of current affairs or providing little nuggets of information gleaned from their tenuous connections. The Coffee Generals were working overtime in those few days, and it was said that sources from within Mubarak's inner circle had divulged his escape from Cairo.

Just before midday I got a phone call from someone right at the top of the army telling me that we would shortly need to spread the news that Mubarak would be leaving. He didn't say to where. I called some people at other TV stations to tell them the news. Some of them spread it, some didn't. I didn't know quite whether to believe it, but my informant was about as senior as it got. For some reason, the army didn't want the news broken in an official statement, but generally disseminated through the media.

At around midday, when the rest of the country was at Friday prayers, the President took a helicopter from the Presidential Palace to El-Nozha airport, and from there took a presidential jet to his residence in Sharm El-Sheikh.

Just before he left, he had a conversation with his Vice President, Omar Suleiman, at the Presidential Palace.

"Do you need any guarantees?" Suleiman asked the President.

"No," Mubarak replied, "why?"

"Do you need to go anywhere abroad?"

"No," vowed the President, "I've done nothing wrong and I want to live in this country and I will live in this country until the end of my life. I choose Sharm El-Sheikh to be the place I spend the rest of my life. I've left everything. Politics, power, everything. I just want to live here."

"You have some time to think about it if you want to do anything else. Some time. Days." Suleiman told him.

The military council were concerned that if Mubarak were to stay in the country, it would cause problems.

I had a crew over at the Presidential Palace, and one of them phoned me up just after prayers. He was walking out of the Presidential Palace to the Republican Guard base connected to the compound. He was with the crew, as well as Omar Suleiman, Zakaria Azmi and Mahmoud Wagdy, the new Interior Minister.

"We don't know what's going on," he explained over the phone, "but they asked us to evacuate the building...they told us get ready, we might be going to Sharm El-Sheikh." Some people in power clearly thought that the President may have to make more speeches there. They may have wanted Mubarak to make the speech stepping down himself, but that would have taken too long and been too complicated. For the sake of simplicity and expediency, they just let Mubarak go.

After a couple of hours, I had learned through my contacts that Mubarak had landed safely in Sharm El-Sheikh. It was the first time since the crisis started that he was on his own. He was without his wife, his children, his advisers, he was totally by himself. Once he made it into his official residence, at about 1:30pm, he picked up the phone and called the Defence Minister, Field Marshal Mohammed Hussein Tantawi. It was a short phone call. He told him, "Hussein, I've decided to give full authority to you and the army. You are now in power."

Tantawi responded, "No Mr President, we can find another way, this wasn't what we wanted…"

"No," Mubarak answered back, "this is my decision. Talk to Omar Suleiman and arrange to have this announced to the public. Take care of yourself, Hussein."

Within a few minutes of Mubarak putting down the phone, one of my contacts in the army called me to let me know Omar Suleiman was currently in a meeting with the Supreme Council. They were preparing an announcement to tell the country, formally, that Mubarak was gone.

Mubarak had wanted a short statement. Suleiman and Tantawi sat and put the statement together. When they had finished, they read it to Mubarak over the phone. Mubarak asked them to check the constitutional and legal aspects of the transfer of power. He didn't want to cause any problems later. They chose Suleiman to read it, rather than a member of the army because they didn't want to give the impression that the President had been deposed in a coup d'etat.

After an hour or so, General Ismail Etman, the army spokesman, came round to my office. He was happy, vibrant. He was in higher spirits than anyone I'd seen for days. He was wearing a short overcoat. He started hurriedly explaining. "It was very hard, to get through these demonstrations, you know, everyone was saluting us! They were happy that we were there!" After I mumbled a polite greeting to him, he opened his jacket and reached in to pull something from the inner pocket. "I've got the statement," he grinned. He pulled out a small digital Betacam tape, not much larger than an audio cassette. "I was just hiding it here because I was afraid of losing it in this crowd," he explained, "I left my car quite far from the building and I had to walk through all those people!"

"Yes," he went on, "Mubarak decided to leave and Omar Suleiman prepared this statement. I'll be waiting here with it until they give the orders to put it on air. They're waiting for Gamal and Alaa to leave Cairo with their families."

It was strange, we were literally sitting on the biggest news story in the world that day, and just had to sit and chat idly, waiting for the next stage. When he was sitting there, Etman pointed out that it would take a year or more to put the country back on track. I agreed, though, thinking about it, that would surely take far longer.

Before the Mubarak family left the Presidential Palace, Alaa went up to Omar Suleiman and asked what they were going to do now.

"Take your mum," Suleiman told him, "and go to Sharm."

We waited. Every few minutes, he would put in a call to the council. Before long he was informed that Gamal and Alaa had made it to the airport and they were just waiting for their mother Suzanne Mubarak to join them. The army had someone following the family the whole time, reporting back to his superiors at the military headquarters. Apparently, the family was loaded up into a helicopter, the blades were whirring, then they suddenly stopped, and Suzanne ran back to the compound.

Suzanne was still in "the villa", one of the palaces in the presidential compound. The villa was something of a mystery, somewhere that nobody else could go. It was reserved exclusively for Mubarak's family and only the closest of close friends. No officials or advisers were allowed in. Even the guards would wait outside when the family was in residence, it was such a private place.

When we heard that they were still waiting at the airport, Etman muttered something about one of the ladies forgetting one of their possessions, perhaps some jewellery or a particularly favoured dress.

As it turned out Suzanne Mubarak refused to leave the villa for more than three hours. She had broken down. Inconsolable with grief for the loss of the life she had grown accustomed to, her world had fallen apart all around her and it was too much to bear. She was found collapsed on the floor, weeping uncontrollably. She couldn't even stand on her own feet. The guards had breached protocol and found her in the villa, on the floor surrounded by all the trinkets and the records of her lifetime.

The guards had to pick her up. Leaning on the young men, they carried her around the house, her tears staining their shoulders as she picked up the few possessions she couldn't bear to part with. In her grief, she kept repeating the same line, over and over, "they had a reason…" When she had composed herself enough to utter something aside from the same hypnotic mantra, she turned to the guards and demanded to know, in a panic, "Do you think they can get in here? Please…don't let them come here! Please, don't let them destroy it…please…look you can stay here, stay in the villa…please…protect it."

After three hours, the guards had managed to calm her down enough for her to compose herself. She wiped away her tears, straightened up her clothes, and headed out the door. After lookng back at the villa one last time, she got in the car and drove to the airport.

Throughout this whole time, I was sitting in my office, waiting with Etman for the orders to broadcast the tape. Though no one knew it at the time, the whole country was waiting for Suzanne Mubarak as she wept in her empty palace.

Suzanne Mubarak was very much the Khedive Ismail of modern Egypt. Like him, she was an advocate of culture in Egypt. She was famed the world over for her support of the opera, architecture, women's rights and literacy, among other endeavours. However, like Khedive Ismail, she would be remembered by history for a life of opulence, corruption and ultimately, failure. During her thirty year tenure as Egypt's First Lady, she alienated many of those at the highest levels of government as she sought to bring about the conditions for Gamal to succeed his father as President of Egypt. Her goal was to reintroduce dynastic succession into Egypt.

Suzanne Thabet was born in 1941 to an Egyptian surgeon and a Welsh nurse in Al-Minya, south of Cairo. In 1957, the 16 year-old Suzanne met Hosni Mubarak, then a dashing air force officer 13 years her senior. The next year, a 17 year-old Suzanne would marry her sweetheart, dropping out of school to follow her new husband.

During her husband's vice presidency and in the first years of his presidency, Suzanne Mubarak kept a low profile, returning to school and eventually gaining an MA in sociology from the American University in Cairo in 1982. Her low profile was in contrast to the outspoken wife of Anwar Sadat, Jehan (whose mother was also British), who was very unpopular in Egypt. She also suffered some health problems which kept her out of the public eye in the 1980s. She became active in public life in 1991, when she began driving the *reading for all* campaign.

By the mid-nineties she would become one the most prominent women in Egypt, taking on a variety of public duties. She was one of the most prominent defenders of women's rights in Egypt, and she insisted that there be 60 female MPs in the Egyptian parliament. As a literacy campaigner, her name adorned hundreds of libraries across Egypt. In the weeks following the toppling of her husband, signs bearing her name in front of the nation's libraries were removed, defaced, or often ripped to shreds, as people sought to cleanse Egypt of the Mubarak name.

As First Lady, she drove a wedge into the highest levels of government: she never got on with Omar Suleiman or Hussein Tantawi. She didn't trust these old men, who she felt were constantly manoeuvring for power behind the back of her husband. The issue of succession had never been settled during Mubarak's reign, and, as he passed his 80th year, it became clear that something would have to be done. Whereas Hosni Mubarak generally favoured his elder son, the quiet businessman Alaa, Suzanne was infatuated with her little boy Gamal. Using all her influence, she did everything she could to make sure Gamal would be able to claim what was rightfully his. All the while, Gamal consistently denied that he ever wanted the presidency.

When Suzanne finally made it to the airport, Etman received the instructions to have the tape broadcast. We left the office together, and walked to the studio. The studio was only two floors down from my office. It took less than a minute to walk the distance. That minute seemed to stretch on forever, and we walked through in silence. Everything that had happened in the past 18 days raced through my mind, the images seemed to blur, until it seemed that I was reliving the whole five years that I spent in the Maspero building. The era of wasted chances and lost opportunities.

Those 18 days characterise the final years of Mubarak's rule. Nobody had the courage to tell Mubarak to take action when he needed to. Nobody had the courage to tell him directly to stand down. Part of the problem is the culture here in Egypt, which is still based on the hierarchy of age. Even when Mubarak called Hussein Tantawi and told him he was stepping down, Tantawi didn't just say yes, thank you. He had to say "Why?" He had to deny that it was what he really wanted. Even at times of national crisis, people still have to dance around the fire, and can't be honest with each other. It was a habit that had been ingrained among the entire ruling elite and, indeed, everyone who had contact with the President. Everyone was being constantly reminded not to upset him, not to make him nervous. Everything had to be sacrificed at the altar of dignity.

We walked into the control room, put the tape in the machine and pressed play. It was 37 seconds long. Emotions were running high, some of the staff in the studio were crying as they worked their machines. They had been overwhelmed with stress, and suddenly, in 37 seconds, the entire weight had been lifted from their shoulders.

The statement was simple:

In the name of God the merciful, the compassionate: citizens, during these very difficult circumstances Egypt is going through, President Hosni Mubarak has decided to step down from the office of president of the republic and has charged the Supreme Council of the Armed Forces to administer the affairs of the country. May God help everybody.

Omar Suleiman had a meeting not long before with Field Marshal Tantawi. They came out with the statement. They decided that Omar Suleiman should be the one to read it out, as per Mubarak's last instructions. He left the office and just read the statement out to the camera which had already been set up in the corridor. Those who watched the video on TV will remember that there was a man just standing there behind Omar Suleiman as he read out his lines. It was unfortunate for the man, he was just in the wrong place at the wrong time.

There is a theory in propaganda, that when people do not want to accept the gravity of a stressful situation, they will make fun of it. It was unsurprising, therefore, that the man became the subject of ridicule across Egypt and the Middle East. Web pages were devoted to him. Mocked up photos were produced, inserting his face behind world leaders like Adolf Hitler, Saddam Hussein, Nasser and Obama. He even found himself photoshopped into films like *Scarface* and *Star Wars*. Songs were sung, "*When I grow up, I don't want to be a teacher, I don't want to be a pilot, I don't want to be an officer and don't want to be the man behind Omar Suleiman!*" It was a way of diffusing the tension, of taking people's minds off the situation. It turned out the man was Hussein Kamel, Omar Suleiman's chief assistant, who had managed Suleiman's office for years. It seems nobody told him to move out the way.

When we finally broadcast the statement, relief swept through my body. I wasn't happy, exactly. I was still upset about what had happened to the people, what had happened to the government. The future was uncertain. I would have preferred a peaceful transition of power, to help fix the problems of this nation. We had a lot of problems, we still do.

I had originally hoped that Mubarak would step aside, though continue as President in name only, then we could have had genuine elections later in the year where the Egyptian people could have dismissed Gamal and his ambitions. I hoped we could have moved from an Egypt ruled for 30 years by one man, with his son waiting in the wings, to a country with a proper democratic system. Unfortunately, after their catastrophic mishandling of the crisis, the government lost all credibility with the public. It will take years to sort out what happened. In an effort to cleanse themselves, the government is now going ahead with show trials to assuage the public, yet corrupt men still remain at the heart of the system.

When the statement was broadcast, the country went wild. The only thing I've seen that was remotely like it was when Egypt won the African Nations Cup in football. People were jubilant, fireworks were being let off. People were singing in the streets, it was an all night party. For one night, it really felt like Egypt was the centre of the world.

EPILOGUE

"I am writing this aboard a plane, which took off 2 hours ago. I left my homeland for skies unknown. I leave with many questions about an uncertain future, unknown for me and for my country in which I was raised, where I found out the meaning of the word homeland, Egypt.

It is the 2nd of April 2011. More than two months have passed since the beginning of the uprising which led to the fall of President Mubarak. I was forced to play a part right in the middle of everything that happened. A responsibility one carries towards what one thinks is part of one's being, and what if part of one's being is one's country? This was my homeland, which I spent all my life adoring and faithfully protecting. This all came at a time when the country was truly in danger of collapsing. I never tired of my duty, nor felt like running away. I carried this responsibility for more than seventy days. If I could do it all over again, I probably would have done exactly the same. I would do so because my only motive was always the love of my homeland, no matter how high the price."

That was a small excerpt from my notes written on my way from Cairo to London on the night of the 2nd of April 2011. The title I chose for my piece was a question "What's next?" I thought the answer to that question would be difficult but I did not imagine that it would be as complicated or mysterious as it turned out to be. Complications in the Egyptian state have reached a phase where no one can even imagine a clear solution. The mystery that revolves around the future of a country that was torn apart by desires, and exposed the fundamental weakness in its political and social structure. New qualities that were concealed within the Egyptian personality have been discovered, the result of the repossession of the concepts and values of six decades past, when the previous phase of Egyptian history began with the 1952 revolution. The shock of watching that violence, the desire for revenge, the relishing of pain inflicted on others and the absence of nobility. Those very different emotions appeared in some Egyptians, contradicting completely everything we know, have come to expect and believe as it relates to our heritage. This is something to think about for those who still call Egypt their home.

When I was a child, I remember being captivated by the story of King Solomon. The king had his *jinn* (spirits – where the English word "genie" comes from) and his people working for him, as he stood leaning on his cane watching over them on a mountainside. When he finally toppled over, the jinn discovered that they had been working for a man who had been dead for some time. It was not until the termites had gnawed through his cane that he fell down, having stood rigid for so long. The people and the jinn had not known they were working for a corpse. In many ways, this old Koranic story is a parable of the end of Mubarak's regime.

When I left my position, or my mission, in Egyptian media it was because I had reached the conclusion that the problems of the media, like the whole state, were not problems that could be solved through quick and easy solutions. The media, like the country, was in deep crisis. The potential collapse of the state media institution, like the other state institutions, was the main reason, but not the only reason, that led to me asking to be relieved of my mission. I would not be able to stave off the avalanche I could see coming. I mentioned those reasons in my resignation statement then, which made some people angry. But in the days, weeks and months that followed, much of what I feared, unfortunately, came to be.

When my office was attacked by some employees of the ERTU asking for special privileges only two days after President Mubarak stepped down, I didn't think it a reason to leave at the time, however; ten weeks later, I felt that maybe it was.

Again I ask "What's next?" I can't help but think of the Egypt of 45 centuries past, as described by Ebor in his Papyrus after the first uprising in the history of Mankind, one led by the Egyptians. Then Egypt lived for a while, for nearly three hundred years in what Egyptologists describe as the years of decadence, the period between the end of the Old Kingdom and the emergence of the Middle Kingdom. Ancient Papyruses elaborated on the misery in which the Egyptians lived because of the disintegration of their kingdom. Bedouins who ruled the Nile Delta became masters, enslaving Egyptians, other Bedouins invaded middle Egypt from what is now Libya, establishing their own kingdom while the south was ruled by the Theban kings. The values and economic system of the Old Kingdom were abandoned as Egypt descended into chaos. As mentioned by the Ptolemaic historian Manetho, Egypt was ruled by seventy kings, each ruling for seventy days.

That is how Egypt was remembered after its first uprising, and I feared that we would see a return to those days after Mubarak, a modern day pharaoh, was felled. There is a great difference between the collapse of a regime and the disintegration of the very foundations of the state itself, which Egypt is witnessing right now. However, many elements of the regime have remained in place, almost like changing one's hardware, but keeping the old software.

Looking back on the things I witnessed, when I was party to the decisions made by the circle of power, it is clear that the regime made some fundamental mistakes. One of them was their political stupidity and disconnection from the public. They had no understanding of the role of media in communicating with the country. Throughout my years inside the state media I tried to stress the concept that is was public property, and in this I did not succeed. It takes more than good intentions and private efforts to achieve something like that. It needed a real political will to put the concept into effect, a political will which was absent. The government had a backward understanding of the role of media. The regime, for the most part, dealt with the media as if it was state property, with its only role being to propagandise for the regime, regardless of what was right or wrong. They did not realise that a proper, effective media can guarantee stability, not undermine it.

The regime's gravest mistake was the belief that there is a contradiction between change and stability. They never understood that change is actually vital for stability, and that after 30 years of rule, there was no other way to maintain stability than to make genuine political changes. However, the narrow, shortsighted pursuit of personal objectives, on the part of those inside the regime, wrecked the country's stability and has forced a far more dangerous monumental change upon the country.

What's next? The question remains and we are still without an answer. I think a step in the right direction would be to look back on our own history again, at what Egypt has passed through before, so we can collectively choose not to go through another reign of decadence, or destitution. This will only come when the concept of unity becomes the solid conviction of the people of Egypt: Muslims, Coptic Christians, Islamists, Salafis, Nubians, Upper Egyptians, liberals, leftists and secularists. There is a real risk of Egypt becoming a divided nation unless the people understand that they must work together.

When Nelson Mandela was released from prison in 1990, he found a country ripped apart by racial division and discrimination. The only feasible path was to unite South Africans of different races to bring about political change. An important aspect of this was the resistance to the temptation for revenge and retribution. Unless Egyptians and their media do not profess false heroism, then there will no way out for the country. There are no rules that

Arab journalists agree upon, and, of course, the same goes for Egyptians. So, in the absence of professionalism and objectivity, and the prevalence of chaos, journalists, together with all those who work in the media must stand together, agree on a position of media ethics, and on the points on which they disagree. As for the state media, may Allah help them unless the state wakes up and recognises the importance of its media, and the concept of genuine public service.

I used to say that Egypt was created to stay. Now I say that it was created to stay, but in a place worthy of its history.